"Good literature can be an inspiring guide to good behavior. Parents who share this book with their children will thank Karen Santorum for the skill and sensitivity with which she chose its contents. And so will the parents' children when, years hence, they read it with their own children."

—GEORGE F. WILL
syndicated columnist

"As a mother, Karen Santorum knows the power of stories to shape and mold our children. In *Everyday Graces*, Karen has compiled a treasure chest of tales that helps us raise the next generation of children into adults of kind compassion. *Everyday Graces* is a must for families that desire their children to become people of character."

—JANET PARSHALL
nationally syndicated talk show host

"Among the casualties of the 'culture war' have been civility, manners, and what we called in my grandparents' generation 'deportment.' Karen Santorum mounts a counter-offensive in *Everyday Graces*, gleaned from classic and contemporary sources that teach what we once held to be common sense and common values. This book belongs in every home in need of reinforcements."

—CAL THOMAS
syndicated columnist

"A powerfully compelling book on the importance of good manners . . . *Everyday Graces* is sure to be a family favorite and one that can and should be passed on from generation to generation."

—*Heart of the Matter Online*

"*Everyday Graces* represents a valuable contribution to the new national trend to emphasize virtues above information, character over skills. Karen Santorum has provided a useful service for all parents who want to encourage more civilized behavior in their children."

—MICHAEL MEDVED
film critic and national radio talk show host

"What I want to say to Mrs. Santorum for giving us this remarkable and stimulating book on the much-neglected subject of manners is: Ma'am, permit me—thank you so very, very much."

—WILLIAM MURCHISON
syndicated columnist and longtime
editor of the *Dallas Morning News*

Everyday Graces

A Child's Book of Good Manners

EDITED, WITH COMMENTARY, BY

Karen Santorum

WITH CONTRIBUTIONS BY *Michael Lamb*

ILLUSTRATIONS BY *Sam Torode*

Cataloging-in-Publication Data:

    Everyday graces : a child's book of good manners / edited, with commentary, by Karen Santorum ; with contributions by Michael Lamb ; illustrated by Sam Torode. — Wilmington, DE : ISI Books, 2003.

        p. ; cm.

    ISBN: 1932236090

       1.   Etiquette — Juvenile literature. 2. Conduct of life — Juvenile literature. I. Santorum, Karen. II. Lamb, Michael. III. Torode, Sam.

BJ1857.C5 E84 2003   2003106613
395.1/22—dc21   CIP

Published in the United States by:

ISI Books
3901 Centerville Road
Wilmington, DE 19807

Book design by Sam Torode

Manufactured in the United States

*This book is lovingly and affectionately dedicated to my dear children,
Elizabeth, John, Daniel, Sarah Maria, Peter, Patrick, and Bella.*

*Thank you for all of the sweet and thoughtful things you do
each and every day to make life beautiful. May you grow up to be
kind and caring adults who see the joy in serving others.*

Contents

XI. CHURCH, WEDDINGS, AND FUNERALS

XII. KINDNESS TOWARDS ANIMALS

XIII. RESPECTING OUR COUNTRY

INTRODUCTION

"INCOMPATIBLE with life."

That's what doctors told my husband and me about the condition of our newborn daughter, Isabella Maria.

Four days after Bella was born, we were told that she had Trisomy 18. We learned that it was similar to Down syndrome — only worse. This genetic disorder causes severe birth defects, and in fact, nine out of ten babies with Trisomy 18 do not survive birth. Of the 10 percent who do survive, 90 percent won't make it to their first birthday.

Our family spent every waking hour at Bella's bedside, and within ten days, she was allowed to come home on hospice care. Rick and I were told to prepare to say good-bye to Bella, that there was no hope.

But we believe there is hope in Christ, so instead of saying good-bye, we decided to give Bella the best life possible for as much time as God would give her. Rick and I, along with our six other children, family, and friends, celebrated Bella's life every day.

On May 13, 2012, we celebrated Bella's fourth birthday. She is a ray of sunshine at the center of our home. Every day she inspires the entire family with her joyful spirit. Bella is loved beyond measure, and she is living proof that her condition is anything but incompatible with life. Bella's smile, laughter, and silliness remind all of us that she is *full* of life.

They said, "Why do anything?" We said, "Just give her a chance." They sent Bella home on hospice care, but we did well-baby care. They said, "Trisomy 18 is a lethal diagnosis." We said, "Bella is God's perfect child — a treasure from heaven." They said, "Bella will never do anything." But she has taught us the most important things in life.

When *Everyday Graces* was first published, I included a chapter about the importance of appreciating people with disabilities. Having been a nurse, I always had a special place in my heart for any person with special needs. But now that I am the mother of a special-needs child, the issue is personal. I am passionate about seeing my little girl, and all people with special needs, treated with dignity and respect.

Treating people with dignity and respect: this, ultimately, is what good manners are about. Manners are not something reserved only for formal affairs; they are the building blocks of good character. Good manners convey, day in and day out, our fundamental respect for others.

Our family's experiences with Bella have only underscored the importance of displaying such respect. I must admit to having been a mama bear with claws out many times when my daughter was not treated well. But as challenging as the journey has been, it has also been a beautiful one, full of kindness and love from so many dear people in our lives. We have been graced with the love, support, and prayers of our family, our friends, our church, and people all over the country. For that, we are eternally grateful.

—*Karen Santorum*
June 30, 2012

NOTE TO PARENTS

WHEN WE SPEAK OF POLITENESS we may think of something that can be easily learned from reading an etiquette book. Such may be the case with simple, isolated behaviors like selecting the proper fork or keeping one's elbows off the table. But true politeness requires more. For it is the mirror of a person's heart and soul — it is an outward expression of inner virtue. And inner virtue is best learned through constant practice and examples.

That is why I wanted to create *Everyday Graces: A Child's Book of Good Manners*. It teaches manners through literature that illustrates the connection between good manners and good character. This book grew out of my frustration at not being able to find a book on manners for children that instructs through stories rather than by rules and dos and don'ts.

Having seven children of our own, my husband and I know the influence stories can have on children. About a week after reading "George Washington and the Cherry Tree" (a story about telling the truth), my son Johnny, who had put a hole in our kitchen wall while practicing his baseball swing, said, "Mommy, I cannot tell a lie: I did it." After this confession, I decided my kids should hear that story about once a week!

One day, I discovered Sarah Maria, our three-year-old who habitually empties all of her drawers before deciding what to wear, stuffing all of her clothes back into her dresser. When I asked her how this change had come about, she told me she did not want to be like "unca." Since I have six brothers, I was not sure to which "uncle" she was referring. Later in the day, I realized that she was referring to "Hunca Munca" in the Beatrix Potter story "The Tale of Two Bad Mice."

There's no doubt that storytelling helps parents lead their children to discern right from wrong. As far back as 450 B.C., the great thinkers were debating how one becomes a good person. Socrates, Plato, and many others since have agreed that children learn best through storytelling. Contemporary moral thinkers such as Robert Coles, William Kilpatrick, Gilbert Meilaender, William J. Bennett, and Vigen Guroian also believe that stories play a critical role in shaping the next generation.

Thus, *Everyday Graces* is a compilation of classic stories, poems, myths, and fables to be read aloud to children. The goal of this book is to cultivate a desire in children to practice good manners and kindness towards others. This desire is reinforced when children recall stories or model their behavior on that of their favorite heroes.

Politeness is not a robe for special occasions; rather, it stems from the very nature of the person in whom reside traits of good, decent, and respectable behavior. A truly polite person strives to practice acts of kindness at all times, in all situations, and with sincerity. She knows that the little acts of kindness — the warm smile, the sympathetic word, and the good deed — are just as important as the big ones. Even when she differs in opinion from others, her words and actions are gracious and disciplined.

We want our children to be successful in everything they do, but our most important goal should be that they become courteous, honest, unselfish, and well-behaved persons. For many parents, the thought of teaching children manners is daunting, especially when added to the other responsibilities of parenthood. But in reality, parents teach manners all the time. When we instruct our children on how to eat and dress, speak with one another, play with siblings and friends, and treat their parents, the elderly, and the sick and needy, we are teaching manners — and there is no place on earth more important than the home for accomplishing this.

Our most effective teaching tool is our own behavior — how we ourselves live and treat others. When virtue is manifest in us, we plant the seeds of love and good manners in our children's hearts. The examples we set for our children are profoundly important for their moral formation. Our children do not need to know that we are perfect, because none of us are; rather, they simply need to know that we too are trying to live decent and respectable lives, treating others by the Golden Rule: "Do unto others as you would have them do to you" (Luke 6:31).

When children use words like "please," "thank you," and "you're welcome," and when they act with kindness and generosity from unselfish motives, family life is enriched. When children learn that they have to put other people first, and that sometimes doing what is right may be costly, they have learned important moral lessons. Children need to see and understand that polite behavior contributes to peace and enjoyment for everyone. Manners are a powerful deterrent to violence, because people who are polite know how to practice restraint.

Ironically, when many people think of good manners they imagine blue-bloods dressed in fine linen and lace at a polo club, sipping rare imported tea with pinkies extended. But good manners are really quite simple. In our everyday activities we can be abusive, selfish, and contentious, or we can be kind, considerate, generous, and cooperative. This choice applies to all, both rich and poor, in every culture. The concept of politeness has been present in all human societies and has enabled civilizations to thrive.

Good manners elevate and strengthen every aspect of family life, worship, the workplace, and even government. There is a strong correlation between politeness and success. Politeness makes a person more likable and respected. In the professional world, good manners are a leading qualification. The lawyer will win arguments in front of the jury with her gentility, the contractor will gain clients through his courteous behavior, the doctor will win her patients' trust with her polite bedside manner, and a business will thrive because of the amicability practiced by its employees.

Unfortunately, in our day, respect and attention to good manners has diminished, whereas individual rights and self-expression have become an obsession. Many people believe they have a right to use obscene language or aggressive behavior. Free and uninhibited self-expression is seen as a virtue; persons are applauded for speaking their mind without regard for the impact of their words on others.

We have seen the fallout in school violence, road rage, and hate crimes. We need to recognize the damage that results from rudeness, hurtful words, and spiteful actions. We need to promote the basic rules of civility as essential to family living and social concord.

We, as parents, are the first and primary teachers of our children. If we insist on courtesy and kindness in our own homes, and if we practice these virtues every day, our children will follow our example. The stories and poems included in this book are intended to serve such ends. I carefully selected them, with particular lessons in mind.

You will read from Lucy Maud Montgomery's *Anne of Green Gables* and find out why speaking your mind isn't always a good idea. Your children will learn about good table manners as you read excerpts from Johanna Spyri's *Heidi* and Lewis Carroll's *Alice in Wonderland*. The art of serving others a pleasant meal is shown in *The Lion, the Witch, and the Wardrobe* by C. S. Lewis. The importance of good grooming is discussed in a story about the battle of Thermopylae. Your children will be touched by the kindness of Sara in Frances

Hodgson Burnett's *A Little Princess*. In "Grace," singer-songwriter Bono beautifully expresses the value of seeing the goodness in everything.

Good sportsmanship is taught in Mary Mapes Dodge's *Hans Brinker* and in "The Battle of Hector and Ajax" from Homer's *Iliad*. Mark Twain's *Tom Sawyer* teaches us that cheating in school is never a good idea. Children will learn why we write letters when they read Rudyard Kipling's "How the First Letter Was Written," and they'll learn how to write letters from Thomas Jefferson and Abraham Lincoln's own correspondence.

These are just a few of the selections contained in this book. There are also fables, myths, and stories about real-life heroes that will inspire children to emulate good behavior. They are instructive, but they are also clever and entertaining. I trust you will find them enjoyable and edifying.

—*Karen Santorum*

CHAPTER ONE

Good Manners at Home

1.
Honor Your Mother and Father

To Allison Cunningham from Her Boy
by Robert Louis Stevenson

For the long nights you lay awake
And watched for my unworthy sake:
For your most comfortable hand
That led me through the uneven land:
For all the storybooks you read:
For all the pains you comforted:

From the sick child, now well and old,
Take, nurse, the little book you hold!
And grant it, heaven, that all who read
May find as dear a nurse at need,
And every child who lists my rhyme,
In the bright, fireside, nursery clime,
May hear it in as kind a voice
As made my childish days rejoice!

Your mother and father have taken care of you since you were a baby. They love you, give much of themselves, sacrifice many things, and would do anything in the world for you. In return, you can show how much you love them by learning to be good.

Manners are small ways of showing goodness. Having good manners means saying "thank you." It means being thoughtful by picking up your toys, setting the table, keeping your room tidy, and asking what you can do to help out. It means pleasantly greeting your mother and father with a "good morning," "good evening," or "hello." Practicing good manners shows that you're a strong person, able to put others before yourself.

P ANSIES

by J. F. Willing, adapted by Karen Santorum

O NCE, THERE WAS A KING who had a beautiful garden. When he went into it one day, he found everything drooping and fading. "Why, what's the matter here?" he asked.

"Oh," the vine sighed, "I cannot grow tall and slender and beautiful like the pine tree, so I don't want to grow any more. There's no use."

The pine said, "I cannot bear fruit like the apple tree. I am good for nothing. I don't want to live any more."

And the apple tree said, "My flowers are just little, simple, common things; they are not beautiful and large like the roses, which everybody praises. I shan't live any longer."

Because everything was finding fault with itself, all the plants looked wretched.

But at last the king came to a pansy flower. It looked up at him as bright and glad and sweet as ever. He said, "Pansy, you don't seem to have fallen into this trouble. They are all finding fault, but you seem to be happy."

"Yes," said the little flower, "I am happy, because I know that when you planted the seed out of which I grew, you didn't want a pine, or an apple tree, or a vine, or a rose. You just wanted a little pansy. So to please you, I am going to be the best little pansy that I can be."

This made the king happy. He had to try hard to bring the other plants out of their discontent, so he was very glad that there was one flower in the garden willing to please him.

Like the little pansy, you must make up your mind to be content, and to grow into the person that you were created to be.

Pansies make people happy. Have you ever noticed how their bright, sweet faces seem to rise toward you when you bend over them in the garden? They look just like happy, contented little people!

I have a friend who gave his little daughter a bed of pansy flowers for a birthday present. She was so delighted with them that when she came home from school, the first thing she did was run out to pet, look at, and talk to them as if they were alive and knew what she said.

One day she told her Mamma that she was sure she could recognize each of them if she were to meet one on the street. "There are no two of them that look alike," she said. "Indeed, Mamma, though they are all lovely, they are no more like each other than the faces of the girls in school. And would you believe it, they seem to know me, and look up and smile whenever I come, as if they were glad to see me!"

I have no doubt that the little girl was happier, and more careful to do the right thing all day in school, because of the time she spent with her pansies.

A sweet-tempered child is the pansy of the home: when she comes in, she brings the sunshine with her. Her parents find the mists of care rolling off their hearts when they hear her sweet, cheerful voice in the hall. Their minds may be full of worry, but when they see their little girl come into a room, as bright as a pansy, their worries flee.

> Behavior is a mirror in which everyone shows his image.
>
> JOHANN WOLFGANG VON GOETHE

I have seen a whole bus full of people brighten up when a pleasant-faced child comes on. She might do something as minor as to be cheerfully willing to stand when there isn't a place to sit, but I always see the weariness leave the people's faces as they watch her. When tired fathers and mothers are away from home, they have only to think of their dear children waiting for them, and they immediately feel refreshed.

So, if you want to be like a pansy, and make everybody in your home brighter and happier, you must learn to be kind and cheerful. Your own Mamma and Daddy, just like the king, will be blessed by your efforts.

It is important that your home is a peaceful and happy place. The bad habits of quarreling or whining interfere with the enjoyment of home life. A simple smile and a cheerful disposition can make an entire day bright. Once in a while, if you are feeling like the vine or the apple tree, remember that your parents love you just the way you are, the way the king loved his little pansy.

THE ROBIN REDBREASTS
by Mrs. Hawkshawe

Two Robin redbreasts built their nest
  Within a hollow tree;
The hen sat quietly at home,
  The cook sang merrily;
And all the little young ones said,
  "Wee, wee, wee, wee, wee, wee!"

One day the sun was warm and bright,
  And shining in the sky,

Cock Robin said, "My little dears,
 'Tis time you learn to fly;"
And all the little young ones said,
 "I'll try, I'll try, I'll try!"

I know a child, and who she is
 I'll tell you by-and-by,
When mamma says, "Do this," or "That,"
 She says, "What for?" and "Why?"
She'd be a better child by far
 If she would say, "I'll try."

God's fourth great commandment is "Honor your father and your mother, that you may have a long life in the land which the Lord, your God, is giving you" (Exodus 20:12). This commandment applies to all parents: biological, adoptive, foster, and anyone assigned to care for you. One way to respect your parents is to respond to them with these simple words: "I'll try."

The Princess and the Goblin
by George MacDonald

In this story, we read about the princess Irene. She has befriended a boy named Curdie, a miner's son, who tells her of an evil world of goblins that have tunneled under her father's castle. The goblins are trying to capture the castle by flooding the entire mountain where Irene and her father live. In this scene, the king is in his castle among guests. Irene is on his lap, concerned about the noises she's hearing.

Chapter 31

"King-papa, do you hear that noise?"

"I hear nothing," said the king.

"Listen," she said, holding up her forefinger.

The king listened, and a great stillness fell upon the company. Each man, seeing that the king listened, listened also, and the harper sat with his harp between his arms, and his fingers silent upon the strings.

"I do hear a noise," said the king at length — "a noise of distant thunder. It is coming nearer and nearer. What can it be?"

They all heard it now, and each seemed ready to start to his feet as he listened. Yet all sat perfectly still. The noise came rapidly nearer.

"What *can* it be?" said the king again.

"I think it must be another storm coming over the mountain," said Sir Walter.

Then Curdie, who at the first word of the king had slipped from his seat, and laid his ear to the ground, rose up quickly, and approaching the king said, speaking very fast:

"Please, Your Majesty, I think I know what it is. I have no time to explain, for that might make it too late for some of us. Will your Majesty give orders that everybody leave the house as quickly as possible and get up the mountain?"

The king, who was the wisest man in the kingdom, knew well there was a time when things must be done and questions left till afterwards. He had faith in Curdie, and rose instantly, with Irene in his arms.

"Every man and woman follow me," he said, and strode out into the darkness.

Before he had reached the gate, the noise had grown to a great thundering roar, and the ground trembled beneath their feet, and before the last of them had crossed the court, out after them from the great hall door came a huge rush of turbid water, and almost swept them away. But they got safe out of the gate and up the mountain, while the torrent went roaring down the road into the valley beneath.

Curdie had left the king and the princess to look after his mother, whom he and his father, one on each side, caught up when the stream overtook them and carried safe and dry.

When the king had got out of the way of the water, a little up the mountain, he stood with the princess in his arms, looking back with amazement on the issuing torrent, which glimmered fierce and foamy through the night. There Curdie rejoined them.

"Now, Curdie," said the king, "what does it mean? Is this what you expected?"

"It is, Your Majesty," said Curdie; and proceeded to tell him about the second scheme of the goblins, who, fancying the miners of more importance to the upper world than they were, had resolved, if they should fail in carrying off the king's daughter, to flood the mine and drown the miners. Then he explained what the miners had done to prevent it. The goblins had, in pursuance of their design, let loose all the underground reservoirs and streams, expecting the water to run down into the mine, which was lower than their part of the mountain, for they had, as they supposed, not knowing of the solid wall close behind, broken a passage through into it. But the readiest outlet the water could find had turned out to be the tunnel they had made to the king's house, the possibility of which catastrophe had not occurred to the young miner until he had laid his ear to the floor of the hall.

Honor your father and your mother, so that you may live long and that it may go well with you.

Deuteronomy 5:16

What was then to be done? The house appeared in danger of falling, and every moment the torrent was increasing.

"We must set out at once," said the king. "But how to get at the horses!"

"Shall I see if we can manage that?" said Curdie.

"Do," said the king.

Curdie gathered the men-at-arms, and took them over the garden wall, and so to the stables. They found their horses in terror; the water was rising fast around them, and it was quite time they were got out. But there was no way to get them out, except by riding them through the stream, which was now pouring from the lower windows as well as the door. As one horse was quite enough for any man to manage through such a torrent, Curdie got on the king's white charger and, leading the way, brought them all in safety to the rising ground.

Having dismounted, Curdie led the horse up to the king. . . .

"But, my child," said the king, "you will be cold if you haven't something more on. Run, Curdie, my boy, and fetch anything you can lay your hands on, to keep the princess warm. We have a long ride before us."

Curdie was gone in a moment, and soon returned with a great rich fur, and the news that dead goblins were tossing about in the current through the house. They had been caught in their own snare; instead of the mine, they had flooded their own country, whence they were now swept up and drowned. Irene shuddered, but the king held her close to his bosom. Then he turned to Sir Walter, and said:

"Bring Curdie's father and mother here."

"I wish," said the king, when they stood before him, "to take your son with me. He shall enter my bodyguard at once, and wait further promotion."

Peter and his wife, overcome, only murmured almost inaudible thanks. But Curdie spoke aloud.

"Please, Your Majesty," he said, "I cannot leave my father and mother."

"That's right, Curdie!" cried the princess. "*I* wouldn't if I were you."

The king looked at the princess and then at Curdie with a glow of satisfaction on his countenance.

"I too think you are right, Curdie," he said, "and I will not ask you again. But I shall have a chance of doing something for you some time."

"Your Majesty has already allowed me to serve you," said Curdie.

"But, Curdie," said his mother, "why shouldn't you go with the king? We can get on very well without you."

"But I can't get on very well without you," said Curdie. "The king is very kind, but I could not be half the use to him that I am to you. Please, Your Majesty, if you wouldn't mind giving my mother a red petticoat! I should have got her one long ago, but for the goblins."

"As soon as we get home," said the king, "Irene and I will search out the warmest one to be found, and send it by one of the gentlemen."

"Yes, that we will, Curdie!" said the princess.

"And next summer we'll come back and see you wear it, Curdie's mother," she added. "Shan't we, king-papa?"

"Yes, my love; I hope so," said the king.

Then turning to the miners, he said, "Will you do the best you can for my servants tonight? I hope they will be able to return to the house to-morrow."

The miners with one voice promised their hospitality.

Then the king commanded his servants to mind whatever Curdie should say to them, and after shaking hands with him and his father and mother, the king and the princess and all their company rode away down the side of the new stream, which had already devoured half the road, into the starry night.

Some people say that the true test of character comes when we are in emergency situations. Curdie never lost his concern for his parents' well-being and safety, showing loyalty to them in a desperate situation. He also acted unselfishly, taking care of the king, Irene, friends, and even the horses.

A Father's Wise Advice to His Son
from Robinson Crusoe *by Daniel Defoe*
adapted by Karen Santorum

I WAS BORN IN THE YEAR 1632, in the city of York, of a good family. My father settled first at Hull, and lived afterwards at York, from whence he had married my mother, whose relations were named Robinson, a very good family in that country.

Being the third son of the family, and not bred to any trade, my head began to be filled very early with rambling thoughts. I would be satisfied with nothing but going to sea, and this inclination led me so strongly against the will, nay, the commands of my father, and against all the entreaties of my mother and other friends, that there seemed to be something fatal in that propension of nature tending directly to the life of misery which was to befall me.

A wise son brings joy to his father, but a foolish son grief to his mother.

PROVERBS 10:1

My father, a wise and grave man, gave me serious and excellent counsel against what he foresaw was my design. He called me one morning into his chamber. He asked me what reasons more than a mere wandering inclination I had for leaving my father's house and my native country. He told me it was men of desperate fortunes on one hand, or of aspiring, superior fortunes on the other, who went abroad upon adventures.

After this, he pressed me earnestly, and in the most affectionate manner, not to play the young man, nor to propell myself into miseries which nature and the station of life I was born in seemed to have provided against; that I was under no necessity of seeking my bread; that he would do well for me, and that if I was not very easy and happy in the world, it must be my mere fate or fault that must hinder it, and that he should have nothing to answer for, having thus discharged his duty in warning me against measures which he knew would be to my hurt.

In a word, he indicated that as he would do very kind things for me if I would stay and settle at home, as he directed, so he would not give me any encouragement to go away. He said he would not cease to pray for me, yet he would venture to say to me that, if I did take this foolish step, God would not bless me, and I would have leisure hereafter to reflect upon having neglected his counsel when there might be none to assist in my recovery.

In this last part of his discourse, which was truly prophetic, I observed tears running down his face, and that when he spoke of my having leisure to repent, and none to assist me, he was so moved that he broke off the discourse, and told me his heart was so full he could say no more.

I was sincerely affected with this discourse — who wouldn't be? — and I resolved not to think of going abroad any more, but to settle at home according to my father's desire. But, alas! A few days wore it all off; and, in short, I wanted to go to sea! I took my mother, and told her of my thoughts about seeing the world.

This put my mother into a great passion. She told me she wondered how I could think of any such thing, after such a discourse with my father, with such kind and tender expressions as she knew my father had used to me; and that, in short, if I would ruin myself, there was no help for me.

For her part, she continued, she would not have so much hand in my destruction; and I should never say that my mother was willing when my father was not. I heard that afterwards my mother reported our

discourse to my father, and that my father, after showing a great concern at it, said to her with a sigh, "That boy might be happy if he would stay at home; but if he goes abroad he will be the most miserable wretch who was ever born. I can give no consent to it."

It was not until almost a year after this that I broke loose, though in the meantime I continued obstinately deaf to all proposals of settling to business, and frequently argued with my father and mother about their being so positively determined against what they knew my inclinations prompted me to.

But being one day at Hull, where I went casually, and without any purpose of making an elopement that time; but, I say, being there, and one of my companions going to sea to London in his father's ship, and prompting me to go with them, with the common allurement of seafaring men, I consulted neither father nor mother any more, nor so much as sent them word of it; but, leaving them to hear of it as they might, without asking God's blessing or my father's, without any consideration of circumstances or consequences, and in an ill hour, God knows, on the 1st of September, 1651, I went on board a ship bound for London.

Never any young adventurer's misfortunes, I believe, began sooner, or continued longer than mine. The ship was no sooner gotten out of the harbor but the wind began to blow, and the waves to rise in a most frightful manner; and, as I had never been at sea before I was most inexpressibly sick in body, and terrified in my mind.

I began now seriously to reflect upon what I had done, and how justly I was overtaken by the judgment of Heaven for my wicked leaving my father's house, and abandoning my duty; all the good counsel of my parents, my father's tears and my mother's entreaties, came now fresh into my mind; and my conscience, which was not yet come to the pitch of hardness to which it has been since, reproached me with the contempt of advice, and the breach of my duty to God and my father.

All this while the storm increased, and the sea, which I had never been upon before, went very high, though nothing like what I have seen many times since; no, nor like what I saw a few days after. But it was enough to affect me then, who was but a young sailor and had never known anything of the matter.

I expected every wave would have swallowed us up, and that every time the ship fell down, as I thought, in the trough or hollow of the sea, we should never rise more; and in this agony of mind I made many vows and resolutions, that if it would please God here to spare my life this one voyage, if ever I got once my foot upon dry land again, I would go directly home to my father, and never run myself into such miseries as these any more. Now I saw plainly the goodness of his observations, how comfortably he had lived all his days, and never had been exposed to tempests at sea, or troubles of shore; and I resolved that I would, like a true repenting prodigal, go home to my father.

This storm was just the beginning of Robinson Crusoe's hardships. Some day you may read the rest of this great story about how he ended up shipwrecked on a deserted island. He was completely alone and had to struggle for survival every day. Seeking shelter, finding food, and protecting himself from the wild animals were constant challenges. He was extremely homesick and wished he had listened to the pleas of his parents.

ICARUS AND HIS FATHER
Greek myth retold by Karen Santorum

ONCE UPON A TIME there was a little boy named Icarus who was the son of an inventor named Daedalus. They lived happily together until one day when both father and son were put into prison on the island of Crete. Icarus had done nothing wrong, but his father was being punished for helping the hero Theseus kill the Minotaur (a creature that was half-man and half-bull), and then escape with the king's daughter.

Daedalus and Icarus were treated fairly by the king and his watchmen. They were given food and water for nourishment, and they could go outside for exercise and fresh air. Icarus enjoyed playing on the beach with the seagulls and watching the ships. He frequently asked his father if they could hide on a ship and escape from the island. He wanted so much to see his friends again, and to play all of his favorite boyhood games. Unfortunately, since they were on an island, Daedalus knew that the king prevented any escape.

One day, as Icarus was playing with the seagulls he noticed that one had fallen and was lying on the sand. When Icarus approached the bird, it lay there motionless and did not resist the boy when he picked it up. He held the delicate bird in his hands and examined its shiny white feathers and strong wings. Icarus whispered to the bird, "It's alright, you're going to be alright, you will fly again." It was at this moment that it occurred to Icarus that if he and his father could somehow fly they could escape from the island.

> Children, obey your parents in the Lord, for this is right.
>
>
>
> EPHESIANS 6:1

He quickly brought the injured bird to his father and asked if they could build two pairs of wings and fly home. Daedalus was a talented inventor, so the thought of flying intrigued him, especially if it meant freedom. He immediately went to work, studying the injured bird's wings and drawing sketches. After several months, father and son were able to gather enough supplies, feathers, and reeds of wood (which they kept hidden in their mattresses), to begin building wings. They shaped the wings with the reeds and attached the feathers with wax and thread.

When they had finished, Daedalus warned his son to only fly at a medium altitude. He said, "Icarus, please stay close to me in the air. Do not fly too high because the heat of the sun will melt the wax on the wings; and do not fly too low because the moisture from the water will make the wings heavy. Both of these things would cause you to fall into the water." Daedalus's heart was heavy with worry for his son, for he knew the risk they were taking. But not to take the risk meant a life of imprisonment. Icarus promised his father that he would listen to his advice and fly with caution.

They waited until just before sunrise, when it was still dark. Off they flew, unnoticed, from the roof of the prison. At first, it was extremely frightening trying to move the wings properly in the wind and navigate in a straight direction over the water. But before long, the wind seemed to cradle them and was lifting them in the air, holding them steadily as they flew.

Icarus was exhilarated with the feeling of flying. He enjoyed the salty sea breeze in his face and the way his body glided through the morning air. The sun was rising in the sky, making the water sparkle. Icarus was so consumed with flying that he forgot his father's warnings. He went with the wind higher and higher into the sky.

Daedalus repeatedly called to his son to fly lower, but Icarus did not hear his father's pleas. He was too far away, and he did not look back at his father or stay close as he had promised. Icarus, feeling the warmth of the sun on his face and enjoying the moment, was not aware of the danger about to befall him. But suddenly, he noticed that his wings were falling apart from the heat of the sun. He quickly lost control and fell into the ocean waters, where he was consumed by the waves.

Daedalus desperately tried to rescue Icarus. He called to him and reached out to him, but the only thing remaining on the water were his son's wings. Icarus had vanished into the depths of the sea.

Daedalus's heart was broken. He nearly sank into the water under the weight of his grief, but the wind lifted him up and carried him home. There he lived with a heavy heart for the rest of his life, longing for the son for whom he would give all his inventions — and freedom itself — to be with again.

This story reminds us of the importance of listening to our parents. They have lived longer than we have and are more knowledgeable about the world. When they instruct us, we should trust and obey them. If Icarus had trusted his father's wise advice, he would not have perished in the sea.

> 'Tis a shame that your family is an honor to you! You ought to be an honor to your family.
>
>
>
> BENJAMIN FRANKLIN
> *Poor Richard's Almanac*

PINOCCHIO
by Carlo Collodi

Once upon a time, there was a piece of wood—that's right, just a common piece of wood. It was going to be made into a table leg by a carpenter. But just as the carpenter lifted his ax to cut this piece of wood, he heard a small voice begging, "Do not strike me so hard." He searched the room to find out where the voice was coming from. Much to his amazement, the carpenter realized that the piece of wood itself was talking!

The carpenter brought the piece of wood to his friend Geppetto, who wanted to turn it into a dancing puppet. Amazingly, the piece of wood insulted Geppetto and struck him in his shins. Geppetto was a gracious man, so he went ahead anyway and turned the wood into an intricate puppet. But the wood was still rude and disrespectful.

The puppet was named Pinocchio, and he talked back, kicked his maker, and even ran away. Pinocchio thought he knew everything and couldn't stand to be corrected. You will read a lot about Pinocchio in this book, because there is so much to be learned from his story of transformation.

In this scene, Pinocchio is sick and is being helped by a fairy. She is trying to give some medicine to Pinocchio, but he is being disagreeable.

CHAPTER 17

SHE THEREFORE DISSOLVED a certain white powder in half a tumbler of water, and offering it to the puppet she said to him lovingly.

"Drink it, and in a few days you will be cured."

Pinocchio looked at the tumbler, made a wry face, and then asked in a plaintive voice:

"Is it sweet or bitter?"

"It is bitter, but it will do you good."

"If it is bitter, I will not take it."

"Listen to me: drink it."

"I don't like anything bitter."

"Drink it, and when you have drunk it I will give you a lump of sugar to take away the taste."

"Where is the lump of sugar?"

"Here it is," said the Fairy, taking a piece from a gold sugar basin.

"Give me first the lump of sugar, and then I will drink that bad bitter water."

"Do you promise me?"

"Yes."

The Fairy gave him the sugar, and Pinocchio having crunched it up and swallowed it in a second, said, licking his lips:

"It would be a fine thing if sugar were medicine! I would take it every day."

"Now keep your promise and drink these few drops of water, which will restore you to health."

Pinocchio took the tumbler unwillingly in his hand and put the point of his nose to it: he then approached it to his lips: he then again put his nose to it, and at last said:

"It is too bitter, too bitter! I cannot drink it."

"How can you tell that, when you have not even tasted it?"

"I can imagine it! I know it from the smell. I want first another lump of sugar . . . and then I will drink it!"

The Fairy then, with all the patience of a good mamma, put another lump of sugar in his mouth, and then again presented the tumbler to him.

"I cannot drink it so!" said the puppet, making a thousand grimaces.

"Why?"

"Because that pillow that is down there on my feet bothers me."

The Fairy removed the pillow.

"It is useless. Even so I cannot drink it."

"What is the matter now?"

"The door of the room, which is half open, bothers me."

The Fairy went and closed the door.

"In short," cried Pinocchio, bursting into tears, "I will not drink that bitter water — no, no, no!"

"My boy, you will repent it."

There will be many times when, like Pinocchio, you'll have to take medicine. It's hard feeling sick and having to take something that you don't like. But remember that your parents give you medicine to make you more comfortable and help you get better! They don't like to see you suffer. Try to be a cooperative patient by doing your best to follow their requests.

I'm Standing in the Corner
by Jack Prelutsky

I'm standing in the corner,
my mom is mad at me,
I'll bet that it's the bubble gum
still stuck to the TV,
or maybe she remembers
that I woke her with my drum,
or could it be the orangeade
in the aquarium?
I wonder if she's angry

that I took apart the phone,
or possibly because of where
she found that ice cream cone.
Maybe it's those vegetables
I hid beneath my bed,
more likely it's a certain word
I accidentally said.
Perhaps I'm being punished
for buttering that bug,
or for the tube of toothpaste
I squeezed out on the rug.
It's probably because I tied
my brother to a tree . . .
I'm standing in the corner,
my mom is mad at me.

When your parents or caregivers have to discipline you, it's because they love you and want you to learn something important. Being part of a family involves learning to consider others. As you become more considerate, your character grows stronger — and you bring peace to your family, friends, and, eventually, the people you will work with.

A GOOD BOY
by Robert Louis Stevenson

I woke before the morning, I was happy all the day,
I never said an ugly word, but smiled and stuck to play.

And now at last the sun is going down behind the wood,
And I am very happy, for I know that I've been good.

My bed is waiting cool and fresh, with linen smooth and fair,
And I must off to sleepsin-by, and not forget my prayer.

I know that, till tomorrow I shall see the sun arise,
No ugly dream shall fright my mind, no ugly sight my eyes,

But slumber hold me tightly till I waken in the dawn,
And hear the thrushes singing in the lilacs round the lawn.

2.
Helping Out at Home

WHY DO I HAVE TO CLEAN MY ROOM?
by Jack Prelutsky

Why do I have to clean my room
when I would rather play?
The crayons scattered on the floor
are hardly in the way.
I almost never trip upon
my basketball or drums,
and I don't pay attention
to the cake and cookie crumbs.
Why do I have to clean my room?
I think my room looks nice.
There's pizza in the corner,
but it's only half a slice.
I'm not at all concerned about
the gravy on the chair,
my piles of model planes and trains,
my stacks of underwear.
I will admit some bits of clay
are sticking to the wall.
I scarcely even notice them
and do not mind at all.
Beneath my bed there's just a wedge
of last week's apple pie,
and yet I have to clean my room . . .
I simply don't know why.

When you were small your parents did everything for you. Now that you are growing up, it's important to help out. You can learn to do the many little things that will prevent big messes later on, like putting your toys away, placing your dirty clothes in the laundry basket, and rinsing your own dishes and loading them in the dishwasher.

The bathroom quickly gets out of control if we don't mind the details. You can help by placing the cap on the toothpaste, returning the towel to the rack, and placing tissues in the trash and toilet paper in the toilet — where it belongs!

PUPPY GOOPS
by Gelett Burgess

Candy in the cushions
Of the easy-chair;
Raisins in the sofa —
How did they get there?
The little Goop who's greedy
Does it every day,
Like a little puppy,
Hiding bones away!

SARAH CYNTHIA SYLVIA STOUT
WOULD NOT TAKE THE GARBAGE OUT
by Shel Silverstein

Sarah Cynthia Sylvia Stout
Would not take the garbage out!
She'd scour the pots and scrape the pans.
Candy the yams and spice the hams.
And though her daddy would scream and shout,
She simply would not take the garbage out.
And so it piled up to the ceilings:
Coffee grounds, potato peelings,
Brown bananas, rotten peas,
Chunks of sour cottage cheese.
It filled the can, it covered the floor,
It cracked the window and blocked the door
With bacon rinds and chicken bones,
Drippy ends of ice cream cones,
Prune pits, peach pits, orange peel,
Gloppy glumps of cold oatmeal,
Pizza crusts and withered greens,
Soggy beans and tangerines,
Crusts of black burned buttered toast,
Gristly bits of beefy roasts . . .
The garbage rolled on down the hall,
It raised the roof, it broke the wall . . .
Orange-colored variety of sweet potatos
Greasy napkins, cookie crumbs,
Globs of gooey bubblegum,
Cellophane from green baloney,
Rubbery blubbery macaroni,
Peanut butter, caked and dry,
Curdled milk and crusts of pie,
Moldy melons, dried up mustard.
Eggshells mixed with lemon custard,
Cold french fries and rancid meat,
Yellow lumps of Cream of Wheat.
At last the garbage reached so high
That finally it touched the sky.

And all the neighbors moved away,
And none of her friends would come to play.
And finally Sarah Cynthia Stout said,
"OK, I'll take the garbage out!"
But then, of course, it was too late
The garbage reached across the state.
From New York to the Golden Gate
And there, in the garbage she did hate,
Poor Sarah met an awful fate.
That I cannot right now relate
Because the hour is much too late.
But children, remember Sarah Stout
And always take the garbage out!

What is one chore that you absolutely hate to do? Why do you hate it so much? Imagine that you refused to do this chore and nobody else did it either. What would happen? Would the results be humorous? Dangerous?

Sarah Cynthia Sylvia Stout just wasn't willing to take the garbage out. As a result, the garbage took over her home and drove her friends away. When you're asked to do an unpleasant chore, like taking out the garbage or cleaning the bathroom, think of what would happen if you were like Sarah and didn't do it.

TOMORROW
from Days with Frog and Toad
by Arnold Lobel

TOAD WOKE UP. "Drat!" he said. "This house is a mess. I have so much work to do."

Frog looked through the window. "Toad, you are right," said Frog. "It is a mess." Toad pulled the covers over his head. "I will do it tomorrow," said Toad. "Today I will take life easy."

Frog came into the house. "Toad," said Frog, "your pants and jacket are lying on the floor."

"Tomorrow," said Toad from under the covers.

"Your kitchen sink is filled with dirty dishes," said Frog.

"Tomorrow," said Toad.

"There is dust on your chairs."

"Tomorrow," said Toad.

"Your windows need scrubbing," said Frog. "Your plants need watering."

"Tomorrow!" cried Toad. "I will do it all tomorrow!

Toad sat on the edge of his bed. "Blah," said Toad. "I feel down in the dumps."

"Why?" asked Frog.

"I am thinking about tomorrow," said Toad.

"I am thinking about all of the many things that I will have to do."

"Yes," said Frog, "tomorrow will be a very hard day for you."

"But Frog," said Toad, "if I pick up my pants and jacket right now, then I will not have to pick them up tomorrow, will I?"

"No," said Frog. "You will not have to."

Toad picked up his clothes. He put them in the closet.

"Frog," said Toad, "if I wash my dishes right now, then I will not have to wash them tomorrow, will I?"

"No," said Frog. "You will not have to."

Toad washed and dried his dishes. He put them in the cupboard.

> If you would reap praise you must sow the seeds, gentle words and useful deeds.
>
>
>
> BENJAMIN FRANKLIN
> *Poor Richard's Almanac*

"Frog," said Toad, "if I dust my chairs and scrub my windows and water my plants right now, then I will not have to do it tomorrow, will I?"

"No," said Frog. "You will not have to do any of it."

Toad dusted his chairs. He scrubbed his windows. He watered his plants.

"There," said Toad. "Now I feel better. I am not in the dumps anymore."

"Why?" asked Frog.

"Because I have done all that work," said Toad. "Now I can save tomorrow for something that I really want to do."

"What is that?" asked Frog.

"Tomorrow," said Toad, "I can just take life easy."

Toad went back to bed. He pulled the covers over his head and fell asleep.

Once you actually start your chores, you'll often be surprised at how quickly you finish. Remember what Toad learned: if you do just a little each day to keep your room neat and tidy, you can save tomorrow for something you really want to do!

MR. NOBODY
author unknown

I know a funny little man,
As quiet as a mouse.
He does the mischief that is done
In everybody's house.
Though no one ever sees his face,
Yet one and all agree
That every plate we break was cracked
By Mr. Nobody.

'Tis he who always tears our books,
Who leaves the door ajar.
He picks the buttons from our shirts,
And scatters pins afar.
That squeaking door will always squeak —
For prithee, don't you see?
We leave the oiling to be done
By Mr. Nobody.

He puts damp wood upon the fire,
That kettles will not boil.
His are the feet that bring in mud
And all the carpets soil.

The papers that so oft are lost —
Who had them last but he?
There's no one tosses them about
But Mr. Nobody.

The fingermarks upon the door
By none of us were made.
We never leave the blinds unclosed
To let the curtains fade.
The ink we never spill! The boots
That lying 'round you see,
Are not our boots — they all belong
To Mr. Nobody.

Just as your parents do so much for you each day, you can respond by doing loving things for your parents. One of the best ways to express your love for your parents is through your actions. Even the smallest thoughtful act — like picking flowers for your mother — will demonstrate your love. Remember what Ralph Waldo Emerson said: "Good manners are made up of small sacrifices."

AMELIA BEDELIA
by Peggy Parish

"OH, AMELIA BEDELIA, your first day of work, and I can't be here. But I made a list for you. You do just what the list says," said Mrs. Rogers.

Mrs. Rogers got into the car with Mr. Rogers.

They drove away.

"My, what nice folks. I'm going to like working here," said Amelia Bedelia.

Amelia Bedelia went inside. "Such a grand house. These must be rich folks. But I must get to work. Here I stand just looking. And me with a whole list of things to do."

Amelia Bedelia stood there a minute longer. "I think I'll make a surprise for them. I'll make lemon-meringue pie. I do make good pies."

So Amelia Bedelia went into the kitchen. She put a little of this and a pinch of that into a bowl. She mixed and she rolled. Soon her pie was ready to go into the oven.

"There," said Amelia Bedelia. She looked at the list again.

Dust the furniture.

"Did you ever hear tell of such a silly thing. At my house we undust the furniture. But to each his own way."

Amelia Bedelia took one last look at the bathroom. She saw a big box with the words *Dusting Powder* on it. "Well, look at that. A special powder to dust with!" exclaimed Amelia Bedelia.

So Amelia Bedelia dusted the furniture. "That should be dusty enough. My, how nice it smells."

"There," said Amelia Bedelia. "That's done."

"Now let's see what this list says."

Amelia Bedelia read,

Change the towels in the green bathroom.

Amelia Bedelia found the green bathroom. "Those towels are very nice. Why change them?" she thought.

Then Amelia Bedelia remembered what Mrs. Rogers had said. She must do just what the list told her. "Well, all right," said Amelia Bedelia.

Amelia Bedelia got some scissors. She snipped a little here and a little there. And she changed those towels.

Put the lights out when you finish in the living room.

Amelia Bedelia thought about this a minute. She switched off the lights. Then she carefully unscrewed each bulb.

And Amelia Bedelia put the lights out. So those things need to be aired out, too. "Just like pillows and babies. Oh, I do have a lot to learn."

Draw the drapes when the sun comes in, read Amelia Bedelia. She looked up. The sun was coming in.

Amelia Bedelia looked at the list again. "Draw the drapes? That's what it says. I'm not much of a hand at drawing, but I'll try."

So Amelia Bedelia sat right down and she drew those drapes.

Amelia Bedelia marked off about the drapes.

"Now what?"

"My pie!" exclaimed Amelia Bedelia. She hurried to the kitchen.

"Just right," she said. She took the pie out of the oven and put it on the table to cool. Then she looked at the list.

The meat market will deliver a steak and a chicken.

Please trim the fat before you put the steak in the icebox.

And please dress the chicken.

"Now I must dress the chicken. I wonder if she wants a he chicken or a she chicken?" said Amelia Bedelia.

Amelia Bedelia went right to work. Soon the chicken was finished.

When the meat arrived, Amelia Bedelia opened the bag. She looked at the steak a long time. "Yes," she said. "That will do nicely."

Amelia Bedelia got some lace and bits of ribbon. And Amelia Bedelia trimmed that fat before she put the steak in the icebox.

Amelia Bedelia heard the door open. "The folks are back," she said. She rushed out to meet them.

"Amelia Bedelia, why are all the light bulbs outside?" asked Mr. Rogers.

"The list just said to put the lights out," said Amelia Bedelia. "It didn't say to bring them back in. Oh, I do hope they didn't get aired too long."

Mrs. Rogers dashed into the bathroom. "Oh, my best towels," she said.

"Didn't I change them enough?" asked Amelia Bedelia.

"Amelia Bedelia, the sun will fade the furniture. I asked you to draw the drapes," said Mrs. Rogers.

"I did! I did! See," said Amelia Bedelia. She held up her picture.

Then Mrs. Rogers saw the furniture. "The furniture!" she cried.

"Did I dust it well enough?" asked Amelia Bedelia. "That's such nice dusting powder."

Mr. Rogers went to wash his hands. "I say," he called. "These are very unusual towels."

Mrs. Rogers dashed into the bathroom. "Oh, my best towels," she said.

"Didn't I change them enough?" asked Amelia Bedelia.

Mrs. Rogers went to the kitchen. "I'll cook the dinner. Where is the rice I asked you to measure?"

"I put it back in the container. But I remember — it measured four and a half inches," said Amelia Bedelia.

"Was the meat delivered?" asked Mrs. Rogers.

"Yes," said Amelia Bedelia. "I trimmed the fat just like you said. It does look nice."

Mrs. Rogers rushed to the icebox. She opened it. "Lace! Ribbons! Oh, dear!" said Mrs. Rogers.

The chicken — you dressed the chicken?" asked Mrs. Rogers.

> The noblest question in the world is, What good may I do in it?
>
> ❧
>
> BENJAMIN FRANKLIN
> *Poor Richard's Almanac*

"Yes, and I found the nicest box to put him in," said Amelia Bedelia.

"Box!" exclaimed Mrs. Rogers.

Mrs. Rogers hurried over to the box. She lifted the lid. There lay the chicken. And he was just as dressed as he could be.

Mrs. Rogers was angry. She was very angry. She opened her mouth. Mrs. Rogers meant to tell Amelia Bedelia she was fired. But before she could get the words out, Mr. Rogers put something in her mouth. It was so good Mrs. Rogers forgot about being angry. "Lemon-meringue pie!" she exclaimed.

"I made it to surprise you," said Amelia Bedelia happily.

So right then and there Mr. and Mrs. Rogers decided that Amelia Bedelia must stay. And so she did.

Mrs. Rogers learned to say undust the furniture, unlight the lights, close the drapes, and things like that.

Mr. Rogers didn't care if Amelia Bedelia trimmed all of his steaks with lace.

All he cared about was having her there to make lemon-meringue pie.

Amelia Bedelia had good intentions, but it's always best to ask for help if the directions aren't clear. When your parents ask you to do something, make sure you understand exactly what they want before you begin.

You can follow Amelia Bedelia's kind-hearted example by doing something extra, beyond what your parents ask you to do. Give them a hug, or ask your grandma to help you make them a lemon-meringue pie. They will be delighted, just as Mr. Rogers was.

3.
Loving Your Family

THE LOVING BROTHERS
by Mother Goose

I love you well, my little brother,
And you are fond of me;
Let us be kind to one another,
As brothers ought to be.
You shall learn to play with me,
And learn to use my toys;
And then I think that we shall be
Two happy little boys.

Brothers and sisters are a blessing to each other. You will have many different friends come and go through your life, but the one constant will be your family. You are walking through life together, so take care of each other and make it a pleasant journey.

BORROWING
by Gelett Burgess

Whose doll is that on the table?
    Whose book is that on the chair?
The knife and the pencils and other utensils,
    Now how do they come to be there?

Didn't you say they were borrowed?
    You'd better take back just a few!
If you lent your playthings, I think you would say things
    If no one returned them to you!

When you and your siblings are playing together, it's important to share. And when you finish using what you borrow, return it to your brother or sister. When you're done playing, don't forget to put your toys away. Family life improves when everyone is kind to each other.

LOVE BETWEEN BROTHERS AND SISTERS
by Isaac Watts

Whatever brawls disturb the street,
    There should be peace at home;
Where sisters dwell, and brothers meet,
    Quarrels should never come.

Birds in their little nests agree;
    And 'tis a shameful sight,
When children of one family
    Fall out and chide and fight.

Hard names at first, and threat'ning words
    That are but noisy breath
May grow to clubs and naked swords,
    To murder and to death.

The devil tempts one mother's son
    To rage against another;
So wicked Cain was hurried on
    Till he had killed his brother.

The wise will make their anger cool,
    At least before 'tis night;
But in the bosom of a fool
    It burns till morning-light.

Pardon, O Lord, our childish rage,
    Our little brawls remove,
That as we grow to riper age
    Our hearts may all be love.

Even when you argue with your siblings, try to work things out and forgive one another. It takes strength and courage to control your temper and forgive. But the more you practice these things, the easier they become.

A True Story about a Girl
by Sara Cone Bryant

ONCE THERE WERE FOUR LITTLE GIRLS who lived in a big, bare house in the country. They were very poor, but they had the happiest times you ever heard of, because they were very rich in everything but money. They had a wonderful, wise father who knew the best stories to tell, and who taught them their lessons in such a beautiful way that it was better than play. Their mother was lovely, merry, and kind;

she was never too tired to help them work or to watch them play. They had all the great green country to play in — dark, shadowy woods, fields of flowers, a river, and a big barn.

One of the little girls was named Louisa. She was very pretty, and ever so strong; she could run for miles through the woods and not get tired. And she had a splendid brain in her little head; it liked study, and it contemplated interesting thoughts all day long.

All the little girls kept diaries. Louisa liked to sit in a corner by herself sometimes, and to write thoughts down in hers. She liked to make up stories out of her own head, and sometimes she composed verses.

When the four little sisters had finished their lessons, and had helped their mother sew and clean, they used to go to the big barn to play. Their favorite play of all was theatricals. Louisa especially liked theatricals better than anything.

> Be kind and compassionate to one another, forgiving each other, just as in Christ God forgave you.
>
>
>
> EPHESIANS 4:32

They made the barn into a theater, and the grown people came to see the plays they acted. They used to climb up on the hay-mow for a stage, and the grown people sat in chairs on the floor. It was great fun. One of the plays they acted was Jack and the Beanstalk. They had a ladder from the floor to the loft, and on the ladder they tied a squash vine all the way up to the loft, to look like the wonderful beanstalk. One of the little girls was dressed up to look like Jack, and she acted that part. When it came to the place in the story where the giant tried to follow Jack, the little girl cut down the beanstalk. Down came the giant tumbling from the loft! The giant was made out of pillows, with a great, fierce head of paper, and funny clothes.

Another story that they acted out was Cinderella. They made a wonderful big pumpkin out of their wheelbarrow, and trimmed it with yellow paper. Cinderella rolled away in it when the fairy godmother waved her wand.

There is one other beautiful story they used to play. It was the story of Pilgrim's Progress. If you have never heard it, you must be sure to read it as soon as you are able to understand the old-fashioned words. The little girls used to put shells in their hats as a sign that they were on a pilgrimage, as the old pilgrims used to do. Then they made journeys over the hill behind the house, and through the woods, and down the lanes; and when the pilgrimage was over they had apples and nuts to eat in the happy land of home.

Louisa loved all these plays, and she created some of her own and wrote them down so that the children could act them out.

But more than fun or writing, Louisa loved her mother, and by and by, as the little girl began to grow into a big girl, she felt very sad to see her mother work so hard. Louisa helped all that she could with the housework, but what her mother really needed was money — for food and clothes, and to pay someone grown up to help in the house.

But there never was enough money for these things, so Louisa's mother grew more and more weary, and sometimes ill. I cannot tell you how much Louisa suffered over this.

The more Louisa thought about it, the more she realized that she cared more about helping her family than anything else in all the world. So she began to work very hard to earn money. She sewed for people, and when she was a little older she taught some little girls their lessons, and then she wrote stories for the papers. Every bit of extra money she earned, she gave to her family. It helped very much, but to Louisa it was so little that she never felt as if she were doing enough.

Every year she grew more unselfish, and every year she worked harder. She liked writing stories best of all that she did, but she did not get much money for them, and some people told her that she was wasting her time.

At last, one day, a publisher asked Louisa, who was now a woman, to write a book for girls. Louisa was not feeling very well, and she was very tired. But whenever she had a chance to work, she always said, "I'll try." So she said, "I'll try," to the publisher.

When she thought about what to write in the book, she remembered the good times she used to have with her sisters in the big, bare house in the country. So she wrote a story with all that in it. She put her dear mother and her wise father in, and all the little sisters, and besides the jolly times and the plays, she put the sad, hard times in — the work and worry and going without things.

When the book was written, she called it *Little Women*, and sent it to the publisher.

The book made Louisa famous! It was so sweet and funny and sad and real, like our own lives, that everybody wanted to read it. Everybody bought it, and much money came from it. After so many years, little Louisa's wish came true: she bought a nice house for her family; she sent one of her sisters to Europe to study; she gave her father books; but best of all, she was able to see to it that her mother, so tired and ill, could have rest and happiness. Never again did her dear mother have to do any hard work, and she had pretty things about her all the rest of her life.

Louisa Alcott, for that was Louisa's name, wrote many beautiful books after this, and she became one of the most famous women in America. But I think the most beautiful thing about her is what I have been telling you: that she loved her family so well that she gave her whole life to make them happy.

Unselfishness is a most important quality in a kind, well-mannered person. An unselfish person acts with consideration for the welfare of others — especially family members. Thoughtful actions are a sign of maturity. Louisa Alcott offers us an example of graceful, selfless living.

THE FAMILY
from Pope John Paul II

IN THE FAMILY . . . husband and wife, adults and children, brothers and sisters accept one another as God's gift and give each other the life and love of God. In the family the healthy and sick stand by each other. Young and old speak up for one another. They try to solve problems together. . . . Lastly, the family is also the place where everyone can experience mutual forgiveness in an atmosphere of love.

Family life is enhanced by mutual kindness. It is not only the big things, but rather the little things that you do — the kind word, the sweet smile, the sharing of your toys — that make your family strong.

4.
Loving Your Home

THE BLUE BOWL
by Blanche Bane Kuder

All day I did the little things,
The little things that do not show;
I brought the kindling for the fire
I set the candles in a row,
I filled a bowl with marigolds,
The shallow bowl you love the best —
And made the house a pleasant place
Where weariness might take its rest.

The hours sped on, my eager feet
Could not keep pace with my desire.
So much to do, so little time!
I could not let my body tire;
Yet, when the coming of the night
Blotted the garden from my sight,
And on the narrow, graveled walks
Between the guarding flower stalks
I heard your step: I was not through
With services I meant for you.

You came into the quiet room
That glowed enchanted with the bloom
Of yellow flame. I saw your face,
Illumined by the firelit space,
Slowly grow still and comforted —
"It's good to be at home," you said.

THE COUNTRY MOUSE AND THE CITY MOUSE
by Aesop, retold by Karen Santorum

THERE WERE ONCE two mice that, despite their differences, were good friends. One mouse lived in the country and the other in the city. Both of them were getting tired of their homes and surroundings and found themselves complaining quite a bit. The city mouse was tired of all the noise and excitement of the city. On the other hand, the country

mouse wished for a greater variety of food than what the countryside had to offer, and he had grown bored with the quiet and slow-paced life of the country.

Thinking he could not take another day of the busy city life, the city mouse went to the country to visit his friend. The country mouse was overjoyed to see him. He immediately prepared a feast of wild berries, sweet plums, corn, barley, and wheat. The two mice sat in the peaceful quiet of the field just outside of the country mouse's home. The city mouse enjoyed the fresh air, the sun, and the gentle breeze. He said that he had never tasted food so fresh and sweet. However, after relaxing for awhile, the city mouse began to miss his assortment of cheeses and the clamoring of dishes in the kitchen of the house where he lived.

So he invited the country mouse to come to stay with him in the city. "Oh, you would not believe what I get to eat everyday," said the city mouse. "I feast daily on the finest cheeses, cakes, honey, nuts, fresh figs, and apples. And since I live in a house, I never have to worry about the wind or the rain."

Upon hearing what the city mouse had to offer, the country mouse became convinced that life in the city was much better than life in the country. So they began their travels immediately. The country mouse was excited to taste the fancy food and experience the good life of the city.

But as they approached the city, the country mouse grew very frightened. The streets were crowded, with heavy horseshoes hitting the ground, carriage wheels bumping along, and huge feet wearing heavy boots and high-heeled shoes. It was enough to make any small creature want to run and hide, for fear that they would perish simply by crossing the street!

The country mouse was relieved when they made it safely to the city mouse's home. It was quite cozy there, in a hole behind the kitchen wall. Instead of straw for a bed, the city mouse had soft, cottony pieces of fabric on which to rest.

"Isn't this great!" said the city mouse. "I couldn't ask for a better home. It's warm and near the food."

The country mouse found himself wishing that this was his home, too, for it was far better than what he had. "What's that wonderful smell?" he asked, his mouth beginning to water.

"Come and I'll show you," said the city mouse. So the two squeezed through the small board that led into the kitchen and scampered up onto the countertop. There they saw the most beautiful sight for a mouse. It was a large piece of delicious-smelling cheese.

They immediately began to nibble at the edges, enjoying every bite, but before long someone came through the kitchen door and right up to the countertop. Off they scurried and hid.

When all was quiet, the two mice ran back into the kitchen, but on their way to the cheese on the countertop, they stopped for a feast on the table. There the country and city mouse each sampled warm bread, fresh figs, and sweet cakes made with cherries. But before they could fill themselves, someone else came into the kitchen, so they had to run and hide again. Not only that, but on their way back to the city mouse's hole, the house cat chased them. It had large claws and looked hungry and fierce. The country mouse could hear his heart beating — he had never been so frightened!

The cat chased them all the way to a small opening in the wall, where they managed to hide. After pawing at the wall for a while, the cat fell asleep and blocked the opening where the two mice had taken refuge.

The cat slept for what seemed like hours. The country mouse longed for his quiet home in the country. He thought about his peaceful meals where he could eat uninterrupted until he was full and not have to risk his life for a bite to eat. He longed to see the moon at night and to feel the cool breeze as it gently moved the fur on his back.

The cat finally woke up. He left his spot, as he knew he could not get into the hideaway where the two mice sat.

The country mouse said, "You can have the city life and all that comes with it. As for me, I prefer my home in the country." So off he ran, and he didn't stop until he reached his cozy home at the bottom of the big oak tree in the country.

Both mice lived happily ever after, for now they both knew that *there's no place like home.*

A PRAYER FOR A LITTLE HOME
by Florence Bone

God send us a little home,
To come back to when we roam.

Low walls and fluted tiles,
Wide windows, a view for miles.

Red firelight and deep chairs,
Small white beds upstairs —

Great talk in little nooks,
Dim colors, rows of books.

One picture on each wall,
Not many things at all.

God send us a little ground,
Tall trees standing round.

Homely flowers in brown sod,
Overhead, thy stars, O God.

God bless thee, when winds blow,
Our home, and all we know.

THE CANDLES
by Hans Christian Andersen

THERE ONCE WAS A BIG WAX CANDLE that knew who it was. "I am made of wax and have been cast, not dipped," it said. "My light is clearer and I burn longer than other candles. I belong in a chandelier or a silver candlestick."

"That must be lovely," said a tallow candle. "I am only made from tallow, but I have been dipped eight times and have a decent-sized waistline; some tallow candles are only dipped twice. I am satisfied! Though I admit it is better to be born in wax than in tallow; but you cannot decide yourself how and where to be born. Wax candles are put in the living room and I have to stay in the kitchen, but that is a good place too, all the food for the whole house is made there."

"There is something more important than food," said the wax candle, "and that is social life. To shine while others shine. There is going to be a ball tonight, any moment they will come for me and my whole family."

> Like a bird that strays from its nest is a man who strays from his home.
>
>
>
> PROVERBS 27:8

Hardly had this been said when the lady of the house came to get the wax candles, but she took the little tallow candle too. She brought it out into the kitchen. There stood a little boy with a basket on his arm; it was filled with potatoes, and a few apples had been put in it, too. All this the kind mistress had given to the poor boy. "Here, my little friend," she said, and she put the tallow candle into his basket. "I know that your mother often works so late into the night." Her little daughter, who was standing nearby, smiled when she heard her mother say "so late into the night."

"We are going to have a party, a ball, and my dress has red bows on it, and I will be allowed to be up, so late into the night," she said joyfully. Her eyes sparkled with expectation, she was so happy. No wax candles can shine like the eyes of a child.

"That was a blessed sight," thought the tallow candle. "I shall never forget it, nor am I likely ever to see such happiness again."

The boy went on his way and the tallow candle went with him.

"I wonder where I am going," it thought. "Probably to people so poor that they don't even have a brass candlestick; while the wax candle sits in silver and is in the finest company. Well, it was my lot to be tallow and not wax."

And the tallow candle was brought to a poor home where a widow lived with her three children. From their rooms, with their low ceilings and narrow windows, one could look across the street into the great house.

"God bless her who gave you this," said the boy's mother when she saw the candle. "It will burn late into the night."

And the candle was lit. "Phew!" it said. "Those sulphur matches smell awful. I am sure they don't dare light the wax candle with such things."

In the rich house also the candles were lit. From the windows their light fell out into the street. Coaches rumbled along the cobblestones as they arrived, bringing the elegantly dressed guests, and soon music could be heard.

"Now the ball is starting," thought the tallow candle, and recalled the little rich girl and how her eyes had sparkled even brighter than wax candles. "I shall never see eyes like those again."

The youngest of the poor woman's children was a girl, too. She put her arms around her brother and sister and whispered to them, "We are going to have hot potatoes for dinner." Her eyes looked bright and happy too, just as happy as the little girl's across the street had looked when she said, "We are going to have a ball tonight, and my dress has red bows on it."

"I wonder," thought the tallow candle, "whether to get hot potatoes for dinner is as good. The two little ones seem equally pleased." The tallow candle sneezed; that is to say, it sputtered, for a tallow candle can't do much to express itself.

The table was set. The potatoes were eaten. How good they tasted!

And then there were apples for dessert. The youngest child recited,

"Dear God, thanks to Your will, I once more my stomach did fill. Amen."

"Did I say it nicely?" the girl asked her mother.

The mother smiled and shook her head. "That you mustn't ask or think about. What is important is to be thankful to God for what He does for us."

The children were put to bed and each given a kiss, and they fell right to sleep. The mother stayed up and sewed late into the night. She had to earn a living for herself and her children. Over in the house of the rich the candles were still burning and the music played. Above in the sky the stars shone, and they shone as brightly on the poor home as on the rich one.

"That was a nice evening," thought the tallow candle. "I wonder if the wax candle has had a better time in the silver candlesticks? That is a question I would like to have answered before I am burned out." Then it thought of the two equally happy faces: one shining in the light of a wax candle and the other in the light of a tallow one.

Well, that is really the end of the story, there is no more, just as there is no more left of either the wax or the tallow candle.

The big wax candle thought it was important to live in a grand home in a silver candlestick. The tallow candle wished it could be important too, like the wax candle. But the tallow candle came to learn that it was just as important to light up nights for the poor family, who had to work hard into the wee hours of the morning. The tallow candle saw the poor children who were full of appreciation for the few things they had. And it realized that even though it wasn't living in a silver candlestick in a grand ballroom, it was content.

Are you happy right where you are? Or do you envy people whose houses and toys seem more fancy and fun than yours? Always remember that the best possession of all is contentment with what you have been given.

Home Is Where There Is One to Love Us
by Charles Swain

Home's not merely four square walls,
Though with pictures hung and gilded;
Home is where Affection calls —
Filled with shrines the Hearth had builded!
Home! Go watch the faithful dove,
Sailing 'neath the heaven above us.
Home is where there's one to love!
Home is where there's one to love us!

Home's not merely roof and room,
It needs something to endear it;
Home is where the heart can bloom,
Where there's some kind lip to cheer it!
What is home with none to meet,
None to welcome, none to greet us?
Home is sweet, and only sweet,
Where there's one we love to meet us!

Our homes provide a cozy place away from the world where we love and are loved. It's fun to be out with our friends playing and going places, but at the end of the day it's always good to come home.

GOD IS THE MAKER OF THE WORLD
by Ralph Waldo Emerson

For flowers that bloom about our feet,
Father, we thank thee.
For tender grass so fresh, so sweet,
Father, we thank thee.
For song of bird and hum of bee,
For all things fair we hear or see,
Father in heaven, we thank thee.

For blue of stream and blue of sky,
Father, we thank thee.
For pleasant shade of branches high,
Father, we thank thee.
For fragrant air and cooling breeze,
For the beauty of the blooming trees,
Father in heaven, we thank thee.

For this new morning with its light,
Father, we thank thee.
For rest and shelter of the night,
Father, we thank thee.
For health and food, for love and friends,
For everything thy goodness sends,
Father in heaven, we thank thee.

An important part of being a well-mannered child is noticing and appreciating everything you have been given. We should take nothing for granted; rather, we should express our deepest gratitude for the beautiful things that surround us.

CHAPTER TWO

Using Words Wisely

1.
Please, Thank You, and Other Kind Words

THE QUEEN'S DECISION
by the Rev. John Todd, retold by Karen Santorum

ONCE UPON A TIME, long ago, the queen of language sent forth a proclamation that a contest would be held for the children in her kingdom. The goal of this contest was to find the sweetest word in the language. To do this, children would be permitted to use the queen's trusty servants: the twenty-six letters of the alphabet. The child who formed the sweetest word would be seated next to the queen, receive a crown of gold, and wear the royal cloak.

Far and wide the alphabet servants sent the proclamation, and many children began to contemplate what word they would form. Everyone kept silent but looked wise, as if to say, "I know something, but I will not tell."

Finally, the day arrived; there waited the queen, the gold crown, and the royal cloak. Her alphabet servants were seated with all the children. Who would find the world's most beautiful word? The queen told them all to carefully write their word on a piece of paper, fold it up, and place it in a special box. She would then draw the papers out one by one, read the words aloud, and call upon their writers to stand up to be questioned. She would then decide upon the merits of each.

So she drew all the children close around her. All were hushed and silent as she put her hand in the box and drew out a paper. Upon opening it, she read aloud, "money." The alphabet servants lined up to spell it, so that everyone could see what the word looked like. Upon seeing the word, the children in the crowd gave a longing sigh.

"Whose is this?" asked the queen.

"It is mine," said an older, well-dressed boy in a loud voice.

"Why do you think this is the sweetest word in the human language?" she asked.

"Because, madam, money is what we all want, what we all work for, and what we all rejoice over. It will buy anything: brightly painted wooden toys, soft stuffed toys, musical toys, wind-up toys, big toys, and little toys. Money will buy fancy cars, trucks that go, candies from all over the world, and ice cream, too. And money will allow me to do whatever I want. With it I can go across the ocean on big ships, visit the circus, and ride on trains. It is the sweetest word ever spoken."

"I beg to differ with you, son." The queen looked intently at him. "You mistreat the meaning of the word 'money.' You say money will do anything and can buy anything; but is that truly so? Will it buy goodness, or strength of character? Will it give you courage or make you kind to others? Will it fill your heart with grace and make you pleasant to be around?

"No, he is a selfish person who thinks only of gaining material things — of buying more and more. For how many times has fortune smiled upon a person, but they have come to no good because they lacked kindness in their hearts? And how many times have people fallen into ruin and been destroyed because they built their life on things bought, instead of paying attention to what was inside of them? It is anything but the sweetest word."

Again she drew from the box. The word was read with great anticipation: "Happy." Upon hearing this, the members of the queen's alphabet beamed with smiles and lined up cheerily for all to see.

"Whose may this be?" asked the queen.

"Mine, madam," said a young girl, her face glowing with excitement.

"And your reasons, Lass?"

"Because that's what my Mother and Father always tell me they want me to be."

"Oh . . . I see," sighed the queen. She set down the piece of paper. "I'm sure your parents mean well. If your happiness is gained through service to others and in living your life in a way that is pleasing to God, then it is a noble thing. However, happiness is not an end in itself; but you will notice that many people treat it as such. The search for happiness as an ultimate good appeals to, and cultivates, supreme selfishness in the heart. It shuts out affections, tramples on the most sacred rights of others, and often fills families with great pain. I cannot allow you the reward."

She then put her hand again into the box and drew out a paper, on which was written the word "Honor." The queen's alphabet proudly formed the new word for everyone to see.

"Who claims this?"

"I do," said a fine-looking young boy, dressed in splendid military garments.

"And what is your plea for your favorite word?" asked the queen.

"Why, madam, it seems to me too plain for argument. The brave boy on the playground, the sailor risking his life on the stormy ocean, the officer saving a young child's life, and the soldier fighting for our country — all are witnesses that *honor* is the word, above all others, that is the sweetest to the human ear."

> Pleasant words are a honeycomb, sweet to the soul and healing to the bones.
>
>
>
> PROVERBS 16:24

"A strong plea, certainly," said the queen. "Honor is a worthy virtue, but I must have time to think further upon it before I decide."

Again the fair hand of the queen drew from the box, and the word was read very quietly: "Please." The alphabet servants did not hear the queen so they did not stand up, and most of the children did not know what word was being considered.

"Whose is this?" said the queen in a low, soft tone.

"I wrote it," said a sweet little girl, almost sinking under the eyes that were turned upon her in utmost curiosity. "And madam queen, there is another phrase that goes hand in hand with 'please' and that is 'thank you,'" she said, ever so softly.

"And can you, my child, tell me the reasons why you think 'please' and 'thank you' are the sweetest words in the world?"

"No, I only feel so, madam."

There was a full pause of silence in the conversation between the queen and the little girl. And smiling, with tears in her eyes, the queen said, "Truly, little one, you feel right."

All the children in the crowd were wondering what word could have possibly moved the queen so. Upon noticing that all of her alphabet servants were seated, the queen asked them, "Please spell the words 'please' and 'thank you,' so that everyone can see."

When the children saw the words, they all smiled — like the sweet little girl, they could instinctively feel the rightness of these words, and they knew they were what the queen was looking for.

The queen stood. "There is no quality in a child or grownup, no beauty of character, no form of kindness, nothing refined, gentle, loving, or good, which is not found in the words 'please' and 'thank you.' For these words bring out the gentleness in a person and show true kindness within a person's heart. These words are truly selfless. They are music to a parent's ears, they help children to play well together, and they convey a deep respect for others. These words initiate polite and kind conversation among people, and encourage peace within communities. There is no language on earth in which 'please' and 'thank you' are not used.

"These *are* the sweetest words on earth. You are a wise child, my dear, for you understand that people appreciate kindness. You know also that kindness begets kindness. Come, little child, wear this red velvet cloak, sit by my side, and receive this golden crown."

Do you know why everyone calls "please" and "thank you" the "magic words"? Because when you use them, wonderful things happen!

POLITENESS
by Gelett Burgess

I think it would be lots of fun
To be polite to everyone;
A boy would doff his little hat,
A girl would curtsey, just like that!

And both would use such words as these:
"Excuse me, Sir," and *"If you please,"*
Not only just at home, you know,
But everywhere that they should go.

When someone thanks you, the polite response is "you're welcome." And if you accidentally bump into someone or do something impolite, you should say "excuse me."

PLEASE

by Alicia Aspinwall

THERE WAS ONCE a little word named "Please" that lived in a small boy's mouth. Pleases live in everybody's mouth, though people often forget they are there.

Now, all Pleases, to be kept strong and happy, should be taken out of the mouth very often, so they can get air. They are like little fish in a bowl, you know, that come popping up to the top of the water to breathe.

The Please I am going to tell you about lived in the mouth of a boy named Dick; but only once in a long while did it have a chance to get out. For Dick, I am sorry to say, was a rude little boy; he hardly ever remembered to say "Please."

"Give me some bread! I want some water! Give me that book!" — that is the way he would ask for things.

His father and mother felt very bad about this. And, as for the poor Please itself, it would sit up on the roof of the boy's mouth day after day, hoping for a chance to get out. It was growing weaker and weaker every day.

The slip of the foot you may soon recover, but a slip of the tongue you may never get over.

BENJAMIN FRANKLIN
Poor Richard's Almanac

This boy Dick had a brother, John. Now, John was older than Dick — he was almost ten; and he was just as polite as Dick was rude. So his Please had plenty of fresh air, and was strong and happy.

One day at breakfast, Dick's Please felt that he must have some fresh air, even if he had to run away. So out he ran — out of Dick's mouth — and took a long breath. Then he crept across the table and jumped into John's mouth!

The Please who lived there was very angry.

"Get out!" he cried. "You don't belong here! This is *my* mouth!"

"I know it," replied Dick's Please. "I live over there in that brother mouth. But alas! I am not happy there. I am never used. I never get a breath of fresh air! I thought you might be willing to let me stay here for a day or so — until I felt stronger."

"Why, certainly," said the other Please, kindly. "I understand. Stay, of course; and when my master uses me, we will both go out together. He is kind, and I am sure he would not mind saying 'Please' twice. Stay, as long as you like."

That noon, at dinner, John wanted some butter; and this is what he said:

"Father, will you pass me the butter, please — please?"

"Certainly," said the father. "But why be so very polite?"

John did not answer. He was turning to his mother, and said,

"Mother, will you give me a muffin, please — please?"

His mother laughed.

"You shall have the muffin, dear; but why do you say 'please' twice?"

"I don't know," answered John. "The words seem just to jump out, somehow. Katie, please — please, some water!"

This time, John was almost frightened.

"Well, well," said his father, "there is no harm done. One can't be too 'pleasing' in this world."

All this time little Dick had been calling, "Give me an egg! I want some milk. Give me a spoon!" in the rude way he had. But now he stopped and listened to his brother. He thought it would be fun to try to talk like John; so he began,

"Mother, will you give me a muffin, m–m–m–?"

He was trying to say "please"; but how could he? He never guessed that his own little Please was sitting in John's mouth. So he tried again, and asked for the butter.

"Mother, will you pass me the butter, m–m–m–?"

That was all he could say.

So it went on all day, and everyone wondered what was the matter with those two boys. When night came, they were both so tired, and Dick was so cross, that their mother sent them to bed very early.

But the next morning, no sooner had they sat down to breakfast than Dick's Please ran home again. He had had so much fresh air the day before that now he was feeling quite strong and happy. And the very next moment, he had another airing; for Dick said,

"Father, will you cut my orange, please?" Why! the word slipped out as easily as could be! It sounded just as well as when John said it — John was saying only one "please" this morning. And from that time on, little Dick was just as polite as his brother.

HOW DO YOU ANSWER THE TELEPHONE?
by Karen Santorum

Mouse picks up the telephone and says, "Squeak, Squeak."
The lion, he just says ROAR!
Frog answers the tellie with a croak, "Speak, Speak."
The sleeping bear yawns and SNORES!

Tell me, how do you answer the telephone?
I really would like to know.
The birds tell me to sing and the tiger says to moan.
And Mister Turtle says to talk . . . R–E–A–L . . . S–L–O–W.

I'll talk with Mrs. Owl who knows everything,
She answers her phone, "WHOOOO'S there?"
The black crow says, "A CALL, A CALL," when his phone rings.
"Just wiggle your nose," says the Hare.

But I think Polly Parrot has got it right.
She says, "Hello, this is Polly."
Of all the things I've heard, this sounds most polite.
So I'll just say, "Hello, this is Wally."

It's important to speak politely when answering the telephone. You might answer by saying, "Hello, this is the Smith residence." Or, "Hello, this is the Smith residence, Molly speaking."

Once the caller asks for someone, say, "One minute please." Or, if you need to take a message, say, "They are unavailable right now — may I take a message?" and write down the caller's name and phone number. It's help-ful to keep a pencil and paper near the telephone.

When you make a call, the way to ask for someone is: "May I please speak with Susie?" Or, "Hello, this is Molly — may I please speak with Susie?"

HELLO, HELLO
by Eve Merriam

Hello, hello, who's calling, please?
Mr. Macaroni and a piece of cheese.

Hello, hello, hello, who's there?
Honey Buzzbee and a big brown bear.

Hello, Hello, will you spell your name?
It's R.A.T. and yours is the same.

Hello, hello, what did you say?
The rain is over, let's go out and play.

Being allowed to answer the phone is a sign of maturity. Now that you're old enough to answer the phone, you should be aware of a few things. Most importantly, if you are alone, don't tell strangers that your parents are gone. Another option is to not pick up the phone at all — you can always let the answering machine get it. If a caller ever makes you feel uncomfortable, give the phone to an adult or just hang up.

HE SHOULD HAVE SAID "THANK YOU" — *or* — THE STORY OF ATALANTA AND HIPPOMENES
Greek myth retold by Karen Santorum

IN ANCIENT GREEK MYTHOLOGY, there were few women more attractive than princess Atalanta. She was famous for her rare combination of beauty and athletic talent.

She was so beautiful that almost every young man in Greece wanted to marry her. But that was the last thing she wanted. She wanted only to hunt, to sail the seas, and to compete in sporting events. And no wonder, for she was faster than anyone except Hermes, the speedy messenger of the gods. She was the first to kill a wild boar at the famous Calydonian Boar Hunt.

The more she achieved in sports, the more she was surrounded by young men who wanted to marry her. Eventually, she had no peace anywhere. Men would shower her with gifts and praise night and day. They would even sleep outside of her house just to be the first to ask her to marry them the following day. Finally, she had had enough. She said a prayer and asked the gods to help her devise a plan to stop all these men from bothering her.

The next morning, when her suitors arrived, she proclaimed, "If you want to marry me, you must defeat me in a foot race tomorrow — but if you lose the race, the gods will strike you dead as soon as I cross the finish line."

Now, you would think that would have solved her problem. Yet the very next morning, they were again lined up to ask Atalanta for her hand in marriage.

Many men died that first day. Word spread throughout the land of their terrible fate. Yet, instead of discouraging men from pestering her, Atalanta's challenge only resulted in more and more of Greece's best young men competing for her — and paying with their lives.

After several days, Aphrodite, the goddess of love, became concerned that all of the finest men in Greece would be killed if something were not done soon. So when a very handsome young man named Hippomenes prayed to her for help in winning the race against Atalanta, she sprang into action.

Just before the race started, she appeared to Hippomenes and handed him three golden apples. "When Atalanta gets ahead of you, roll one of these apples out in front of her," she instructed.

During the first part of the race, Hippomenes and Atalanta ran side by side — but it wasn't long before Atalanta took the lead. Out came the first apple, which Hippomenes tossed in front of her.

When she saw this magnificent, radiant golden apple, she slowed down to scoop it up with her right hand. As she did, Hippomenes sped by her. But she was too fast, and caught up with him again as they passed the halfway point in the race.

Again Hippomenes threw an apple, and again Atalanta slowed down and scooped it up, this time with her left hand.

But his lead was still not secured. As the finish line came into sight, she passed him a third time. He pulled out the final apple and rolled it past her on the road.

This time, she had to stop to adjust the two apples she already had so that she could pick up the third. That provided all the time Hippomenes needed. He bolted past her and on to victory!

There was a great celebration as the crowd carried the couple off to the temple to marry. Even Atalanta was joyful that these horrible races had finally come to an end. Hippomenes was a hero and enjoyed all of the lavish attention that was showered upon him.

Everyone was happy except Aphrodite. She waited and watched Hippomenes for hours after the race as the celebration continued, but not once did he pause to thank her for what *she* had done. The more that people praised him, the angrier Aphrodite became.

Finally, the wedding ceremony began. As the couple came to the altar, Aphrodite appeared. "I gave you a gift that not only saved your life, but won you the greatest prize in the land. Could you find not one moment during the time when all were praising you to thank me? You are not worthy of the gift you have been given."

And with those words she turned them both into lions and banished them to serve the gods forever.

Aphrodite was kind to give Hippomenes the golden apples. He could have expressed his appreciation by saying "thank you." Expressing gratitude is important.

The Fairy
from Tales of Mother Goose *by Charles Perrault*
translated by Charles Welsh

Once upon a time there was a widow who had two daughters. The elder was so much like her, both in looks and character, that whoever saw the daughter saw the mother. They were both so disagreeable and so proud that there was no living with them. The younger, who was the very picture of her father for sweetness of temper and virtue, was one of the most beautiful girls ever seen. As people naturally love their own likeness, this mother doted on her elder daughter, and at the same time had a great aversion for the younger. She made her eat in the kitchen and work continually.

Among other things, this unfortunate child had to go twice a day to draw water more than a mile and a half from the house, and bring home a pitcherful of it. One day, as she was at this fountain, there came to her a poor woman, who begged of her to let her drink.

"Oh, yes, with all my heart, Goody," said this pretty little girl. Rinsing the pitcher at once, she took some of the clearest water from the fountain, and gave it to her, holding up the pitcher all the while, that she might drink the easier.

The good woman having drunk, said to her, "You are so pretty, so good and courteous, that I cannot help giving you a gift." For this was a fairy, who had taken the form of a poor countrywoman, to see how far the civility and good manners of this pretty girl would go. "The gift I will give you," continued the Fairy, "is that, at every word you speak, there shall come out of your mouth either a flower or a jewel."

Well done is better than well said.

BENJAMIN FRANKLIN
Poor Richard's Almanac

When this pretty girl returned, her mother scolded at her for staying so long at the fountain. "I beg your pardon, mamma," said the poor girl, "for not making more haste."

And in speaking these words there came out of her mouth two roses, two pearls, and two large diamonds.

"What is it I see there?" said her mother, quite astonished. "I think pearls and diamonds come out of the girl's mouth! How happens this, my child? "

This was the first time she had ever called her "my child."

The girl told her frankly all the matter, not without dropping out great numbers of diamonds.

"Truly," cried the mother, "I must send my own dear child thither. Fanny, look at what comes out of your sister's mouth when she speaks. Would you not be glad, my dear, to have the same gift? You have only to go and draw water out of the fountain, and when a poor woman asks you to let her drink, to give it to her very civilly."

"I should like to see myself going to the fountain to draw water," said this ill-bred minx.

"I insist you shall go," said the mother, "and that instantly."

She went, but grumbled all the way, taking with her the best silver tankard in the house.

She no sooner reached the fountain than she saw coming out of the wood, a magnificently dressed lady, who came up to her, and asked to drink. This was the same fairy who had appeared to her sister, but she had now taken the air and dress of a princess, to see how far this girl's rudeness would go.

"Am I come hither," said the proud, ill-bred girl, "to serve you with water, pray? I suppose this silver tankard was brought purely for your ladyship, was it? However, you may drink out of it, if you have a fancy."

"You are scarcely polite," answered the fairy, without anger. "Well, then, since you are so disobliging, I give you for a gift that at every word you speak there shall come out of your mouth a snake or a toad."

So soon as her mother saw her coming, she cried out —

"Well, daughter?"

"Well, mother?" answered the unhappy girl, throwing out of her mouth a viper and a toad.

" Oh, mercy!" cried the mother, "what is it I see?" It is her sister who has caused all this, but she shall pay for it," and immediately she ran to beat her. The poor child fled away from her, and went to hide herself in the forest near by.

The King's son, who was returning from the chase, met her, and seeing her so beautiful, asked her what she did there alone and why she cried.

"Alas! Sir, my mother has turned me out of doors."

The King's son, who saw five or six pearls and as many diamonds come out of her mouth, desired her to tell him how that happened. She told him the whole story. The King's son fell in love with her, and, considering that such a gift was worth more than any marriage portion another bride could bring, conducted her to the palace of the King, his father, and there married her.

As for her sister, she made herself so much hated that her own mother turned her out of doors. The miserable girl, after wandering about and finding no one to take her in, went to a corner of the wood, and there died.

Kind words and deeds are what politeness is all about, and the two go hand-in-hand. It was courteous for the younger daughter to offer the poor woman a drink, and to offer it in a friendly way. When you have a friend over, it's always nice to offer him or her something to drink. It's also considerate to serve your friend before serving yourself.

POLITENESS
by A. A. Milne

If people ask me
I always tell them,
"Quite well, thank you, I'm very glad to say."
If people ask me

I always answer
"Quite well, thank you, how are you today?"
I always answer,
I always tell them,
If they ask me
Politely. . . .
BUT SOMETIMES

I wish

That they wouldn't.

Even the best of us do not feel like being polite all of the time. Sometimes if we have had a bad day, being polite is not easy. But this is still no excuse for bad manners.

If you smile and are polite even when things are not going well, your positive effort will pay off — you'll start to feel a little calmer and better. Your effort may pay off in other ways, too, as the next story shows.

THE WORTH OF POLITENESS
from a story by Alex M. Gow
adapted by Karen Santorum

LATE ONE SATURDAY AFTERNOON, two ladies were returning home when one of them lost a glove. She remembered that she had none suitable for church the next day, so she proposed turning into Walnut Street to buy a pair. According to a summer rule, the stores closed early; but one door was open. It was a small knickknack store, and at any other time they would not have visited it to buy gloves. But they had no other choice.

A modest young girl was leaving the store just as they entered, and the owner of the store stood ready to lock the door behind her. The young girl was weary after a long, hard day of standing hour upon hour. But when the women asked to see the store's gloves, the young girl still replied kindly, "Please walk with me and I will show you where they are." She showed as much patience and willingness to help as if the work day had just begun, or as if the store had been her own.

The gloves were bought, along with some other little articles that lay in sight on the counter. On receiving the money, the young girl said

"Thank you," as if the favor had been one done to herself instead of her customers.

When the ladies left the store, one of them said to the other, "That's what I call true politeness. Let's go there again when we're out shopping!"

Though they had never been in the store before, after that day they returned again and again. Each time, they were treated with the same polite and patient desire to please. The women then told all their friends about it. In the end, the store gained a multitude of new and happy customers — all because of one girl's politeness.

Good manners take relatively little effort compared to the benefits they reap.

Tell Him So
author unknown

If you hear a kind word spoken
　　Of some worthy soul you know,
It may fill his heart with sunshine
　　If you only tell him so.

If a deed, however humble,
　　Helps you on your way to go,
Seek the one whose hand has helped you,
　　Seek him out and tell him so!

If your heart is touched and tender
　　Toward a sinner, lost and low,
It might help him to do better
　　If you only tell him so!

Oh, my sisters, oh, my brothers,
　　As o'er life's rough path you go,
If God's love has saved and kept you,
　　Do not fail to tell men so!

2.
Taming the Tongue

ANNE OF GREEN GABLES
by Lucy Maud Montgomery

Here's an excerpt from a delightful story about a little girl named Anne Shirley — Anne with an "e" at the end, as she's always quick to declare. Anne is a melodramatic and imaginative girl who is always getting herself into predicaments. She's an orphan who is accidentally sent to live with two elderly people, Marilla and Matthew Cuthbert. The Cuthberts had requested a boy from the orphanage so that they could have help with their farm work — but they found themselves with Anne instead.

Anne so desperately wants to have a real home that she pleads with them to keep her. Matthew loves Anne and wants her to stay, but Marilla needs more convincing. Eventually, due to Matthew's persistence, Marilla reluctantly decides to give Anne a chance. In this scene, Anne is introduced to Marilla's best friend, Mrs. Rachel Lynde — a woman who prides herself on speaking her mind.

CHAPTER 9

ANNE WAS OUT in the orchard when Mrs. Rachel came, wandering at her own sweet will through the lush, tremulous grasses splashed with ruddy evening sunshine; so that good lady had an excellent chance to talk her illness fully over, describing every ache and pulse-beat with such evident enjoyment that Marilla thought even grippe must bring its compensations. When the details were exhausted, Mrs. Rachel introduced the real reason of her call.

"I've been hearing some surprising things about you and Matthew."

"I don't suppose you are any more surprised than I am myself," said Marilla. "I'm getting over my surprise now."

"It was too bad there was such a mistake," said Mrs. Rachel sympathetically. "Couldn't you have sent her back?"

"I suppose we could, but we decided not to. Matthew took a fancy to her. And I must say I like her myself — although I admit she has her faults. The house seems a different place already. She's a real bright little thing."

Marilla said more than she had intended to say when she began, for she read disapproval in Mrs. Rachel's expression.

"It's a great responsibility you've taken on yourself," said that lady gloomily, "especially when you've never had any experience with children. You don't know much about her or her real disposition, I suppose, and there's no guessing how a child like that will turn out. But I don't want to discourage you I'm sure, Marilla."

"I'm not feeling discouraged," was Marilla's dry response. "When I make up my mind to do a thing it stays made up. I suppose you'd like to see Anne. I'll call her in."

Anne came running in presently, her face sparkling with the delight of her orchard rovings; but, abashed at finding herself in the unexpected presence of a stranger, she halted confusedly inside the door. She certainly was an odd-looking little creature in the short tight wincey dress she had worn from the asylum, below which her thin legs seemed ungracefully long. Her freckles were more numerous and obtrusive than ever; the wind had ruffled her hatless hair into over-brilliant disorder; it had never looked redder than at that moment.

"Well, they didn't pick you for your looks, that's sure and certain," was Mrs. Rachel Lynde's empathetic comment. Mrs. Rachel was one of those delightful and popular people who pride themselves on speaking their mind without fear or favour. "She's terrible skinny and homely, Marilla. Come here, child, and let me have a look at you. Lawful heart, did anyone ever see such freckles? And hair as red as carrots! Come here, child, I say."

Anne "came there," but not exactly as Mrs. Rachel expected. With one bound she crossed the kitchen floor and stood before Mrs. Rachel, her face scarlet with anger, her lips quivering, and her whole slender form trembling from head to foot.

"I hate you," she cried in a choked voice, stamping her foot on the floor. "I hate you — I hate you — I hate you —" a louder stamp with each assertion of hatred. "How dare you call me skinny and ugly? How dare you say I'm freckled and redheaded? You are a rude, impolite, unfeeling woman!"

"Anne!" exclaimed Marilla in consternation.

But Anne continued to face Mrs. Rachel undauntedly, head up, eyes blazing, hands clenched, passionate indignation exhaling from her like an atmosphere.

"How dare you say such things about me?" she repeated vehemently. "How would you like to have such things said about you? How would you like to be told that you are fat and clumsy and probably hadn't a spark of imagination in you? I don't care if I do hurt your feelings by saying so! I hope I hurt them. You have hurt mine worse than they were ever hurt before, even by Mrs. Thomas' intoxicated husband. And I'll never forgive you for it, never, never!"

Stamp! Stamp!

"Did anybody ever see such a temper!" exclaimed the horrified Mrs. Rachel.

"Anne, go up to your room and stay there until I come up," said Marilla, recovering her powers of speech with difficulty.

> A gentle answer turns away wrath, but a harsh word stirs up anger.
>
>
>
> PROVERBS 15:1

Anne, bursting into tears, rushed to the hall door, slammed it until the tins on the porch wall outside rattled in sympathy, and fled through the hall and up the stairs like a whirlwind. A subdued slam above told that the door of the east gable had been shut with equal vehemence.

"Well, I don't envy you your job bringing *that* up, Marilla," said Mrs. Rachel with unspeakable solemnity.

Marilla opened her lips to say she knew not what of apology or deprecation. What she did say was a surprise to herself then and ever afterwards.

"You shouldn't have twitted her about her looks, Rachel."

"Marilla Cuthbert, you don't mean to say that you are upholding her in such a terrible display of temper as we've just seen?" demanded Mrs. Rachel indignantly.

"No," said Marilla slowly, "I'm not tring to excuse her. She's been very naughty and I'll have to give her a talking to about it. But we must make allowances for her. She's never been taught what is right. And you were too hard on her, Rachel."

Marilla could not help tacking on that last sentence, although she was again surprised at herself for doing it. Mrs. Rachel got up with an air of offended dignity.

"Well, I see that I'll have to be very careful what I say after this, Marilla, since the fine feelings of orphans, brought from goodness knows where, have to be considered before anything else. On, no, I'm not vexed — don't worry yourself. I'm too sorry for you to leave any room for anger in my mind. You'll have your own troubles with that child. But if you'll take my advice — which I suppose you won't do, although I've brought up ten children and buried two — you'll do that 'talking to' you mention with a fair-sized birch switch. I should think that would be the most effective language for that kind of a child. Her temper matches her hair I guess. Well, good evening, Marilla. I hope you'll come down to see me often as usual. But you can't expect me to visit here again in a hurry, if I'm liable to be flown at and insulted in such a fashion. It's something new in my experience."

Whereat Mrs. Rachel swept out and away — if a fat woman who always waddled could be said to sweep away — and Marilla with a very solemn face betook herself to the east gable.

On the way upstairs she pondered uneasily as to what she ought to do. She felt no little dismay over the scene that had just been enacted. How unfortunate that Anne should have displayed such temper before Mrs. Rachel Lynde, of all people! Then Marilla suddenly became aware of an uncomfortable and rebuking consciousness that she felt more humiliation over this than sorrow over the discovery of such a serious defect in Anne's disposition. And how was she to punish her? The amiable suggestion of the birch switch — to the efficiency of which all of Mrs. Rachel's own children could have borne smarting testimony — did not appeal to Marilla. She did not believe she could whip a child. No, some other method of punishment must be found to bring Anne to a proper realization of the enormity of her offence.

Marilla found Anne face downward on her bed, crying bitterly, quite oblivious of muddy boots on a clean counterpane.

"Anne," she said, not ungently.

No answer.

"Anne," with greater severity, "get off that bed this minute and listen to what I have to say to you."

Anne squirmed off the bed and sat rigidly on a chair beside it, her face swollen and tear-stained and her eyes fixed stubbornly on the floor.

"This is a nice way for you to behave, Anne! Aren't you ashamed of yourself?"

"She hadn't any right to call me ugly and redheaded," retorted Anne, evasive and defiant.

"You hadn't any right to fly into such a fury and talk the way you did to her, Anne. I was ashamed of you — thoroughly ashamed of you. I wanted you to behave nicely to Mrs. Lynde, and instead of that you have disgraced me. I'm sure I don't know why you should lose your temper like that just because Mrs. Lynde said you were redhaired and homely. You say it yourself often enough."

"Oh, but there's such a difference between saying a thing yourself and hearing other people say it," wailed Anne. "You may know a thing is so, but you can't help hoping other people don't quite think it is. I suppose you think I have an awful temper, but I couldn't help it. When she said those things something just rose right up in me and choked me. I had to fly at her."

"Well, you made a fine exhibition of yourself I must say. Mrs. Lynde will have a nice story to tell about you everywhere — and she'll tell it, too. It was a dreadful thing for you to lose your temper like that, Anne."

"Just imagine how you would feel if somebody told you to your face that you were skinny and ugly," pleaded Anne tearfully.

An old remembrance suddenly rose up before Marilla. She had been a very small child when she had heard one aunt say of her to another, "What a pity she is such a dark, homely little thing." Marilla was every day of fifty before the sting had gone out of that memory.

"I don't say that I think Mrs. Lynde was exactly right in saying what she did to you, Anne," she admitted in a softer tone. "Rachel is too outspoken. But that is no excuse for such behavior on your part. She was a stranger and an elderly person and my visitor — all three very good reasons why you should have been respectful to her. You were rude and saucy and" — Marilla had a saving inspiration of punishment — "you must go to her and tell her you are very sorry for your bad temper and ask her to forgive you."

In this exchange, Anne was wrong to lose her temper and say the hurtful things she did. But Mrs. Rachel Lynde was also wrong to have spoken unkindly. Unfortunately, not all adults have good manners, either. There is nothing good about speaking your mind without regard for the person whom you're speaking about. What's noble is the ability to control our tongues and think before we speak.

What should happen after hurtful words have been spoken, by a child or an adult? This next scene is a good example of the answer.

CHAPTER 10

"OH, MRS. LYNDE, I am so extremely sorry," she said with a quiver in her voice. "I could never express all my sorrow, no, not if I used up a whole dictionary. You must just imagine it. I behaved terribly to you and I've disgraced the dear friends, Matthew and Marilla, who have let me stay at Green Gables although I'm not a boy. I'm a dreadfully wicked and ungrateful girl, and I deserve to be punished and cast out by respectable people forever. It was very wicked of me to fly into a temper because you told me the truth. It was the truth; every word you said was true. My hair is red and I'm freckled and skinny and ugly. What I said to you was true, too, but I shouldn't have said it. Oh, Mrs. Lynde, please, please, forgive me. If you refuse, it will be a lifelong sorrow on a poor little orphan girl. Would you inflict such sorrow, even if she had a dreadful temper? Oh, I am sure you wouldn't. Please say you forgive me, Mrs. Lynde."

Anne clasped her hands together, bowed her head, and waited for the word of judgment.

> Reckless words pierce like a sword, but the tongue of the wise brings healing.
>
>
>
> PROVERBS 12:18

When you apologize, ask forgiveness from your heart. You don't have to get down on your knees and make a speech like Anne did! But do look the person in the eyes and speak sincerely.

Another way to apologize is by writing a note. The following is one of the most famous literary apologies, in the form of a poem.

THIS IS JUST TO SAY
by William Carlos Williams

I have eaten
the plums
that were in
the icebox

and which
you were probably
saving
for breakfast

Forgive me
they were delicious
so sweet
and so cold

THE UGLY DUCKLING
by Hans Christian Andersen
adapted by Karen Santorum

IT WAS SO BEAUTIFUL out in the country. It was summer. The oats were still green, but the wheat was turning yellow. Down in the meadow the grass had been cut and made into haystacks. The old castle, with its deep moat surrounding it, lay bathed in sunshine. Between the heavy walls and the edge of the moat there was a narrow strip of land covered by a whole forest of burdock plants. Their leaves were large and some of the stalks were so tall that a child could stand upright under them and imagine that he was in the middle of the wild and lonesome woods. Here a duck had built her nest. While she sat waiting for the eggs to hatch, she felt a little sorry for herself and hardly anybody came to visit her. The other ducks preferred swimming in the moat to sitting under a dock leaf and gossiping.

Finally the eggs began to crack. "Peep . . . Peep," they said one after another. The egg yolks had become alive and were sticking out their heads.

"Quack . . . Quack . . . ," said their mother. "Look around you." And the ducklings did; they glanced at the green world about them, and that was what their mother wanted them to do, for green was good for their eyes.

"How big the world is!" piped the little ones, for they had much more space to move around in now than they had inside the egg.

"Do you think that is the whole world?" quacked their mother. "The world is much larger than this. Are you all here?" The duck got up and turned around to look at her nest. "Oh no, the biggest egg hasn't hatched yet; and I'm so tired of sitting here! I wonder how long it will take?" she wailed, and sat down again.

"What's new?" asked an old duck who had come visiting.

"One of the eggs is taking so long," complained the mother duck. "It won't crack. But take a look at the others. They are the sweetest little ducklings you have ever seen; and every one of them looks exactly like their father. I have sat on it so long that I guess I can sit a little longer, at least until they get the hay in," replied the mother duck.

"Suit yourself," said the older duck.

At last the big egg cracked too. "Peep . . . Peep," said the young one, and tumbled out. He was big and very ugly.

The duck looked at him. "He's awfully big for his age," she said. "He doesn't look like any of the others. I wonder if he could be a turkey? Well, we shall soon see. Into the waters he will go, even if I have to kick him to make him do it."

The next day the mother duck took her whole brood to the moat.

One after another, the little ducklings plunged into the water. For a moment their heads disappeared, but then they popped up again and the little ones floated like so many corks. Their legs knew what to do without being told. All of the new brood swam very nicely, even the ugly one.

"He is no turkey," mumbled the mother. "See how beautifully he uses his legs and how straight he holds his neck. He is my own child and, when you look closely at him, he's quite handsome . . . Quack! Quack! Follow me and I'll take you to the hen yard and introduce you to everyone. Don't walk, waddle like well-brought up ducklings. Keep your legs far apart, just as your mother and father have always done. Bow your heads and say, 'Quack!'" And that was what the little ducklings did.

Other ducks gathered about them and said loudly, "What do we want that gang here for? Aren't there enough of us already? Pooh! Look how ugly one of them is! He's the last straw!" And one of the ducks flew over and bit the ugly duckling on the neck.

"Leave him alone!" shouted the mother. "He hasn't done anyone any harm."

"He's big and he doesn't look like everybody else!" replied the duck who had bitten him. "And that's reason enough to beat him."

"Very good-looking children you have," remarked another duck. "All of them are beautiful except one. He didn't turn out very well. I wish you could make him over again."

"That's not possible," answered the mother duck. "He may not be handsome, but he has good character and swims as well as the others, if not a little better. Perhaps he will grow handsomer as he grows older and becomes a bit smaller." She smoothed his neck for a moment and then added, "Besides, he's a drake; and it doesn't matter so much what he looks like. He is strong and I am sure he will be able to take care of himself."

"Well, the others are nice," said the old duck.

The poor little duckling, who had been the last to hatch and was so ugly, was bitten and pushed and made fun of by the other ducks. The turkey rustled his feathers as if he were a full-rigged ship under sail, and strutted up to the duckling. He gobbled so loudly at him that his own face got all red.

The poor little duckling did not know where to turn. How he grieved over his own ugliness, and how sad he was! The poor creature was mocked and laughed at by the whole hen yard.

That was the first day; and each day that followed was worse than the one before. The poor duckling was chased and mistreated by everyone, even his own sisters and brothers, who quacked again and again, "If only the cat would get you, you ugly thing!"

Even his mother said, "I wish you were far away." The other ducks bit him and hens pecked at him. The little girl who came to feed the fowls kicked him.

At last the duckling ran away. It ran over the tops of bushes, frightening all the little birds so that they flew up into the air. "They, too, think I'm ugly," thought the ugly duckling, and closed his eyes — but he kept on running.

Finally he came to a great swamp where wild ducks lived; and here he stayed for the night, for he was too tired to go any farther.

In the morning he was discovered by the wild ducks. They looked at him and one of them asked, "What kind of bird are you?"

The ugly duckling bowed in all directions, for he was trying to be as polite as he knew how.

"You are ugly," said the wild ducks, "but that is no concern of ours, as long as you don't try to marry into our family."

The poor duckling wasn't thinking of marriage. All he wanted was to be allowed to swim among the reeds and drink a little water when he was thirsty.

After a few days he left the swamp. Across the fields and the meadows he went, but a wind had come up and he found it hard to make his way against it.

Toward evening he came upon a poor little hut. It was so wretchedly crooked that it looked as if it couldn't make up its mind which way to fall and that was why it was still standing. Suddenly he noticed that the door was off its hinges, making a crack; and he squeezed himself through it and was quickly inside.

An old woman lived in the hut with her cat and her hen.

In the morning the hen and the cat discovered the duckling. The cat meowed and the hen clucked.

"What is going on?" asked the old woman, and looked around. She couldn't see very well, and when she found the duckling she thought it was a fat, full-grown duck. "What a fine catch!" she exclaimed. "Now we shall have duck eggs, unless it's a drake. We'll give it a try."

So the duckling was allowed to stay for three weeks on probation, but he laid no eggs. The cat was the master of the house and the hen the mistress. They always referred to themselves as "we and the world," for they thought that they were half the world — and the better half at that. The duckling thought that he should be allowed to have a different opinion, but the hen did not agree.

"Can you lay eggs?" she demanded.

"No," answered the duckling.

"Then keep your mouth shut."

And the cat asked, "Can you arch your back? Can you purr?"

"No."

"Well, in that case, you have no right to have an opinion." The duckling was sitting in a corner and was in a bad mood. Suddenly he recalled how lovely it could be outside in the fresh air when the sun shone: a great longing to be floating in the water came over the duckling, and he could not help talking about it.

"You have no idea how delightful it is to float in the water, and to dive down to the bottom of a lake and get your head wet," said the duckling.

"What is the matter with you?" asked the hen. "You have nothing to do, that's why you get ideas like that. Lay eggs or purr, and such notions will disappear."

"You don't understand me!" wailed the duckling.

"And if I don't understand you, who will? I hope you don't think that you are wiser than the cat or the old woman — not to mention myself. Don't give yourself airs! Thank your Creator for all He has done for you. Aren't you sitting in a warm room? Now get to work: lay some eggs, or learn to purr and arch your back."

"I think I'll go out into the wide world," replied the duckling.

"Go right ahead!" said the hen.

And the duckling left. He found a lake where he could float in the water and dive to the bottom. There were other ducks, but they ignored him because he was so ugly.

Autumn came and the leaves turned yellow and brown, then they fell from the trees. The wind caught them and made them dance. The clouds were heavy with hail and snow. A raven sat on a fence and screeched, "Ach! Ach!" because it was so cold.

One evening just as the sun was setting gloriously, a flock of beautiful birds came out from among the rushes. Their feathers were so white that they glistened; and they had long graceful necks. They were swans. They made a very loud cry, then they spread their powerful wings. They were flying south to a warmer climate, where the lakes were not frozen in the winter. Higher and higher they circled. The ugly duckling turned round and round in the water like a wheel and stretched his neck up toward the sky; he felt a strange longing. He screeched so piercingly that he frightened himself.

Oh, he would never forget those beautiful birds, those happy birds. When they were out of sight the duckling dove down under the water to the bottom of the lake; and when he came up again he was beside himself. He did not know the name of those birds or where they were going, and yet he felt that he loved them as he had never loved any other creatures. He did not envy them. It did not even occur to him to wish he were so handsome himself. He would have been happy if the other ducks had let him stay in the hen yard: that poor, ugly bird!

The weather grew colder and colder. The duckling had to swim round and round in the water, to keep just a little space for himself that wasn't frozen. Each night his hold became smaller and smaller. On all sides of him the ice creaked and groaned. At last he was too tired to swim any more. He sat still. The ice closed in around him.

> Do not let any unwholesome talk come out of your mouths, but only what is helpful for building others up according to their needs.
>
>
>
> EPHESIANS 4:32

Early the next morning a farmer saw him and with his clogs broke the ice to free the duckling. The man put the bird under his arm and took it home to his wife, who brought the duckling back to life.

It would be too horrible to tell of all the hardship and suffering the duckling experienced that long winter. It is enough to know that he did survive. When again the sun shone warmly and the larks began to sing, the duckling was lying among the reeds in the swamp. Spring had come!

He spread out his wings to fly. How strong and powerful they were! Before he knew it, he was flying far from the swamp. The apple trees were blooming and lilac bushes stretched their flower-covered branches over the water. Everything was so beautiful: so fresh and green. Out of a forest of rushes came three swans. They ruffled their feathers and floated so lightly on the water. The ugly duckling recognized the birds and felt again that strange sadness come over him.

"I shall fly over to them, those royal birds! And they can hack me to death because I, who am so ugly, dare to approach them! What difference does it make? It is better to be killed by them than to be bitten by the other ducks, and pecked by the hens, or to suffer through another winter."

And he lighted on the water and swam toward the magnificent swans. When they saw him they ruffled their feathers and started to swim in his direction. They were coming to meet him.

The poor creature bent his head humbly while he waited for the swans. But what was that he saw in the water? It was his own reflection; and he was no longer an awkward, clumsy, gray bird, so ungainly and so ugly. He was a swan!

It does not matter that one has been born in the hen yard as long as one has lain in a swan's egg.

He was thankful that he had known so much want, and gone through so much suffering, for it made him appreciate his present happiness and loveliness of everything about him all the more. The swans made a circle around him and caressed him with their beaks.

Some children came out into the garden. They had bought bread with them to feed the swans. All the children joyfully clapped their hands.

Cake and bread were cast on the water for the swans. Everyone agreed that the new swan was the most beautiful of them all. The older swans bowed toward him.

He felt so shy that he hid his head beneath his wing. He was happy, but not proud, for a kind heart can never be proud. He thought of the time when he had been mocked and persecuted. And now everyone said that he was the most beautiful of the most beautiful birds. And the lilac bushes stretched their branches right down to the water for him. The sun shone so warm and brightly. He ruffled his feathers and raised his slender neck, while out of joy in his heart, he thought, "Such happiness I did not dream of when I was the ugly duckling."

Hurtful words separated the ugly duckling from his family. It's important to think before we speak. Remember the Golden Rule: "Do unto others as you would have them do unto you." When you're about to say something to someone, ask yourself, "Is this something that I would like someone to say to me?"

Controlling the Tongue
by Geoffrey Chaucer

My son, keep well thy tongue, and keep thy friend.
A wicked tongue is worse than a fiend;
My son, from a fiend men may them bless.

My son, God of his endless goodness
Walled a tongue with teeth and lips eke,
For man should him avise what he speak.
Hath many a man been split, as clerkes teach;
But for little speech avisely
Is no man shent, to speak generally.
My son, thy tongue shouldst thou restrain
At all time, but when thou dost thy pain
To speak of God, in honour and prayer.
The first virtue, son, if thou wilt lere,
Is to restrain and keep well thy tongue;
Thus learn children when that they been young.
My son, of muckle speaking evil-avised,
Where less speaking had enough sufficed,
Cometh muckle harm; thus was me told and taught.
In muckle speech sin wanteth nought.
Wost thou whereof a rakel tongue serveth?
Right as a sword forcutteth and forcarveth
An arm a-two, my dear son, right so
A tongue cutteth friendship all a-two.

*This is an old poem, which may sound funny today because of its words.
But it reminds us that the tongue can be a dangerous weapon. Carefully
choose the words you use.*

JOSEPH'S COAT
author unknown

IT WAS NIPPING COLD for November. Winter had arrived before
schedule. "My, this coat feels good!" Joseph gave a little flying leap
to express how good it felt. His thin legs seemed to lose themselves upward, his happy face, mounted on a thin little neck, to lose itself downward in the huge new coat.

Mother was happy today, too, as she watched him down the road.
"Nobody will look at his back," she thought. "They'll just look at his face,
and say, 'My that boy's warm, I know!'"

But somebody looked at his back. At the junction of the roads, a little
way on, the minister's boy and his particular friends swung in behind
Joseph. They were all warm, too. The minister's boy's coat was new, too,

but a different "new" from Joseph's. It had a fur collar that turned up about his ears, and it was exactly broad enough and long enough.

All at once somebody shouted. It was the minister's boy. "Oh, look! Joseph's coat — Joseph's coat o' many colors! Look there! Look there!"

Suddenly Joseph was no longer warm; a nipping cold struck through to his neck.

"Joseph's coat! Joseph's coat!"

He knew there was something the matter with it, and it must be with the behind of it, for that was all those boys could see. All the leap had come out of Joseph's thin little legs, all the joy out of his heart. He went on because you couldn't get to school without going on. But that was all — just went on. At the schoolhouse he waited around, instinctively facing front to folks, until they had all gone in. Then he took off his "new" coat and looked at the behind. Then he knew.

There was a long straight seam in the middle, and on each side of it the thick cloth had faded to a different shade, a distinctly different shade. Two colors really, one on each side of that long straight seam — a cruel little trick of the sun. Joseph was only eight, but he saw at once why they had called it Joseph's coat of many colors.

The next day Joseph waited behind a wall at the junction of roads until the minister's boy and his friends had come and gone. Then he slipped out and followed them. That helped a little — he tried to think it helped a little. But there were recesses and meetings — of course he might stay inside; you don't have to wear an overcoat when you stay in.

Joseph stayed in. Through the window he could see the minister's boy having a splendid time. The third day he saw something else. He saw the minister's boy in *his* coat — the multi-colored coat Aunt Caroline had sent — strutting about the yard amid the others' shouts of delight. Some of the others tried it on and strutted. Joseph just sat in his seat and looked at them as tears rolled down his cheeks.

The next day he turned Aunt Caroline's coat inside out and wore it so. He waited till he got nearly to the fork in the road before turning it inside out; he wasn't going to make Mother feel bad, too. She had lined the coat anew with shiny black cotton stuff all of one color. Joseph felt a little better; this would help.

But it only made things worse. The minister's boy and his particular friends instantly saw the ridiculousness of that inside-out little coat. "Look at it! Look at it — inside out! Wearin' it inside out!" The joke was just too good!

There was just one other thing to do, and Joseph did it the next day.

The place where the roads forked was about halfway from Joseph's home to the schoolhouse; so he went warm halfway the next day. The other half he shivered along, very small indeed, and very cold indeed, outside of the Aunt Caroline coat. For he had left Aunt Caroline's coat folded up behind a stone wall. Going home that afternoon, he was warm the last half of his way, anyway. It helped to be half warm.

For a day or two the sun and the wind conspired together to befriend little Joseph. But the fourth day the wind blew and the sun rested. There was snow, too, in fine steely flakes, and Joseph's teeth chattered, and he ran on stiff little legs, and blew on stiff little fingers. He kept looking ahead to the last half of going home. He wished he had pushed the Aunt Caroline coat farther in under the stones out of the way of the snow.

"Joseph Merriam," called the teacher on the day after the snowstorm. She had her roll book and pencil waiting, but she got no answer. It was strange for Joseph Merriam not to answer the roll call; he was one of her little steadies. "Joseph is not here, I see; can anyone tell me if he is sick? He must be sick." "Yes'm, he is. He's got pneumonia dreadfully," someone answered. "There were lights in his house all night, my father said."

> The worst wheel of the cart makes the most noise.
>
> 🕭
>
> BENJAMIN FRANKLIN
> *Poor Richard's Almanac*

For many nights there were lights, and for many mornings the doctor's sleigh. Joseph laid in his bed, saying wild, mixed-up words in a weak little voice. "I'm almost to the stone wall; then I'll be warm!"

"Joseph's coat o' many colors — Joseph's coat o' many colors!"

"I don't want Mother to know they laughed; don't anybody tell Mother."

The minister's boy heard of those wild little words, and pieced them together into a story. He remembered who had cried, "Joseph's coat o' many colors!" tauntingly, cruelly. And now — oh, now he remembered that Joseph had not worn any overcoat at all those last days that he went to school! *No coat.* The heart of the minister's boy contracted with an awful fear. He took to haunting Joseph's house in all his free minutes — waiting at the gate for the doctor to come out, and shivering with something besides cold at his brief answers. The answers grew worse and worse.

Going to bed was so difficult for the minister's boy. He lay in his own bed, remembering that other little bed of Joseph's. When remembering was too great a torture, the minister's boy crept out of bed and dressed himself. Out into the clear, cold starlight, down the frozen road, he crept toward Joseph's lighted windows. He was not aware of being cold anywhere but in his soul — he shivered there.

A long time he stood waiting for he knew not what. Then someone came out of the house. It was not the doctor; it was the minister. The boy could not see his face, but you don't have to see your own father's face. They went back down the dim night road together, and together into the minister's study.

"I've killed him," the boy said. "I've killed Joseph. I did it."

The minister's face was curiously lighted in spite of this awful confession of his son. The light persisted.

"Sit down, Philip," he said, for the boy was shaking like a leaf. "Now tell me." All the story, piece by piece — the boy told it all.

"So it was I — I killed him. I — I didn't expect to — "

Silence for a little while. Then:

"Did you think Joseph was dead, Philip? He came very close indeed to it; but the crisis is past, and he will get well. I waited to know."

"You mean — I — haven't?"

"I mean you haven't, thank God." Philip was overjoyed and full of thanks with the news of Joseph's improved condition.

When, after a long while, the boy was slipping away, the minister called to him gently.

"Come back a moment, Philip."

"Yes, I'm back, Father. I know what you're thinking of. Father, may I — punish myself this time — for making fun of a boy — a *little* boy? It needs a good deal o' punishin', but I'll do it — please let me do it, Father! Please — please try me, anyway."

And because the minister was a wise minister, he nodded his head.

When little Joseph got well, he wore to school a beautiful warm coat with a soft furry collar that went up — up — around his ears. It was very thick and warm and handsome, and all of a color. Joseph wore it all the way.

The rest of the winter the minister's boy wore to school an Aunt Caroline coat of many colors.

William Shakespeare, one of the greatest writers who ever lived, once wrote, "These words are razors to my wounded heart." This story shows how much words can hurt.

THE CHATTERBOX
by Ann and Jane Taylor

From morning till night it was Lucy's delight,
To chatter and talk without stopping;
There was not a day but she rattled away,
Like water forever a dropping!

As soon as she rose, while she put on her clothes,
'Twas vain to endeavor to still her;
Nor once did she lack, to continue her clack,
Till again she laid down on her pillow.

You'll think now, perhaps, that there would have been gaps,
If she had not been wonderful clever;
That her sense was so great, and so witty her pate,
That it would be forthcoming forever:

But that's quite absurd, for have you not heard,
That much tongue, and few brains, are connected?
That they are suppos'd, to think least who talk most,
And their wisdom is always suspected?

While Lucy was young, if she'd bridled her tongue,
With a little good sense and exertion;
Who knows but she might now have been our delight,
Instead of our jest and aversion!

It's not polite to go on talking without letting others get a word in. To do so sends the message that you think you know everything, and that you don't care what others think. Always be a good listener.

THE TALKATIVE TORTOISE
by Bidpai, retold by Karen Santorum

ONCE UPON A TIME, a tortoise lived in a pond with two ducks, who were her good friends. She enjoyed the company of the ducks because she could talk with them to her heart's content. The tortoise liked to talk. She always had something to say, and she liked to hear herself say it.

After many years of this pleasant living, a dry season came and the pond became very low; finally it dried up. The two ducks saw that they could no longer live there, so they decided to fly to another region, where there was more water. They went to the tortoise to bid her good-bye.

"Oh, don't leave me behind!" begged the tortoise. "Take me with you; I will die if I am left here."

"But you cannot fly!" said the ducks. "How can we take you with us?"

"Take me with you! Take me with you!" said the tortoise.

The ducks felt so sorry for her, that, after much thought, they conceived of a way to take her. "We have come up with a possibility," they said, "if only you can manage to keep still long enough. We will each take hold of one end of a stout stick, and you must take the middle in your mouth; then we will fly up in the air and carry you with us. But remember not to talk! If you open your mouth, you will be lost."

The tortoise said she would not say a word. She would not so much as move her mouth; and she was very grateful. So the ducks brought a strong little stick and took hold of the ends, while the tortoise bit firmly on the middle. Then the two ducks rose slowly into the air and flew away with their burden.

When they were above the treetops, the tortoise wanted to say, "How high we are!" But she remembered, and kept still. When they passed the church steeple she wanted to say, "What is that which shines?" But she remembered, and held her peace.

Then they came over the village square, and the people looked up and saw them. "Look at the ducks carrying a tortoise!" they shouted; and every one ran to look. The tortoise wanted to say, "What business is it of yours?" But she didn't. Then she heard the people shout, "Isn't that *strange*! Look at it! Look!"

At that, the tortoise grew so angry that she could not think of anything but that she wanted to say, "Hush, you foolish people!" So she opened her mouth — and fell to the ground.

And that was the end of the tortoise.

Have you ever heard someone say, "Bite your tongue"? This is often very good advice — learning when not to say what's on your mind can keep you out of a lot of trouble!

Cyrano Meets His Match
from Cyrano de Bergerac *by Edmond Rostand*
adapted by Michael Lamb

It is said that many years ago, in France, there lived a man who was both a poet and a great swordsman. He was also one of his country's greatest braggarts. His name was Cyrano de Bergerac. Cyrano also had one other claim to fame: he had an extremely large nose. As a boy, he was often teased about it. But when he was older, if a man merely mentioned his nose or looked at it carelessly, he would have to answer to Cyrano's sword. To cross swords with Cyrano was certain death, and therefore no man dared focus any attention on the great man's nose. The following play dramatizes what happened when a young cadet, named Christian, did just that.

ONE DAY, a group of Cyrano's friends sat waiting for him in a small Paris restaurant. These men were cadets in the regiment of Carbon de Castel-Jaloux. One of them was a handsome young recruit named Christian de Neuvillette. Just the evening before, Cyrano had single-handedly defeated nearly a hundred men who were attempting to murder one of his friends.

De Bergerac's swordsmanship had been magnificent and the cadets were eager to hear the story of the night's events. Cyrano, who was never one to shy away from singing his own praises, was more than happy to tell the tale. Christian de Neuvillette, the new recruit, viewed this as being far too much bragging. He leaned towards one of the cadets to softly ask a question.

Christian: What can one do when a man grows too boastful?

Cadet: Show him that others also have courage.

Christian: And in turn show the braggart his own flaws.

Cadet: Of course!!

Christian: Thank you.

All cadets (except Christian): The story, Cyrano, tell us the story. Tell us how it is that so many dead rogues litter the streets.

Cyrano: The story?

All cadets: Yes, the story, now, the story.

Cyrano: Oh — my story (the cadets draw up chairs and benches; they lean forward, while Christian sits back in a corner chair). Well, I went alone to meet them. In the sky, the moon shone like a great white watch, when suddenly the heavenly watchmaker began to draw a wad of cotton clouds about the face of this bright timepiece, and the night became the darkest night the world had known. The streets were evil holes of blackness. You could see no further than —

Christian: Your nose!

(The silence is tremendous. Everyone is startled and rises. The cadets turn to Cyrano, who has stopped abruptly.)

Cyrano: Who is that man?

A cadet (in a low voice): A raw recruit who came to us this morning.

Cyrano: This morning? Very well. (He turns white, then red, and seems about to hurl himself upon Christian.) I — ! (He controls himself with a great effort and resumes in a strained voice.) As I was saying — well, the night was dark. (General astonishment. The cadets take their seats again and watch Cyrano intensely.) I walked, thinking that in some dark corner they were waiting for us ready to take me —

Christian: By the nose.

Cyrano (in a choked voice): Take me and cut my throat, pull out my teeth and cast my body in the river Seine. Perhaps I was unwise to poke —

Christian: Your nose —

Cyrano: To poke along these dark alleys and unfamiliar streets. Suddenly there was a rapping upon —

Christian: Your nose.

Cyrano (mopping perspiration from his brow): Upon the pavement, they were coming. "Duty calls," I said, "March on! Go forward, Cyrano!" When from the shadows a sword flashed —

Christian: Upon your nose.

Cyrano: I sprang and swiftly parried it. I found myself —

Christian: Nose against nose.

Cyrano (leaping at him): By thunder!

(All the cadets expect murder, but, reaching Christian, Cyrano again masters himself and goes on.)

Cyrano: I found myself pitted against a hundred cutthroats who stank —

Christian: To make you hold your nose.

Cyrano (pales, but smiles coldly): Who stank of onions and sweat. I rushed, head down —

Christian: Nosing the scent.

Cyrano: Head down, and charged! I ran through two, ripped one, and slashed another. Then someone shouted — Ugh! — and I went —

Christian: Honk! (as he blows his nose).

Cyrano (bursting out): Out! Heaven help you! Out! All of you! (The cadets rush towards the door, leaving the building. Cyrano and Christian stand face to face.)

Cyrano: Embrace me!

Christian: Sir —

Cyrano: You are brave.

Christian: Oh! But —

Cyrano: Yes, you are very brave and I like you for that.

Christian: But I feel —

Cyrano: I say, embrace me.

Christian (impulsively grasping his hands): You'll never know how very much your friendship means to me.

Cyrano: Isn't this friendship sort of sudden?

Christian: Forgive me, I wish I could express my admiration.

Cyrano: But all those noses?

Christian: Let me take them back.

In the Book of Proverbs, it says, "He that is slow to anger is better than the mighty, and he that rules his spirit is better than he that taketh a city." Because Cyrano controlled his anger, he and Christian became the best of friends and went on to share many adventures.

LETTER TO HIS SON
by Lord Chesterfield

TALK OFTEN, BUT NEVER LONG: in that case, if you do not please, at least you are sure not to tire your hearers.

Tell stories very seldom, and absolutely never but where they are very apt and very short. Omit every circumstance that is not material, and beware of digressions. To have frequent recourse to narrative betrays great want of imagination.

Never hold anybody by the button, or the hand, in order to be heard out; for if people are not willing to hear you, you had much better hold your tongue than them.

Avoid as much as you can, in mixed companies, argumentative conversations. But if the conversation grows warm and noisy, endeavor to put an end to it, by some genteel levity or joke.

Above all things, and upon all occasions, avoid speaking of yourself, if it be possible. Such is the natural pride and vanity of our hearts that it perpetually breaks out, even in people of the best parts.

Always look people in the face when you speak to them: not doing it is thought to imply conscious guilt; besides that you lose the advantage of observing by their countenances what impression your discourse makes upon them. In order to know people's real sentiments, I trust much more to my eyes than to my ears: for they can say whatever they have a mind I should hear; but they can seldom help looking what they have no intention that I should know.

Never give nor receive scandal willingly; for though the defamation of others may for the present gratify the malignity of the pride of our hearts, cool reflection will draw very disadvantageous conclusions from such a disposition; and in the case of scandal, as that of robbery, the receiver is always thought as bad as the thief.

But to conclude this long letter; all the above mentioned rules, however carefully you may observe them, will lose half their effect, if unaccompanied by kindness and the Graces. Whatever you say, if you say it with a supercilious, cynical face, or an embarrassed countenance, or a silly, disconcerted grin, will be ill received. If, into the bargain, you mutter it, or utter it, indistinctly and ungracefully, it will be still worse received. If your air and address are vulgar, awkward, and *gauche*, you may be esteemed indeed, if you have great intrinsic merit; but you will never please; and without pleasing, you will rise but heavily. Venus, among the ancients, was synonymous with the Graces, who were always supposed to accompany her; and Horace tells us that even Mercury, the God of Arts and Eloquence, would not do without the Graces.

Lord Chesterfield offers wise advice about speaking. When you talk to someone, look into his eyes and speak clearly. Listen well, don't brag, and don't gossip about others.

3.
Telling the Truth

MERCURY AND THE WOODMAN
by Aesop

ONCE A GOOD, hard-working Woodman was chopping away at a tree by the bank of a deep river. His hand slipped and his hatchet fell into the water. He couldn't dive to get it and he was a poor man who couldn't afford to lose his useful tool. So he was very sad and sat with his head in his hands.

Mercury saw him and felt sorry for him, so when the Woodman told him what had happened he offered to help. Mercury dived in and came up with a solid gold hatchet.

"Is this yours?" he said.

"I wish it were," said the Woodman, "but to be honest, it's not."

"Is this yours?" said Mercury, after he had dived again and come up with a silver one.

"No," replied the Woodman, "that's not mine either."

"Well, is this it?" said Mercury and he brought up the man's old hatchet.

"Yes, it is," said the man, "and it was mighty kind of you to get it for me. Thank you."

"I knew it was all the time," said Mercury, "and you are an honest man. Here, take this gold one and this silver one, too, as a reward for telling the truth."

The Woodman was so pleased that he ran home to tell all his friends.

One of them ran right away to the riverbank, threw his hatchet in the water and started to cry.

Mercury came as before and dived, bringing up a golden hatchet.

"Is this yours?" he asked.

"Yes! Yes!" shouted the greedy liar, and grabbed for it.

"I happen to know that it is not," said Mercury.

He flew off, leaving the man sitting there on the bank with no gold hatchet and his own down at the bottom of the river.

Our words reflect our character. It's always best to tell the truth, no matter what the consequences may be. Sometimes, it's tempting to think that if we lie and no one finds out, we won't be punished. But this isn't so, because our conscience will punish us. God sees everything we do and he hears everything we say, so we should always try to act in a way that pleases him.

TRUTH THE BEST
by Elizabeth Turner

Yesterday Rebecca Mason,
In the parlour by herself,
Broke a handsome china basin,
Placed upon the mantelshelf.

Quite alarmed, she thought of going
Very quietly away,
Not a single person knowing
Of her being there that day.

But Rebecca recollected
She was taught deceit to shun;
And the moment she reflected,
Told her mother what was done;
Who commended her behaviour,
Loved her better, and forgave her.

Sooner or later, everyone breaks something! Our initial desire is to run away or hide what was broken. But, if you confess right away, you'll minimize negative feelings about your accident. When you break something, make a sincere apology and offer to pay to fix or replace it.

GEORGE WASHINGTON AND THE CHERRY TREE
retold by Karen Santorum

LONG AGO, there lived a little boy whose name was George Washington. He lived on a farm in Virginia. On his sixth birthday, his father gave him a special present. It was a hatchet with a hand-carved wooden handle and a sharp metal blade on top. To George, this was the best present a boy could ever get. It meant that he was growing up, for his father now trusted him with a fine, sharp tool.

George said "Thank you!" as he hugged and kissed his father, and he promised to be very careful with the hatchet. Then off he went to play, bringing his hatchet with him.

George headed to the woodpile, anxious to try out his new hatchet. He picked up and piled some twigs. Much to his surprise, the hatchet sliced right through them without any effort. Then, with just a few whacks, George chopped a log into several pieces.

> Kings take pleasure in honest lips; they value a man who speaks the truth.
>
>
>
> PROVERBS 16:13

He went to the vineyard and cut some dead vines that had fallen to the ground. Then he headed to the large family garden, where he chopped off a large cabbage, two big purple eggplants, a squash, and five ears of corn for his mother to prepare for dinner. George tucked the vegetables into the pouch he made with his shirt and ran them inside to his mother.

"Mother, I thought these vegetables would be quite nice for dinner," said George.

"Oh, my goodness, George, I do hope that you are hungry. But thank you, son, for your thoughtfulness," said his mother.

George's father, who was sitting at the table having a cup of tea and reading a book, said, "Careful with the hatchet, son. And please don't go into the orchard with it."

George hurried out the door wondering what else he could cut with his new hatchet. It was a lovely spring day, but George did not notice the warm sun on his face, or the fragrant spring air, or the gentle breeze that tugged at his shirt — he was having too much fun pretending to be a great woodcutter. He was imagining that he had a log house to build, and firewood to chop before the winter blizzard roared through the farm. There was work to do, and George had to hurry to get it done in time. He cut sticks along the way and even struck an old fence post.

Before long, George realized that he had wandered into his father's prized fruit orchard. It was a beautiful sight at this time of year. All of the apple, pear, peach, and plum trees were blossoming and getting ready to produce the delicious fruit that Mr. Washington grew so well. Every tree was special to George's father, but there was one in particular that he loved. It was a small tree, given to Mr. Washington as a gift, sent on a ship from England. It was a tree that would bear fruit new to this country: a small round fruit, red in color, with a taste so sweet and wonderful, called a *cherry*. George's father nursed all of the trees in his orchard with a loving eye and gentle touch, but he cared especially for his dear little cherry tree. The Washington family looked forward to tasting the cherries and using them in pies, jams, and muffins.

> A man of integrity runs with truth, not with the times; with right, and not with might.
>
>
>
> WILLIAM PENN

George wandered through the orchard for a few minutes before deciding he'd better go home — he was sorely tempted to try his hatchet on the fruit trees.

But his curiosity got the better of him.

George looked at the trunk of a tall old pear tree in the distance. His eyes followed the grand tree's form right up to the top, where the sun was glistening through the fine green leaves.

"I wonder if that tree is easy to cut," he thought, as he walked slowly toward the tree. Before he knew it, he was swinging the hatchet right into the tree.

Thank goodness, the bark on the tree was thick and hard. Probably it was made that way to protect it from curious boys like George. The hatchet barely left a mark.

George then came upon an apple tree. "Well, this tree isn't nearly as big as the pear tree," he thought. And with the hatchet wrapped tightly in his small hands, George swung back his arms and plunged the sharp blade into the apple tree. The hatchet not only went into the bark, but it got stuck. George tugged and tugged to pull it out.

"It would take forever to chop this tree down," George said to himself. He then saw the small cherry tree.

It was just the right size. George ran up to it and swung the hatchet. Much to his surprise, the sharp blade of the hatchet went halfway into the tree and came out with ease. Forgetting his father's wishes, George took another swing that brought the little cherry tree to the ground.

For a moment, just a moment, George felt proud that he had cut down a tree all by himself. But then a horrible feeling came over him, the kind of sick feeling you get when you realize you've done something wrong.

George thought of how his father loved him and would do anything for him. He thought about his father's immense joy when the cherry tree arrived, and the joy they had felt planting it together. And then he remembered how his father had told him not to go into the orchard with the hatchet.

George quickly knelt on the ground and pulled the tree up to a standing position, desperately hoping that somehow, magically, the tree would mend. He held it there for a moment, wishing he could go back in time and take back the damage he had done.

Tears rolled down his cheeks when he realized that there was nothing he could do to bring the tree back. Sad and ashamed, George sat in the field with his head resting on his folded arms. Eventually, he summoned the courage to walk home, ever so slowly, to face his parents at their evening meal.

George was especially quiet as he helped his mother prepare dinner. Without being told, he set the table, poured the water into the glasses, cut the vegetables, and even took the bread from the oven. His mother wondered why George was so eager to help.

Then Mr. Washington came slowly through the door. He did not give them his usual cheerful greeting; he just sank into the blue living room chair. He sat quietly, disappointment, sadness, and anger in his face. George could see his father through the crack in the kitchen door. His heart raced and he felt dizzy. How was he going to face his father and look him in the eye again after what he had done?

Finally, after a few minutes, the silence was broken. Mr. Washington stood up and walked into the kitchen. As George listened to the sound of his father's footsteps nearing the kitchen door, his anxiety mounted and he wanted nothing more than to run away as fast as he could into the fields.

Mr. Washington stood sternly at the kitchen table. He looked at Mrs. Washington, then at George, who stood at his chair. "George, do you know who cut down my cherry tree?" Mr. Washington's voice was stern.

George turned white as a sheet and took a big breath. He summoned all his courage. He looked his father in the eye and said, "Father, I cannot tell a lie. I cut down the cherry tree with my hatchet. I am so sorry. Please forgive me." With those words George could no longer hold back the tears.

George waited for his punishment. Three minutes felt like three hours, as he waited for his father's response.

After thinking awhile, Mr. Washington sat down in the kitchen chair and said, "Come here, George." He put George on his lap and held him in his strong arms. "My dear boy, I would rather lose a thousand cherry trees than have my son be a liar."

George never forgot his father's words about the importance of always speaking the truth. He grew up to be an honest, noble man full of courage, and a great blessing to his family, our country, and the world.

George would rather be punished than tell a lie. He was wrong to chop down the tree, but he was brave for owning up to the truth. This same strength made George Washington an honorable general in the Revolutionary War and one of our country's greatest presidents.

"Honesty is the best policy," Washington wrote to a future president, James Madison, in 1785. "This applies to public as well as to private life, to States as well as individuals."

CHAPTER THREE

Table Manners

1.
Be Considerate at the Table

WHOLE DUTY OF CHILDREN
by Robert Louis Stevenson

A child should always say what's true
And speak when he is spoken to,
And behave mannerly at table,
At least as far as he is able.

Try to practice being polite and attentive at every meal. You can even practice good table manners when you are having a tea party, or while you're in the tree house having lunch with your friends.

NEVER POKE YOUR UNCLE WITH A FORK
by Jack Prelutsky

Never poke your uncle with a fork,
never kick your uncle in the shins,
never bop your uncle with a cork . . .
these are all unpardonable sins.
If you grab your uncle by the nose,
if you put potatoes on his lap,
if you drop spaghetti on his clothes,
he will make you go and take a nap.
When you're at the table, precious child,
if you start to misbehave, and act
thoroughly undisciplined and wild,
he will gnash his teeth, and that's a fact.

If you jab your uncle with a spoon,
if you prod your uncle with a bone,
you will leave the table very soon,
and have to eat your dinner all alone.

If you shouldn't poke you're uncle with your fork, what should you do with it? A traditional American way of using utensils is to cut your food with your knife in your right hand and your fork in your left, with the fork's tines facing down. Once the food is cut, place the knife on top of the plate with the blade facing you, and pass the fork back into your right hand for eating. A traditional European way of eating is a bit different: you cut your food as described above, but instead of transferring the fork, you eat while holding your knife in your right hand, fork in the left, tines up or down depending on what you're eating. The European way actually allows you to eat with more ease since you can use the knife to guide the food (especially those peas!) onto your fork. Remember to hold your fork and knife with your index finger on the back of the utensil when cutting.

BEFORE TEA
by A. A. Milne

Emmeline
Has not been seen
For more than a week. She slipped between
The two tall trees at the end of the green . . .
We all went after her. *"Emmeline!"*

"Emmeline,
I didn't mean —
I only said that your hands weren't clean."
We went to the trees at the end of the green . . .
But Emmeline
Was not to be seen.

Emmeline
Came slipping between
The two tall trees at the end of the green.
We all ran up to her. "Emmeline!
Where have you been?

Where have you been?
Why, it's more than a week!" And Emmeline
Said, "Sillies, I went and saw the Queen.
She said my hands are *purfickly* clean!"

Develop the habit of washing your hands before meals — especially if you've been out catching frogs or digging up worms! If your clothes are dirty, change into something clean before sitting down to eat.

HOW TO EAT SOUP
by Gelett Burgess

Whenever you are eating soup
Remember not to be a Goop!
And if you think to say this rhyme,
Perhaps 'twill help you every time:
Like little boats that put to sea,
I push my spoon AWAY from me;
I do not tilt my dish, nor scrape
The last few drops, like a hungry ape!
Like little boats, that, almost filled,
Come back without their cargoes spilled,
My spoon sails gently to my lips,
Unloading from the SIDE, like ships.

In addition to pushing your soup spoon away from you, and bringing it to your mouth and sipping it from the side, remember to lean forward a little so that any drops that don't make their way into your mouth will return to the bowl and not the table! When you finish your soup, place the spoon on the underplate, or, if there isn't one, simply place it inside the bowl.

THE GOOP PICNIC
by Gelett Burgess

They came to the best sort of place for a rest,
    On the grass, with the trees overhead,
They sat down in a bunch and they opened their lunch,
    And they had a be–autiful spread!

And when they were done, and they'd had all their fun,
    They proved they were Goops, or were blind;
For they picked up their wraps and they left all their scraps
    For the *next* picnic party to find!

Picnics are so much fun! It's wonderful to sit on a blanket under the wide blue sky. Enjoy the scenery, the sun, and the breeze — and remember to gather up and dispose of your trash when you're done.

THE STORY OF AUGUSTUS WHO WOULD NOT HAVE ANY SOUP
by Dr. Heinrich Hoffmann

Augustus was a chubby lad;
Fat ruddy cheeks Augustus had;
And every body saw with joy,
The plump and hearty healthy boy.
He ate and drank as he was told,
And never let his soup get cold.
But one day, one cold winter's day,
He scream'd out — "Take the soup away!
O take, the nasty soup away!
I won't have any soup today!"

How lank and lean Augustus grows!
Next day he scarcely fills his clothes,
Yet, though he feels so weak and ill,
The naughty fellow cries out still —
"Not any soup for me, I say:
O take the nasty soup away!
I won't have any soup today!"

The third day comes: Oh! What a sin!
To make himself so pale and thin.
Yet, when the soup is put on table,
He screams, as loud as he is able,
"Not any soup for me, I say:
I won't have any soup today!"

Look at him, now the fourth day's come!
He scarcely weighs a sugar-plum;
He's like a little bit of thread,
And on the fifth day he was — dead!

Your parents serve you healthy foods because they love you. They want you to grow up strong and to have a long, full life. So when the vegetables are served be polite and try a bite!

ANNE OF GREEN GABLES
by Lucy Maud Montgomery

Chapter 22

"AND WHAT ARE YOUR EYES popping out of your head about now?" asked Marilla, when Anne had just come in from a run to the post office. "Have you discovered another kindred spirit?"

Excitement hung around Anne like a garment, shone in her eyes, kindled in every feature. She had come dancing up the lane, like a wind-blown sprite, through the mellow sunshine and lazy shadows of the August evening.

"No, Marilla, but oh, what do you think? I am invited to tea at the manse tomorrow afternoon! Mrs. Allan left the letter for me at the post office. Just look at it, Marilla. 'Miss Anne Shirley, Green Gables.' That is the first time I was ever called 'Miss.' Such a thrill as it gave me! I shall cherish it for ever among my choicest treasures."

"Mrs. Allan told me she meant to have all the members of her Sunday school class to tea in turn," said Marilla, regarding the wonderful event very coolly. "You needn't get in such a fever over it. Do learn to take things calmly, child."

For Anne to take things calmly would have been to change her nature. All "spirit and fire and dew," as she was, the pleasures and pains of life came to her with trebled intensity. Marilla felt this and was vaguely troubled over it, realizing that the ups and downs of existence would probably bear hardly on this impulsive soul and not sufficiently understanding that the equally great capacity for delight might more than compensate. Therefore Marilla conceived it to be her duty to drill Anne into a tranquil uniformity of disposition as impossible and alien to her as to a dancing sunbeam in one of the brook shallows. She did not make much headway, as she sorrowfully admitted to herself. The downfall of some dear hope or plan plunged Anne into "deeps of affliction." The fulfilment thereof exalted her to dizzy realms of delight. Marilla had almost begun to despair of ever fashioning this waif of the world into her model little girl of demure manners and prim deportment. Neither would she have believed that she really liked Anne much better as she was.

Anne went to bed that night speechless with misery because Matthew had said the wind was round northeast and he feared it would be a rainy day tomorrow. The rustle of the poplar leaves about the house worried her, it sounded so like pattering rain drops; and the dull, faraway roar of the gulf, to which she listened delightedly at other times, loving its strange, sonorous, haunting rhythm, now seemed like a prophecy of storm and disaster to a small maiden who particularly wanted a fine day. Anne thought that the morning would never come.

But all things have an end, even nights before the day on which you are invited to take tea at the manse. The morning, in spite of Matthew's predictions, was beautiful, and Anne's spirits soared to their highest.

"Oh, Marilla, there is something in me today that makes me just love everybody I see," she exclaimed as she washed the breakfast dishes. "You don't know how good I feel! Wouldn't it be nice if it could last? I believe I could be a model child if I were just invited out to tea every day. But oh, Marilla, it's a solemn occasion too. I feel so anxious. What if I shouldn't behave properly? You know I never had tea at a manse before, and I'm not sure that I know all the rules of etiquette, although I've been studying the rules given in the Etiquette Department of the *Family Herald* ever since I came here. I'm so afraid I'll do something silly or forget to do something I should do. Would it be good manners to take a second helping of anything if you wanted to very much?"

"The trouble with you, Anne, is that you're thinking too much about yourself. You should just think of Mrs. Allan and what would be nicest and most agreeable for her," said Marilla, hitting for once in her life on a very sound and pithy piece of advice. Anne instantly realized this.

"You are right, Marilla. I'll try not to think about myself at all."

Anne evidently got through her visit without any serious breach of "etiquette" for she came home through the twilight, under, a great, high-sprung sky gloried over with trails of saffron and rosy cloud, in a beatified state of mind and told Marilla all about it happily, sitting on the big red sandstone slab at the kitchen door with her tired curly head in Marilla's gingham lap.

People all over the world enjoy afternoon teas. There is something wonderful about friends sharing a hot cup of tea together. Children often start this practice early in life with their miniature porcelain tea sets, serving tea to their bears and dolls.

Because Anne was the one invited to tea, she was the guest. The person doing the inviting is called the hostess, the one who pours the tea. Afternoon teas last for about an hour. Girls usually wear dresses, and boys a jacket and tie. The food at a tea party is different from that served at a picnic or dinner. You'll find an assortment of cakes, cookies, and scones. Cucumber sandwiches are also common — they may not sound very appetizing, but try a bite. You can even try hosting your own tea party sometime!

PIPPI LONGSTOCKING
by Astrid Lindgren

In the story that follows, you'll read about a young girl named Pippi. She has no parents and lives with her pet monkey, named Mr. Nilsson, and her horse. Her neighbors, Tommy and his sister Annika, are very curious about Pippi so they befriend her. Pippi is a spunky girl who likes adventure and knows very little about good manners. In this excerpt, Pippi is invited to a coffee party.

CHAPTER 9

TOMMY'S AND ANNIKA'S mother had invited a few ladies to a coffee party, and as she had done plenty of baking, she thought Tommy and Annika might invite Pippi over at the same time. The children would entertain each other and give no trouble to anyone.

Tommy and Annika were overjoyed when their mother told them and immediately dashed over to Pippi's to invite her. Pippi was in the garden, watering the few flowers still in bloom with an old rusty watering can. As it was raining cats and dogs that day Tommy told Pippi her watering seemed hardly necessary.

"Yes, that's what you say," said Pippi grudgingly, "but I've lain awake all night thinking what fun it was going to be to get up and water, and I'm not going to let a little rain stand in my way."

Now Annika came forth with the delightful news about the coffee party.

"A coffee party! *Me!*" cried Pippi, and she was so excited that she began to water Tommy instead of the rosebush she intended to sprinkle.

"Oh, what will happen? Oh, I'm so nervous. What if I can't behave myself?"

"Of course you can," said Annika.

"Don't you be too certain about that," said Pippi. "You can be sure I'll try, but I have noticed several times that people don't think I know how to behave even when I'm trying as hard as I can. At sea we were never so fussy about things like that. But I promise that I'll take special pains today so you won't have to be ashamed of me."

"Good," said Tommy, and he and Annika hurried home again in the rain.

"This afternoon at three o'clock, don't forget," cried Annika, peeking out from under the umbrella.

At three o'clock a very stylish young lady walked up the steps of the Settergrens' house. It was Pippi Longstocking. For this special occasion she had unbraided her pigtails, and her red hair hung like a lion's mane around her. With red crayon she had painted her mouth fiery red, and she had blackened her eyebrows so that she looked almost dangerous. With the crayon she had also painted her fingernails, and she had put big green rosettes on her shoes.

"I should imagine I'll be the most stylish person of all at this party," she said contentedly to herself as she rang the doorbell.

In the Settergrens' living room sat three fine ladies, and with them Tommy, Annika, and their mother. A wonderful coffee table had been spread, and in the fireplace a fire was burning brightly. The ladies were talking quietly with one another, and Tommy and Annika were sitting on the sofa, looking at an album. Everything was so peaceful.

Suddenly the peace was shattered.

"Atten-shun!" A piercing cry came from the hall, and the next minute Pippi Longstocking stood in the doorway. She had cried out so loudly and so unexpectedly that the ladies had jumped in their seats.

"Forward march!" came the next command, and Pippi, with measured steps, walked up to Mrs. Settergren.

"Halt!" She stopped. "Arms forward, one, *two*," she cried and with both hands gripped one of Mrs. Settergren's and shook it heartily.

"Knees bend!" she shrieked and curtsied prettily. Then she smiled at Mrs. Settergren and said in her ordinary voice, "You see, I am really very shy, so if I didn't give myself some commands I'd just stand in the hall and not dare to come in."

Then she rushed up to the other ladies and kissed them on the cheek.

"Charming, charming, upon my honor!" said she, for she had once heard a stylish gentleman say that to a lady. Then she sat down in the best chair she could find. Mrs. Settergren had intended the children to have their party up in Tommy's and Annika's room, but Pippi stayed calmly in her chair, slapped herself on the knee, and said, looking at the coffee table, "That certainly looks good. When do we begin?"

At that moment Ella, the maid, came in with the coffee pot, and Mrs. Settergren said, "Please come and have some coffee."

"First!" cried Pippi and was up by the table in two skips. She heaped as many cakes as she could onto a plate, threw five lumps of sugar into a coffee cup, emptied half the cream pitcher into her cup, and was back in her chair with her loot even before the ladies had reached the table.

Pippi stretched her legs out in front of her and placed the plate of cakes between her toes. Then she merrily dunked cakes in her coffee cup and stuffed so many in her mouth at once that she couldn't have uttered a word no matter how hard she tried. In the twinkling of an eye she had finished all the cakes on the plate. She got up, struck the plate as if it were a tambourine, and went up to the table to see if there were any cakes left. The ladies looked disapprovingly at her, but that didn't bother her. Chatting gaily, she walked around the table, snatching a cake here and a cake there.

> That everyone may eat and drink, and find satisfaction in all his toil — this is the gift of God.
>
>
>
> ECCLESIASTES 3:13

"It certainly was nice of you to invite me," she said. "I've never been to a coffee party before."

On the table stood a large cream pie, decorated in the center with a piece of red candy. Pippi stood with her hands behind her back and looked at it. Suddenly she bent down and snatched the candy with her teeth. But she dived down a little too hastily, and when she came up again her whole face was covered with whipped cream.

"Goody!" laughed Pippi. "Now we can play blindman's buff, for we've certainly got a blind man all made to order! I can't see a thing!"

She stuck out her tongue and licked away the cream. "This was indeed a dreadful accident," said she. "And the pie is all ruined now anyway, so I may as well eat it all up at once."

She dug into it with the pie server, and in a few minutes the whole pie had disappeared. Pippi patted her stomach contentedly. Mrs. Settergren had gone out into the kitchen so she knew nothing about the accident to the cream pie, but the other ladies looked very sternly at Pippi. No doubt they would have liked a little pie too. Pippi noticed that they looked disappointed and decided to cheer them up.

"Now you mustn't feel bad about such a little accident," she said comfortingly. "The main thing is that we have our health. And at a coffee party you should have fun."

She then picked up a sugar bowl and tipped all the lump sugar in it out on the floor. "Well, my goodness!" she cried. "Now look what I've done! How could I make such a mistake? I thought this was the granulated sugar. Bad luck seems to follow me today."

Thereupon she took a sugar spoon out of another bowl and began to sprinkle granulated sugar all over the floor. "I hope you notice," she said,

"that this is the kind of sugar you sprinkle on things. So it's perfectly all right for me to do this. Because why should there be the kind of sugar to sprinkle on things if somebody doesn't go and sprinkle it? — that's what I'd like to know.

"Have you ever noticed what fun it is to walk on a floor that has had sugar sprinkled all over it?" she asked the ladies. "Of course it's even more fun when you're barefoot," she added as she pulled off her shoes and stockings. "You ought to try it too, because nothing's more fun, believe me!"

At that moment Mrs. Settergren came in, and when she saw the sugar all over the floor she took Pippi firmly by the arm and led her over to the sofa to Tommy and Annika. Then she went over to the ladies and invited them to have more coffee. That the cream pie had disappeared only made her happy, because she thought the ladies had liked it so much that they had eaten it all.

Pippi, Tommy, and Annika sat talking quietly on the sofa. The fire crackled on the hearth. The ladies drank their coffee, and all was quiet and peaceful again. And as so often happens at coffee parties, the ladies began to talk about their servant problems. Apparently they had not been able to get very good servants, for they were not at all satisfied with them, and they agreed that it really was better not to have any servants at all. It was much more satisfactory to do things yourself because then you at least knew that things were done right.

Pippi sat on the sofa listening, and after the ladies had been talking a while she said, "Once my grandmother had a servant named Malin. She had chilblains on her feet, but otherwise there was nothing wrong with her. The only annoying thing was that as soon as company came she would rush at them and bite their legs. And bark! Oh, how she would bark! You could hear it all through the neighborhood, but it was only because she was playful. Only, of course, strangers didn't always understand that. The dean's wife, an elderly woman, came to see Grandmother once soon after Malin first came, and when Malin came dashing at her and bit her in the ankle, the dean's wife screamed so loudly that it scared Malin, so that her teeth clamped together and she couldn't get them apart. There she sat, stuck to the dean's wife's ankle until Friday. And Grandmother had to peel the potatoes herself. But at least it was well done. She peeled so well that when she was done there were no potatoes left — only peelings. But after that Friday the dean's wife never came to call on Grandmother again. She just never could take a joke. And poor Malin who was always so good-natured and happy! Though for that matter she was a little touchy at times, there's no denying that. Once when Grandmother poked a fork in her ear she howled all day."

Pippi looked around and smiled pleasantly. "Yes, that was Malin for you," she said and twiddled her thumbs.

The ladies acted as if they had heard nothing. They continued to talk.

"If my Rosa were only clean," said Mrs. Bergren, "then maybe I could keep her. But she's a regular pig — "

"Say, you ought to have seen Malin," Pippi interrupted. "Malin was so outrageously dirty that it was a joy to see her, Grandmother said. For the longest time Grandmother thought she had a very dark complexion but, honest and true, it was nothing but dirt that would wash off. And once at a bazaar at the City Hotel she got first prize for the dirt under her nails. Mercy me, how dirty that girl was!" said Pippi happily. Mrs. Settergren looked at her sternly.

"Can you imagine!" said Mrs. Granberg. "The other evening when Britta was going out she borrowed my blue satin dress without even asking for it. Isn't that dreadful?"

"Yes, indeed," said Pippi, "she certainly seems to be cut from the same piece of cloth as Malin, from what you say. Grandmother had a pink undershirt that she was specially fond of. But the worst of it was that Malin liked it too. And every morning Grandmother and Malin argued about who was to wear the undershirt. At last they decided it would be fair to take turns and each wear it every other day. But imagine how tricky Malin could be! Sometimes she'd come running in when it wasn't her turn at all and say, 'No mashed turnip today if I can't wear the pink woolen undershirt!' Well, what was Grandmother to do? Mashed turnip was her very favorite dish. There was nothing for it but to give Malin the shirt. As soon as Malin got the shirt she went out into the kitchen as nice as could be and began to mash turnip so that it spattered all over the walls."

There was silence for a little while, and then Mrs. Alexandersson said, "I'm not absolutely certain but I strongly suspect that my Hulda steals. In fact I've noticed that things disappear."

"Malin," began Pippi, but Mrs. Settergren interrupted her. "Children," she said decidedly, "go up to the nursery immediately!"

"Yes, but I was only going to tell that Malin stole too," said Pippi. "Like a raven! Everything she could lay her hands on. She used to get up in the middle of the night and steal; otherwise she couldn't sleep well, she said. Once she stole Grandmother's piano and tucked it into her own top bureau drawer. She was very clever with her hands, Grandmother said."

Tommy and Annika took hold of Pippi and pulled her out of the room and up the stairs. The ladies began their third cups of coffee, and Mrs. Settergren said, "It's not that I want to complain about my Ella, but she does break the china."

A red head appeared over the stair rail.

"Speaking of Malin," said Pippi, "maybe you are wondering if she used to break any china. Well, she did. She set apart one day a week just to break china. It was Tuesday, Grandmother said. As early as five o'clock on Tuesday morning you could hear this jewel of a maid in the kitchen, breaking china. She began with the coffee cups and glasses and little things like that and then went on to the soup bowls and dinner plates, and she finished up with platters and soup tureens. There was such a crash bang in the kitchen all morning that it was a joy to hear it, Grandmother said. And if Malin had any spare time late in the afternoon, she would go into the drawing room with a little hammer and knock down the antique East Indian plates that were hanging on the walls. Grandmother bought new china every Wednesday," said Pippi and disappeared up the stairs as quickly as a jack-in-the-box.

But now Mrs. Settergren's patience had come to an end. She ran up the stairs, into the nursery, and up to Pippi, who had just begun to teach Tommy to stand on his head.

"You must never come here again," said Mrs. Settergren, "if you can't behave any better than this."

Pippi looked at her in astonishment and her eyes slowly filled with tears. "That's just what I was afraid of," she said. "That I couldn't behave properly. It's no use to try; I'll never learn. I should have stayed on the ocean."

She curtsied to Mrs. Settergren, said good-bye to Tommy and Annika, and went slowly down the stairs.

The ladies were now getting ready to go home too. Pippi sat down in the hall near the shelf where rubbers were kept and watched the ladies putting on their hats and coats.

"Too bad you don't like your maids," said she. "You should have one like Malin. Grandmother always said there was nobody like her. Imagine! One Christmas when Malin was going to serve a little roast pig, do you know what she did? She had read in the cookbook that roast pig must be served with frilled paper in the ears and an apple in the mouth. But poor Malin didn't understand that it was the pig who was supposed to have the apple. You should have seen her when she came in on Christmas Eve with her best apron on and a big Gravenstein apple in her mouth. 'Oh, Malin, you're crazy!' Grandmother said to her, and Malin couldn't say a word in her own defense, she could only wiggle her ears until the frilled paper rustled. To be sure, she tried to say something, but it just sounded like blubb, blubb, blubb. And of course she couldn't bite people in the leg as she usually did, and it would be a day when there was a lot of company. Poor little Malin, it wasn't a very happy Christmas Eve for her," said Pippi sadly.

> Eat to live and not live to eat.
>
>
>
> BENJAMIN FRANKLIN
> *Poor Richard's Almanac*

The ladies were now dressed and said a last good-bye to Mrs. Settergren. And Pippi ran up to her and whispered, "Forgive me because I couldn't behave myself. Good-bye!"

Then she put on her large hat and followed the ladies. Outside the gate their ways parted. Pippi went toward Villa Villekulla and the ladies in the other direction.

When they had gone a little way they heard someone panting behind them. It was Pippi who had come racing back.

"You can imagine that Grandmother mourned when she lost Malin. Just think, one Tuesday morning when Malin had had time to break only about a dozen teacups she ran away and went to sea. And Grandmother had to break the china herself that day. She wasn't used to it, poor thing, and she got blisters all over her hands. She never saw Malin again. And that was a shame because she was such an excellent maid, Grandmother said."

Pippi left, and the ladies hurried on, but when they had gone a couple of hundred feet, they heard Pippi, from far off, yelling at the top of her lungs, "SHE NEVER SWEPT UNDER THE BEDS!"

When you arrive at a party, politely greet the host or hostess upon entering the room. Don't draw attention to yourself like Pippi.

She found the best and most comfortable chair and sat in it, when she should have offered it to someone else. She was also first in line at the coffee table, and took much more than her share of cream and sugar. She monopolized the conversation, and didn't go to the nursery when the hostess demanded she leave the room. What a guest!

When you're at a party, enjoy the opportunity to talk with others and listen to what they say. Before leaving, thank the host or hostess. Everyone will be so pleased that they will be sure to invite you again!

A MAD TEA PARTY
from Alice in Wonderland *by Lewis Carroll*
adapted by Michael Lamb

THERE WAS A TABLE set out under a tree in front of the house, and the March Hare and the Mad Hatter were having tea at it. A Dormouse was sitting between them, fast asleep, and the other two were using it as a cushion, resting their elbows on it and talking over its head. "Very uncomfortable for the Dormouse," thought Alice; "only it's asleep, I suppose it doesn't mind."

The table was a large one, but the three were all crowded together at one corner of it. "No room! No room!" they cried out when they saw Alice coming. "There's plenty of room!" said Alice indignantly, and she sat down in a large armchair at one end of the table.

"Have some wine," the March Hare said in an encouraging tone. Alice looked all around the table, but there was nothing on it but tea. "I don't see any wine," she remarked.

"There isn't any," said the March Hare.

"Then it wasn't very civil of you to offer it," said Alice angrily.

"It wasn't very civil of you to sit down without being invited," said the March Hare.

"I didn't know it was your table," said Alice. "It's laid out for a great many more than three."

"Your hair wants cutting," said the Hatter. He had been looking at Alice for some time with great curiosity, and this was his first speech.

"You should learn not to make personal remarks," Alice said with some severity; "it's very rude."

The Hatter opened his eyes very wide on hearing this; but all he said was "Why is a raven like a writing-desk?"

"Come, we shall have some fun now!" thought Alice. "I'm glad they've begun asking riddles. — I believe I can guess that," she added aloud.

"Do you mean that you think you can find out the answer to it?" said the March Hare.

"Exactly so," said Alice.

"Then you should say what you mean," the March Hare went on.

"I do," Alice hastily replied; "at least — at least I mean what I say — that's the same thing, you know."

"Not the same thing a bit!" said the Hatter. "Well, you might just as well say that 'I see what I eat' is the same thing as 'I eat what I see'!"

"You might just as well say," added the March Hare, "that 'I like what I get' is the same thing as 'I get what I like'!"

"You might just as well say," added the Dormouse, which seemed to be talking in its sleep, "that 'I breathe when I sleep' is the same thing as 'I sleep when I breathe'!"

"It is the same thing with you," said the Hatter; and here the conversation dropped, and the party sat silent for a minute, while Alice thought over all she could remember about ravens and writing-desks, which wasn't much.

The Hatter was the first to break the silence. "What day of the month is it?" he said, turning to Alice; he had taken his watch out of his pocket and was looking at it uneasily, shaking it every now and then and holding it to his ear.

Alice considered a little, and then said "The fourth."

"Two days wrong!" sighed the Hatter.

The March Hare took the watch and looked at it gloomily, then dipped it into his cup of tea.

Alice had been looking over his shoulder with some curiosity. "What a funny watch!" she remarked. "It tells the day of the month, and doesn't tell what o'clock it is!"

"Why should it?" muttered the Hatter. "Does your watch tell you what year it is?"

"Of course not," Alice replied very readily: "but that's because it stays the same year such a long time."

"Which is just the case with mine," said the Hatter.

Alice felt dreadfully puzzled. The Hatter's remark seemed to have no meaning in it, and yet it was certainly English. "I don't quite understand," she said, as politely as she could.

"The Dormouse is asleep again," said the Hatter, and he poured a little hot tea upon its nose. The Dormouse shook its head impatiently, and said, without opening its eyes, "Of course, of course; just what I was going to remark myself."

"Have you guessed the riddle yet?" the Hatter said, turning to Alice again.

"No, I give up," Alice replied. "What's the answer?"

"I haven't the slightest idea," said the Hatter.

"Nor I," said the March Hare.

Alice sighed wearily. "I think you might do something better with the time," she said, "than waste it asking riddles with no answers."

This story of the mad tea party gives us a good example of how not to act when we're dining!

Dining should be a cheerful and comfortable experience. It is a special time in the day when the family comes together for nourishment and conversation. In order to have a pleasant meal, it is important to be attentive and courteous to our parents, brothers, and sisters. Try to talk about happy things during mealtime, and avoid arguments. Be grateful for the food you are given, as well as the portion.

ICE CREAM
from Frog and Toad All Year
by Arnold Lobel

ONE HOT SUMMER DAY Frog and Toad sat by the pond. "I wish we had some sweet, cold ice cream," said Frog. "What a good idea," said Toad. "Wait right here, Frog. I will be back soon." Toad went to the store. He bought two big ice-cream cones.

Toad licked one of the cones. "Frog likes chocolate best," said Toad, "and so do I."

Toad walked along the path. A large, soft drop of chocolate ice cream slipped down his arm. "This ice cream is melting in the sun," said Toad.

Toad walked faster. Many drops of melting ice cream flew through the air. They fell down on Toad's head. "I must hurry back to Frog!" he cried.

More and more of the ice cream was melting. It dripped down on Toad's jacket. It splattered on his pants and on his feet. "Where is the path?" cried Toad. "I cannot see!"

Frog sat by the pond waiting for Toad. A mouse ran by.

"I just saw something awful!" cried the mouse. "It was big and brown!"

"Something covered with sticks and leaves is moving this way!" cried a squirrel.

"Here comes a thing with horns!" shouted a rabbit. "Run for your life!" "What can it be?" asked Frog.

Frog hid behind a rock. He saw the thing coming. It was big and brown. It was covered with sticks and leaves. It had two horns.

"Frog," cried the thing. "Where are you?" "Good heavens!" said Frog. "That thing is Toad!"

Toad fell into the pond. He sank to the bottom and came up again. "Drat," said Toad. "All of our sweet, cold ice cream has washed away."

"Never mind," said Frog. "I know what we can do." Frog and Toad quickly ran back to the store. Then they sat in the shade of a large tree and ate their chocolate ice-cream cones together.

On a hot summer day, ice cream melts quickly! This story reminds us that eating can be messy at times. No need to worry — just wipe your face with a napkin, and remember to go to the bathroom and wash up when you're done. If a bit of food gets stuck between your teeth, you can remove it later with a toothpick.

2.
Eat in Moderation and Be Generous to Others

THE LION, THE WITCH, AND THE WARDROBE
by C. S. Lewis

This next story comes from one of the best-loved series of all time, The Chronicles of Narnia *by C. S. Lewis. Four children, Peter, Lucy, Susan, and Edmund, leave their home in London during World War II to stay with a kindly professor in his country manor. One day, while playing hide and seek, they discover a magical wardrobe (what a clothes closet is called in England) that is actually a portal into another world. Through the wardrobe they enter into Narnia — a cold, snowy land put under the spell of perpetual winter by the White Witch.*

In the excerpt below, Edmund betrays his brother and sisters to the White Witch. She brings him under her spell by feeding him highly addictive Turkish Delight sweets.

CHAPTER 4

"MY POOR CHILD," the Queen said, "how cold you look! Come and sit with me here on the sledge and I will put my mantle round you and we will talk."

Edmund did not like this arrangement at all but he dared not disobey; he stepped onto the sledge and sat at her feet, and she put a fold of her fur mantle round him and tucked it well in.

"Perhaps something hot to drink?" said the Queen. "Should you like that?"

"Yes please, your Majesty," said Edmund, whose teeth were chattering.

The Queen took from somewhere among her wrappings a very small bottle which looked as if it were made of copper. Then, holding out her arm, she let one drop fall from it onto the snow beside the sledge. Edmund saw the drop for a second in mid-air, shining like a diamond. But the moment it touched the snow there was a hissing sound and there stood a jeweled cup full of something that steamed. The dwarf immediately took this and handed it to Edmund with a bow and a smile; not a very nice smile. Edmund felt much better as he began to sip the hot drink. It was something he had never tasted before, very sweet and foamy and creamy, and it warmed him right down to his toes.

"It is dull, Son of Adam, to drink without eating," said the Queen presently. "What would you like best to eat?"

"Turkish Delight, please, your Majesty," said Edmund.

The Queen let another drop fall from her bottle onto the snow, and instantly there appeared a round box, tied with green silk ribbon, which, when opened, turned out to contain several pounds of the best Turkish Delight. Each piece was sweet and light to the very center and Edmund had never tasted anything more delicious. He was quite warm now, and very comfortable.

While he was eating the Queen kept asking him questions. At first Edmund tried to remember that it is rude to speak with one's mouth full, but soon he forgot about this and thought only of trying to shovel down as much Turkish Delight as he could, and the more he ate the more he wanted to eat, and he never asked himself why the Queen should be so inquisitive. She got him to tell her that he had one brother and two sisters, and that one of his sisters had already been in Narnia and had met a Faun there, and that no one except himself and his brother and his sisters knew anything about Narnia. She seemed especially interested in the fact that there were four of them, and kept on coming back to it. "You are sure there are just four of you?" she asked. "Two Sons of Adam and two Daughters of Eve, neither more nor less?" and Edmund, with his mouth full of Turkish Delight, kept on saying, "Yes, I told you that before," and forgetting to call her "Your Majesty," but she didn't seem to mind now.

At last the Turkish Delight was all finished and Edmund was looking very hard at the empty box and wishing that she would ask him whether he would like some more. Probably the Queen knew quite well what he was thinking; for she knew, though Edmund did not, that this was enchanted Turkish Delight and that anyone who had once tasted it would want more and more of it, and would even, if they were allowed, go on eating it till they killed themselves. But she did not offer him any more.

Instead, she said to him, "Son of Adam, I should so much like to see your brother and your two sisters. Will you bring them to see me?"

"I'll try," said Edmund, still looking at the empty box.

"Because, if you did come again — bringing them with you of course — I'd be able to give you some more Turkish Delight. I can't do it now, the magic will only work once. In my own house it would be another matter."

"Why can't we go to your house now?" said Edmund. When he had first got onto the sledge he had been afraid that she might drive away with him to some unknown place from which he would not be able to get back; but he had forgotten about that fear now.

"It is a lovely place, my house," said the Queen. "I am sure you would like it. There are whole rooms full of Turkish Delight, and what's more, I have no children of my own. I want a nice boy whom I could bring up as a Prince and who would be King of Narnia when I am gone. While he was Prince he would wear a gold crown and eat Turkish Delight all day long; and you are much the cleverest and handsomest young man I've ever met. I think I would like to make you the Prince — some day, when you bring the others to visit me."

"Why not now?" said Edmund. His face had become very red and his mouth and fingers were sticky. He did not look either clever or handsome, whatever the Queen might say.

"Oh, but if I took you there now," said she, "I shouldn't see your brother and your sisters. I very much want to know your charming relations. You are to be the Prince and — later on — the King; that is understood. But you must have courtiers and nobles. I will make your brother a Duke and your sisters Duchesses."

"There's nothing special about *them*," said Edmund, "and, anyway, I could always bring them some other time."

"Ah, but once you were in my house," said the Queen, "you might forget all about them. You would be enjoying yourself so much that you wouldn't want the bother of going to fetch them. No. You must go back to your own country now and come to me another day, *with them*, you understand. It is no good coming without them."

"But I don't even know the way back to my own country," pleaded Edmund.

"That's easy," answered the Queen. "Do you see that lamp?" She pointed with her wand and Edmund turned and saw the same lamp-post under which Lucy had met the Faun. "Straight on, beyond that, is the way to the World of Men. And now look the other way" — here she pointed in the opposite direction — "and tell me if you can see two little hills rising above the trees."

"I think I can," said Edmund.

"Well, my house is between those two hills. So next time you come you have only to find the lamp-post and look for those two hills and walk through the wood till you reach my house. But remember — you must bring the others with you. I might have to be very angry with you if you came alone."

"I'll do my best," said Edmund.

"And, by the way," said the Queen, "you needn't tell them about me. It would be fun to keep it a secret between us two, wouldn't it? Make it a surprise for them. Just bring them along to the two hills — a clever boy like you will easily think of some excuse for doing that — and when you come to my house you could just say 'Let's see who lives here' or something like that. I am sure that would be best. If your sister has met one of the Fauns, she may have heard strange stories about me — nasty stories that might make her afraid to come to me. Fauns will say anything, you know, and now — "

"Please, please," said Edmund suddenly, "please couldn't I have just one piece of Turkish Delight to eat on the way home?"

"No, no," said the Queen with a laugh, "you must wait till next time." While she spoke, she signaled to the dwarf to drive on, but as the sledge swept away out of sight, the Queen waved to Edmund, calling out, "Next time! Next time! Don't forget. Come soon."

If Edmund had not been so selfish, he would not have fallen under the wicked spell of the White Witch. In this second scene, the other children have taken refuge in Mr. and Mrs. Beaver's home. Here, in contrast to Edmund's greediness for sweets, we see generosity at the table.

CHAPTER 7

"So you've come at last!" Mrs. Beaver said, holding out both her wrinkled old paws. "At last! To think that ever I should live to see this day! The potatoes are on boiling and the kettle's singing and I daresay, Mr. Beaver, you'll get us some fish."

"That I will," said Mr. Beaver, and he went out of the house (Peter went with him), and across the ice of the deep pool to where he had a little hole in the ice which he kept open every day with his hatchet. They took a pail with them. Mr. Beaver sat down quietly at the edge of the hole (he didn't seem to mind it being so chilly), looked hard into it, then suddenly shot in his paw, and before you could say Jack Robinson had whisked out a beautiful trout. Then he did it all over again until they had a fine catch of fish.

Meanwhile the girls were helping Mrs. Beaver to fill the kettle and lay the table and cut the bread and put the platter in the oven to heat and draw a huge jug of beer for Mr. Beaver from a barrel which stood in one corner of the house, and to put on the frying-pan and get the dripping hot. Lucy thought the Beavers had a very snug little home though it was not at all like Mr. Tumnus's cave. There were no books or pictures, and instead of beds there were bunks, like on board ship, built into the wall. And there were hams and strings of onions hanging from the roof, and against the walls were gum boots and oilskins and hatchets and pairs of shears and spades and fishing-rods and fishing-nets and sacks. And the cloth on the table, though very clean, was very rough.

Just as the frying-pan was nicely hissing Peter and Mr. Beaver came in with the fish which Mr. Beaver had already opened with his knife and cleaned out in the open air. You can think how good the new-caught fish smelled while they were frying and how the hungry children longed for them to be done and how very much hungrier still they had become before Mr. Beaver said, "Now we're nearly ready." Susan drained the potatoes and then put them back in the empty pot to dry on the side of the range while Lucy was helping Mrs. Beaver to dish up the trout, so that in a very few minutes everyone was drawing up their stools (it was three-legged stools in the Beavers' house except for Mrs. Beaver's own special rocking chair beside the fire) and preparing to enjoy themselves. There was a jug of creamy milk for the children (Mr. Beaver stuck to beer) and a great big lump of deep yellow butter in the middle of the table from which everyone took as much as he wanted to go with his potatoes, and all the children thought — and I agree with them — that there's nothing to beat good freshwater fish if you eat it when it has been alive half an hour ago and has come out of the pan half a minute ago. And when they had finished the fish Mrs. Beaver brought unexpectedly out of the oven a great and gloriously sticky marmalade roll, steaming hot, and at the same time moved the kettle onto the fire, so that when they had finished the marmalade roll the tea was made and ready to be poured out. And when each person had got his (or her) cup of tea, each person shoved back his (or her) stool so as to be able to lean against the wall and gave a long sigh of contentment.

"And now," said Mr. Beaver, pushing away his empty beer mug and pulling his cup of tea toward him, "if you'll just wait till I've got my pipe lit up and going nicely — why, now we can get to business. It's snowing again," he added, cocking his eye at the window. "That's all the better, because it means we shan't have any visitors; and if anyone should have been trying to follow you, why he won't find any tracks."

Mr. and Mrs. Beaver gave their guests a warm welcome. By preparing a snack, warm meal, or hot cup of tea, you can make someone feel welcome in your home. When your friends visit, offer them something to eat and drink. And when you visit them and they offer you the same, be sure to thank them for their generosity.

Lucy and Susan also offered to help Mrs. Beaver in the kitchen. Your help preparing a meal and setting the table will be welcomed in your own home and in your friends' homes.

CHOCOLATE CAKE
based on "The Plum Cake" by Ann and Jane Taylor
adapted by Karen Santorum

"Oh, I've got a chocolate cake, what a feast I'll gladly make,
I'll eat, and I'll stuff, and I'll cram;
Morning, and noon, and night — it is my great delight;
What a happy young boy I am."

Thus said little George, and beginning to gorge,
He dug into the cake and applied;
His fingers and thumbs, while making chocolate cake crumbs,
His fingers hunting, and digging beside.

But so sad to tell, a misfortune befell,
Which ruined all of his fun;
After eating his fill, he was taken so ill,
That he trembled for what he had done.

As he grew worse and worse, the doctor and nurse,
To cure his disorder were sent,

And rightly you think, he had medicine to drink,
Which made George for his stuffing repent.

And while on the bed he rolled his sore head,
Impatient with stomachache and pain,
He'd learned a good lesson from his sweet chocolate cake.
"Don't be such a glutton again."

Remember to eat slowly and enjoy your food. Chew your food quietly with your mouth closed, and never talk with your mouth full. Unlike little George, if you would like some dessert, just ask: "May I please have some cake?"

THE DOG AND THE SHADOW
by Aesop

ONE DAY A DOG managed to find a big piece of meat. While he was walking along looking for a good spot to sit down quietly to his meal, he crossed a bridge over a clear stream. Looking down, he saw his own reflection in the water.

Because he was a greedy brute, he decided that there was a dog down there in the water who had a piece of meat which he could grab. So he barked his fiercest bark, and grabbed for the other dog's meat.

What he had in his mouth fell into the stream, and he found out too late that he not only didn't have any extra meat — he didn't have any meat at all.

THE MOUSE AND THE WEASEL
by Aesop

A POOR SKINNY LITTLE MOUSE had worked and worked to make a hole in a corn basket so he could get in and have all he wanted to eat.

He finally made it, and when he got inside he stuffed and crammed himself with so much corn he became as fat as a butterball. When he had much more than enough he thought he'd leave, but oh no; he was much too big around the middle now and he couldn't get out at all.

A weasel, who was sitting on the sidelines, just passing the time of day watching the Mouse, said, "Mouse, if you want to get out of there you had better start reducing back to the skinny fellow you used to be."

If we only eat what we need to feel full, not only will we look healthy — we'll feel better, too!

WHERE LUNCH BOXES GROW ON TREES
from Ozma of Oz *by L. Frank Baum*
adapted by Michael Lamb

DOROTHY HAD MET two new friends: Billina, a hen who could talk, and Tiktok, an amazing mechanical man. They had walked quite a while together and decided that it was time to rest. Dorothy was quite hungry. She then remembered the lunchbox she had picked off the lunchbox tree. Only in the Land of Oz, she thought, does one find lunchboxes growing on trees.

Dorothy sat down and opened her tin lunchbox. In the cover she found a small tank that was full of very nice lemonade. It was covered by a cup, which might also, when removed, be used to drink the lemonade. Within the lunchbox were three slices of turkey, two slices of cold ham, some lobster salad, four slices of bread and butter, some custard pie, an orange, nine large strawberries, and some nuts and raisins. Singularly enough, the nuts in this lunchbox grew already cracked, so that Dorothy had no trouble in picking out their meats to eat.

She spread the feast upon the rock beside her and began her dinner, first offering some of it to Tiktok, who declined because, as he said, he was merely a machine. Afterward she offered to share with Billina, but the hen murmured something about "dead things" and said she preferred her bugs and ants.

"Who do the lunchbox trees belong to?" the child asked Tiktok, while engaged in eating her meal.

"They belong to the royal family of Ev," Tiktok replied. "King Evoldo, of Ev, allows all the people of his land to eat from them and share in the goodness of the lunch box trees. You will find the royal "E" stamped upon the bottom of every lunchbox." Dorothy turned the lunchbox over and at once discovered the royal mark upon it, just as Tiktok had said.

When Dorothy ate with others, she always offered to share her food with them. They appreciated her kindness and were, in turn, polite to her.

The King of the Golden River
by John Ruskin

This is a story of three brothers. The youngest brother, Gluck, learned a secret from the King of the Golden River — how to turn a river into gold by dropping three drops of holy water into the source of the river. However, a person only gets one chance to accomplish this task.

The two wicked older brothers, having squandered their fortunes, took the secret that Gluck learned and attempted the quest themselves. The first to try was Hans. He stole holy water from a church after the good priest refused to give it to him. Hans made it to the river, but when he dropped the stolen holy water into it, he was turned to a black stone.

When Hans didn't return, the second brother, Schwartz, decided to try. He knew that Hans had stolen the holy water and thought that this was the reason for his fate. So Schwartz took some of Gluck's money and went to a corrupt priest, who sold him some holy water. Like his brother before him, he encountered opportunities to show kindness toward others on his journey to the river, but, like Hans, he helped no one. When he dropped the water in the river, he too turned into a black stone.

CHAPTER 5

WHEN GLUCK FOUND that Schwartz did not come back, he was very sorry, and did not know what to do. He had no money, and was obliged to go and hire himself again to the goldsmith, who worked him very hard, and gave him very little money. So, after a month or two, Gluck grew tired, and made up his mind to go and try his fortune with the Golden River. "The little King looked very kind," thought he. "I don't think he will turn me into a black stone." So he went to the priest, and the priest gave him some holy water as soon as he asked for it. Then Gluck took some bread in his basket, and the bottle of water, and set off very early for the mountains.

If the glacier had occasioned a great deal of fatigue to his brothers, it was twenty times worse for him, who was neither so strong nor so practiced on the mountains. He had several very bad falls, lost his basket and bread, and was very much frightened at the strange noises under the ice.

He lay a long time to rest on the grass, after he had got over, and began to climb the hill just in the hottest part of the day. When he had climbed for an hour, he got dreadfully thirsty, and was going to drink like his brothers, when he saw an old man coming down the path above him, looking very feeble, and leaning on a staff. "My son," said the old man, "I am faint with thirst, give me some of that water." Then Gluck looked at him, and when he saw that he was pale and weary, he gave him the water; "Only pray don't drink it all," said Gluck. But the old man drank a great deal, and gave him back the bottle two-thirds empty. Then he bade him good speed, and Gluck went on again merrily. And the path became easier to his feet, and two or three blades of grass appeared upon it, and some grasshoppers began singing on the bank beside it; and Gluck thought he had never heard such merry singing.

Then he went on for another hour, and the thirst increased in him so that he thought he should be forced to drink. But, as he raised the flask, he saw a little child lying panting by the roadside, and it cried out piteously for water. Then Gluck struggled with himself, and determined to bear the thirst a little longer; and he put the bottle to the child's lips, and it drank it all but a few drops. Then it smiled on him, and got up, and ran down the hill; and Gluck looked after it, till it became as small as a little star, and then turned and began climbing again. And then there were all kinds of sweet flowers growing on the rocks, bright green moss, with pale pink starry flowers, and soft belled gentians, more blue than the sky at its deepest, and pure white transparent lilies. And crimson and purple butterflies darted hither and thither, and the sky sent down such pure light, that Gluck had never felt so happy in his life.

Yet, when he had climbed for another hour, his thirst became intolerable again; and, when he looked at his bottle, he saw that there were only five or six drops left in it, and he could not venture to drink. And, as he was hanging the flask to his belt again, he saw a little dog lying on the rocks, gasping for breath — just as Hans had seen it on the day of his ascent. And Gluck stopped and looked at it, and then at the Golden River, not five hundred yards above him; and he thought of the dwarf's words, "that no one could succeed, except in his first attempt"; and he tried to pass the dog, but it whined piteously, and Gluck stopped again. "Poor beastie," said Gluck, "it'll be dead, when I come down again, if I don't help it." Then he looked closer and closer at it, and its eyes turned on him so mournfully that he could not stand it. "Confound the King, and his gold too," said Gluck; and he opened the flask, and poured all the water into the dog's mouth.

The dog sprang up and stood on its hind legs. Its tail disappeared, its ears became long, longer, silky, golden; its nose became very red, its eyes became very twinkling; in three seconds the dog was gone, and before Gluck stood his old acquaintance, the King of the Golden River.

"Thank you," said the monarch; "but don't be frightened, it's all right"; for Gluck showed manifest symptoms of consternation at this reply to his last observation. "Why didn't you come before," continued the dwarf, "instead of sending me those rascally brothers of yours, for me to have the trouble of turning into stones? Very hard stones they make too."

"Oh, dear me!" said Gluck, "have you really been so cruel?"

"Cruel!" said the dwarf, "they poured unholy water into my stream: do you suppose I'm going to allow that?"

"Why," said Gluck, "I am sure, sir — your Majesty, I mean — they got the water out of the church font."

"Very probably," replied the dwarf; "but," and his countenance grew stern as he spoke, "the water which has been refused to the cry of the weary and dying is unholy, though it had been blessed by every saint in heaven; and the water which is found in the vessel of mercy is holy, though it had been defiled with corpses."

> They broke bread in their homes and ate together with glad and sincere hearts.
>
>
>
> Acts 2:46–47

So saying, the dwarf stooped and plucked a lily that grew at his feet. On its white leaves there hung three drops of clear dew. And the dwarf shook them into the flask which Gluck held in his hand. "Cast these into the river," he said, "and descend on the other side of the mountains into the Treasure Valley. And so good speed."

As he spoke, the figure of the dwarf became indistinct. The playing colors of his robe formed themselves into a prismatic mist of dewy light: he stood for an instant veiled with them as with the belt of a broad rainbow. The colors grew faint, the mist rose into the air; the monarch had evaporated.

And Gluck climbed to the brink of the Golden River, and its waves were as clear as crystal, and as brilliant as the sun. And, when he cast the three drops of dew into the stream, there opened where they fell, a small whirlpool, into which the waters descended with a musical noise.

Gluck stood watching it for some time, very much disappointed, because not only was the river not turned into gold, but its waters seemed much diminished in quantity. Yet he obeyed his friend the dwarf, and descended the other side of the mountains, towards the Treasure Valley; and, as he went, he thought he heard the noise of water working its way under the ground. And, when he came in sight of the Treasure Valley, behold, a river, like the Golden River, was springing from a new cleft of the rocks above it, and was flowing in innumerable streams among the dry heaps of red sand.

And as Gluck gazed, fresh grass sprang beside the new streams, and creeping plants grew, and climbed among the moistening soil. Young flowers opened suddenly along the riversides, as stars leap out when twilight is deepening, and thickets of myrtle and tendrils of vine cast lengthening shadows over the valley as they grew. And this the Treasure Valley became a garden again, and the inheritance, which had been lost by cruelty, was regained by love.

And Gluck went, and dwelt in the valley, and the poor were never driven from his door: so that his barns became full of corn, and his house of treasure. And, for him, the river had, according to the dwarf's promise, become a River of Gold.

And, to this day, the inhabitants of the valley point out the place where the three drops of holy dew were cast into the stream, and trace the course of the Golden River under the ground, until it emerges in the Treasure Valley. And at the top of the cataract of the Golden River, are still to be seen two black stones, round which the waters howl mournfully every day at sunset; and these stones are still called by the people of the valley the Black Brothers.

Gluck was compassionate. He put his own needs aside in order to generously fulfill the needs of others. He also put the lives of the old man, the child, and even the dog above his desire for gold.

When you are with others, follow Gluck's example and attend to their needs before your own. Especially at mealtime, serve others first and make sure everyone has been served before you reach for seconds.

3.
Appreciate What You Are Served

PINOCCHIO
by Carlo Collodi

We return to the story of Pinocchio the wooden puppet. He was ravenous with hunger and begging for food in the village late at night. After having a basin of water dumped on his head, he went home soaking wet and fell asleep in front of the fire.

CHAPTER 7

POOR PINOCCHIO, whose eyes were still half shut from sleep had not as yet discovered that his feet were burnt off. The moment, therefore, that he heard his father's voice he slipped off his stool to run and open the door; but after stumbling two or three times he fell his whole length on the floor.

And the noise he made in falling was as if a sack of wooden ladles had been thrown from a fifth story.

"Open the door!" shouted Geppetto from the street.

"Dear Papa, I cannot," answered the puppet, crying and rolling about on the ground.

"Why cannot you?"

"Because my feet have been eaten."

"And who has eaten your feet?"

"The cat," said Pinocchio, seeing the cat, who was amusing herself by making some shavings dance with her forepaws.

"Open the door, I tell you!" repeated Geppetto. "If you don't, when I get into the house you shall have the cat from me!"

"I cannot stand up, believe me. Oh, poor me, poor me! I shall have to walk on my knees for the rest of my life!"

Geppetto, believing that all this lamentation was only another of the puppet's tricks, thought of a means of putting an end to it, and climbing up the wall he got in at the window.

He was very angry, and at first he did nothing but scold; but when he saw his Pinocchio lying on the ground and really without feet he was quite overcome. He took him in his arms and began to kiss and caress him and to say a thousand endearing things to him, and as the big tears ran down his cheeks, he said, sobbing:

"My little Pinocchio! How did you manage to burn your feet?"

"I don't know, Papa, but believe me it has been an infernal night that I shall remember as long as I live. It thundered and lightened, and I was very hungry, and then the Talking Cricket said to me: 'It serves you right; you have been wicked and you deserve it,' and I said to him: 'Take care, Cricket!' . . . and he said: 'You are a puppet and you have a wooden head,' and I threw the handle of a hammer at him, and he died, but the fault was his, for I didn't wish to kill him, and the proof of it is that I put an earthenware saucer on a brazier of burning embers, but a chicken flew out and said: 'Adieu until we meet again, and many compliments to all at home': and I got still more hungry, for which reason that little old man in a nightcap opening the window said to me, 'Come underneath and hold out your hat,' and poured a basinful of water on my head, because asking for a little bread isn't a disgrace, is it? And I returned home at once, and because I was always very hungry I put my feet on the brazier to dry them, and then you returned, and I found they were burnt off, and I am always hungry, but I have no longer any feet! *Ih! Ih! Ih! Ih!* . . ." And poor Pinocchio began to cry and to roar so loudly that he was heard five miles off.

Geppetto, who from all this jumbled account had only understood one thing, which was that the puppet was dying of hunger, drew from his pocket three pears, and giving them to him said:

"These three pears were intended for my breakfast; but I will give them to you willingly. Eat them, and I hope they will do you good."

"If you wish me to eat them, be kind enough to peel them for me."

"*Peel them?*" said Geppetto, astonished. "I should never have thought, my boy, that you were so dainty and fastidious. That is bad! In this world we should accustom ourselves from childhood to like and to eat everything, for there is no saying to what we may be brought. There are so many chances! . . ."

"You are no doubt right," interrupted Pinocchio, "but I will never eat fruit that has not been peeled. I cannot bear rind."

So that good Geppetto fetched a knife, and arming himself with patience peeled the three pears, and put the rind on a corner of the table.

Having eaten the first pear in two mouthfuls, Pinocchio was about to throw away the core; but Geppetto caught hold of his arm and said to him:

"Do not throw it away; in this world everything may be of use."

"But core I am determined I will not eat," shouted the puppet, turning upon him like a viper.

"Who knows! There are so many chances! . . ." repeated Geppetto without losing his temper.

And so the three cores, instead of being thrown out of the window, were placed on the corner of the table together with the three rinds.

Having eaten, or rather having devoured the three pears, Pinocchio yawned tremendously, and then said in a fretful tone:

"I am as hungry as ever!"

"But, my boy, I have nothing more to give you!"

"Nothing, really nothing?"

"I have only the rind and the cores of the three pears."

"One must have patience!" said Pinocchio. "If there is nothing else, I will eat a rind."

And he began to chew it. At first he made a wry face; but then one after another he quickly disposed of the rinds; and after the rinds even the cores, and when he had eaten up everything he clapped his hands on his sides in his satisfaction, and said joyfully:

"Ah! Now I feel comfortable."

"You see now," observed Geppetto, "that I was right when I said to you that it did not do to accustom ourselves to be too particular or too dainty in our tastes. We can never know, my dear boy, what may happen to us. There are so many chances! . . ."

> Better a dry crust with peace and quiet than a house full of feasting, with strife.
>
>
>
> PROVERBS 17:1

Geppetto gave Pinocchio the pears intended for his own breakfast, but Pinocchio was ungrateful. Instead of saying "thank you," Pinocchio demanded that Geppetto peel them — without even saying "please"!

But you can respond with gratitude to the food set before you. Remember to thank God for the food you're about to eat, and be sure to thank the people who prepared it for you.

THE ADVENTURES OF HUCKLEBERRY FINN
by Mark Twain

CHAPTER I

YOU DON'T KNOW ABOUT ME without you have read a book by the name of *The Adventures of Tom Sawyer*; but that ain't no matter. That book was made by Mr. Mark Twain, and he told the truth, mainly. There was things which he stretched, but mainly he told the truth. That is nothing. I never seen anybody but lied one time or another, without it was Aunt Polly, or the widow, or maybe Mary. Aunt Polly — Tom's Aunt Polly, she is — and Mary, and the Widow Douglas is all told about in that book, which is mostly a true book, with some stretchers, as I said before.

Now the way that the book winds up is this: Tom and me found the money that the robbers hid in the cave, and it made us rich. We got six thousand dollars apiece all gold. It was an awful sight of money when

it was piled up. Well, Judge Thatcher he took it and put it out at interest, and it fetched us a dollar a day apiece all the year round — more than a body could tell what to do with. The Widow Douglas she took me for her son, and allowed she would sivilize me; but it was rough living in the house all the time, considering how dismal regular and decent the widow was in all her ways; and so when I couldn't stand it no longer I lit out. I got into my old rags and my sugar-hogshead again, and was free and satisfied. But Tom Sawyer he hunted me up and said he was going to start a band of robbers, and I might join if I would go back to the widow and be respectable. So I went back.

The widow she cried over me, and called me a poor lost lamb, and she called me a lot of other names, too, but she never meant no harm by it. She put me in them new clothes again, and I couldn't do nothing but sweat and sweat, and felt all cramped up. Well, then, the old thing commenced again. The widow rung a bell for supper, and you had to come on time. When you got to the table you couldn't go right to eating, but you had to wait for the widow to tuck down her head and grumble a little over the victuals, though there wasn't really anything the matter with them — that is, nothing only everything was cooked by itself. In a barrel of odds and ends it is different; things get mixed up, and the juice kind of swaps around, and the things go better.

Huck didn't understand why the widow Douglas wanted to pray before eating. He thought she was praying to make the food edible!

Heidi
by Johanna Spyri

Heidi was an orphan, and her aunt no longer wanted to care for her. She was given to her grandfather, who lived alone in the Swiss Alps and had a reputation for being tough, uncaring, and cruel. But Heidi discovered that her grandfather was really a kind and gentle soul who took good care of her. She loved living in the mountains and playing with the goats, and she became friends with Peter, a goatherd. In this scene, Heidi and Peter are watching the goats and having a picnic lunch.

HEIDI JUMPED UP and ran round among the goats. It was new and extremely amusing to her to see how the little creatures leaped about and played together, and Heidi made the personal acquaintance of each, for every one had a quite distinct individuality and its own peculiar ways.

Meanwhile Peter had brought out the bag and nicely arranged all four of the pieces of bread and cheese on the ground in a square, the larger pieces on Heidi's side, the smaller ones on his side; he knew just how many he had. Then he took the little bowl and milked sweet, fresh milk from Schwanli into it and placed it in the middle of the square. Then he called Heidi, but he had to call longer for her than for the goats, because she was so interested and pleased with the playing and frolicking of her new playmates that she saw and heard nothing else.

But Peter knew how to make himself understood. He called till he made the rocks above echo; and Heidi appeared, and the table he had laid looked so inviting that she danced round it for joy.

"Stop jumping; it is time to eat," said Peter. "Sit down and begin."

Heidi sat down.

"Is the milk mine?" she asked, looking with satisfaction at the neat square and the bowl in the middle.

"Yes," answered Peter, "and the two large pieces of bread and cheese are yours, too; and when you have drunk all the milk, you can have another bowlful from Schwanli, and then it is my turn."

"And where will you get your milk?" Heidi wanted to know.

"From my goat — from Schnecke. Go to eating!" commanded Peter once more.

Heidi began with her milk, and as soon as she set down her empty bowl Peter rose and filled it again. Heidi broke some of her bread into it; the rest, a piece still larger than all Peter's bread, she handed over to him, with all her large portion of cheese, and said, "You may have that, I have enough."

Peter looked at Heidi in speechless amazement, for never in his life had he been able to say such a thing or give anything away. He hesitated a little, for he could not really believe that Heidi was in earnest. She went on offering the bread and cheese, and when he did not take it, she laid it down on his knee. Then he saw that she meant it for him, seized the prize, nodded his thanks, and then made the most satisfactory dinner of his goat-herding life.

TOAD AND FROG
author unknown

"Croak," said the toad,
"I'm hungry I think,
Today I've had nothing to eat or drink;
I'll crawl to a garden and jump through the pales,
And there I'll dine nicely on slugs and on snails."

"Ho, ho!" said the frog,
"Is that what you mean?
Then I'll hop away to the next meadow stream,
There I will drink, and eat worms and slugs too,
And then I shall have a good dinner like you."

When eating at a friend's house, remember that people eat many different types of foods: Italian, Chinese, Indian, and so on. You'll probably like what you're served, but if not, you don't have to let your hosts know it. Even if you think something doesn't look appetizing, try a little. You may find a new ethnic food that will become a favorite!

CHICKEN NICKEL
by Aaron Zenz

ONCE THERE WAS A BIRD who loved to eat spaghetti. His name was Chicken Nickel.

He loved spaghetti so much that he would eat it every day for every meal. In fact, he even named his pet fish "Noodle."

Chicken Nickel ate his spaghetti in a very odd way. Instead of eating it with tomato sauce, he poured on chocolate syrup.

Chomp, chomp, chomp, delicious!

And instead of meatballs, he covered his spaghetti with oranges.

Munch, munch, munch, mmmmm . . .

And instead of drinking milk with his dinner, he would grab his fishbowl and drink fish-water.

Slurp, slurp, slurp, ahhhhh!

One day, he was eating his spaghetti as usual — *mmm, mmm, mmm.*

With his chocolate sauce — *chomp, chomp, chomp.*

And his oranges — *munch, munch, munch.*

And his fish-water — *slurp, slurp, GLUMP, slurp.*

Huh?

Chicken Nickel felt a glump go down. He looked at Noodle's bowl, and it was —

EMPTY! Oh no! He had swallowed the fish!

"Noodle! Noodle!" cried Chicken Nickel. He wanted to save his pet. But how?

Think, Chicken Nickel, think. Use your noodle . . . That's it!

Chicken Nickel grabbed a piece of spaghetti from his plate. He opened his beak wide. He held on tight to one end of the noodle and hung the other end down his throat.

Chicken Nickel waited until he felt Noodle grab one end of the spaghetti. Then he slowly pulled it up, up, up until his fish was safe!

Hooray!

It was a wonderful reunion.

Chicken Nickel still loves spaghetti. And he still eats it with chocolate sauce. And he still has it with oranges.

But, instead of fish-water . . .

. . . he always drinks his milk.

4.
Setting the Table

DANIEL PLACE'S GIFT
by Rick Santorum

IT WAS GOING TO BE one of the most important days of Daniel Place's life. His daughter — the daughter of a carpenter, no less — was going to marry a prince from the far away land of Paterjohn. Daniel had never visited this magnificent kingdom, but he had heard stories of the refinement and elegance of the people who lived there.

Ever since the wedding had been announced, Daniel had worried that the parents and guests of the prince would not approve of his humble home and simple wedding plans. Over the last few months he had worked hard to earn more money to spruce up his house and rent a nice hall to hold a fine feast. But he was still worried, because his daughter, Anne Marie, told him that the people in Paterjohn did not eat as crudely as did the people of his village.

So for weeks he worked hard to carve wooden plates and cups. He also made knives and simple versions of forks and spoons. He used the finest wood and the best design he could find, but they were still quite plain.

The day before the wedding, he presented his special gift to Anne Marie as she and her mother were setting up the tables and chairs for the wedding banquet. Unbeknownst to Daniel, earlier that day the king had given Anne Marie a lovely set of dinnerware to use at the wedding feast. The king did so out of kindness, for he knew that there was no such finery in this village. Now, his daughter saw that her father's gift did not approach the quality of the king's gift, but she also saw the love behind it.

She smiled and embraced her father. "Daddy, they are so beautiful. Could we use them tomorrow at our wedding banquet?"

"Do you really like them that much?" asked her father.

"More than any gift I have ever received," she replied.

As was the custom in that rather backwards land, Anne Marie and her father took the plates, cups, knives, forks, and spoons and set them near the door where people entered. Everyone would take a plate and cup, but many of the people from this small village would not bother taking the silverware, preferring to eat with their fingers.

As is the case so often in our lives, an angel was watching this exchange between a loving father and a devoted daughter. He was so moved by what he saw that later that night, when all were asleep, he went to the banquet hall. He took out the unsophisticated wooden plates and transformed them into bone china so fine that they were superior to anything ever before seen in this or any other land.

To make sure all the guests would appreciate their beauty, he placed one on the table in front of every chair in the hall. He then took the cups, changed them into crystal goblets, and placed them in a position of honor above the plate on the right.

The angel then turned the utensils into luminous sterling silver. But where should he put them for all to see?

He thought that since most people cut with their right hand, the knife should be to the right of the plate. He placed the knives very close to the plates, with their sharp sides against the edges of the plates so that no one would be cut reaching for them.

Since the fork is used to hold food while cutting, he placed it on the left side of the plate.

As for the spoon, most people use it with their right hand while they are eating their soup, which is served before the rest of the meal. So the angel determined that the spoon must go in the easiest spot to begin with: to the right of the knife.

The little angel felt proud because the table looked so lovely. But as he admired his work, one thing kept bothering him. The fork, the fork to the left of the plate, looked so lonely.

"What can I do?" he asked himself. "I don't have any silverware left to place next to it. I have done so much work, yet it is still not complete!" And the little angel started to cry. He pulled a handkerchief out of his pocket to wipe his tears.

Suddenly, he stopped crying. "That's it! I can put a nicely folded handkerchief on each plate so that people can wipe their faces when they are eating!" And so napkins were invented.

The next day, after the charming wedding ceremony at the village church, Daniel followed the bride and groom into the hall. Instead of wild applause for the couple, everyone had gathered around the tables with awe on their faces as they pointed at what was in front of them.

Daniel's heart sank. "I have humiliated my daughter at her own wedding," he thought to himself. Just then the king came striding toward him from the back of the room. The crowd parted and grew quiet as he approached Daniel and the wedding party.

Daniel's heart was pounding so hard that it nearly knocked loose the flower pinned on his jacket. The king held his hand high in the air to assure every ear would turn his way.

"Loyal subjects of Paterjohn," he proclaimed. "I arrived here yesterday believing that we provided to our guests the most elegant hospitality in the world. I was wrong. This banquet and these tables are the finest I have ever seen. I order from this day forward that all tables in Paterjohn must be set as my dear daughter-in-law's family has done for this incredible wedding feast."

All shouted, "Hurray!" And so it was done. Ever since that lovely wedding day, tables have been set just the way the angel arranged Daniel Place's utensils.

And that's why it is called a "place setting."

When arranging the table, you can add little touches to make the setting more beautiful — such as putting flowers in a vase or placing candles in candleholders on the table. Remember to place a napkin in the middle of each plate (though there's an exception to this rule, as you'll see in the next poem). You can even fold the napkins in fancy shapes. Be creative and add your own unique flair to the table!

If you are confused about how to arrange the plates, knives, spoons, forks, napkins, and glasses, just sing this song to the tune of the nursery rhyme, "Hey Diddle Diddle."

HEY DIDDLE DIDDLE
by Elizabeth Santorum

Hey Diddle Diddle, the plate's in the middle,
Now on the right goes the spoon,
The napkin is left, beside the fork,
Keep going you're going to eat soon.

Hey Diddle Diddle, the plate's in the middle,
The knife is left of the spoon,
The glass is above it, now you've got it right,
You're going to eat lunch by noon.

DOROTHY IN THE LAND OF UTENSIA
from The Emerald City of Oz *by L. Frank Baum*
retold by Michael Lamb

AN ARMY OF SPOONS had captured Dorothy, Toto, and Bellina the hen. A row of spoons had surrounded all three of them. The spoons stood straight up and carried swords and muskets. Dorothy laughed at the queer things. "Who are you?" she asked. "We're the Spoon Brigade," said their leader, "and you are our prisoners. We are from the Land of Utensia, soldiers of King Kleaver, and we obey only his orders, which are to bring all prisoners to him as soon as they are captured. So step lively, my girl, and march."

By and by they left the woods and entered a big clearing, in which was the Kingdom of Utensia. Standing all around the clearing were a good many cookstoves, ranges, and grills, of all sizes and shapes, and besides these there were several kitchen cabinets and cupboards and a few kitchen tables. These things were crowded with utensils of all sorts: frying pans, kettles, forks, knives, basting and soup spoons, sifters, colanders, flat irons, rolling pins, and many others.

When the Spoon Brigade appeared with the prisoners a wild shout arose, and many of the utensils hopped off their stoves or their benches and ran crowding around Dorothy, the hen, and the dog.

"Stand back!" cried the Captain sternly, and he led his captives through the curious throng until they came before a big range that stood in the center of the clearing. Beside this range was a butcher's block upon which lay a great cleaver with a keen edge.

"Wake up, your Majesty," said the Captain. "Here are prisoners." Hearing this, King Kleaver sat up and looked at Dorothy sharply. "Gristle and fat!" he cried. "Where did this girl come from?"

"I found her in the forest and brought her here a prisoner," replied the Captain.

"Why did you do that?" inquired the King, puffing his pipe lazily.

"To create some excitement," the Captain answered. "It is so quiet here that we are all getting rusty for want of amusement. For my part, I prefer to see stirring times."

"Naturally," returned the cleaver, with a nod. "I have always said, Captain, that you are a sterling officer and a solid citizen, bowled and polished. But what do you expect me to do with these prisoners?"

"That is for you to decide," declared the Captain.

"To be sure; to be sure," muttered the cleaver. "As you say, we have had dull times since the grindstone left us. Command my Counselors and the Royal Courtiers to attend me, as well as the High Priest and the Judge. We'll then decide what can be done."

The utensils all lined up in their proper positions, the forks on the left, knives and spoons on the right.

When all the Counselors and the Courtiers had assembled — and these seemed to include most of the inhabitants of the kingdom — the King rapped on the block for order and said:

"Friends and fellow utensils! Our worthy Commander of the Spoon Brigade, Captain Dipp, has captured the three prisoners before you and brought them here for — for — I don't know what for. So I ask your advice how to act in this matter, and what fate I should mete out to these captives. Judge Sifter, stand on my right. It is your business to sift this affair to the bottom. High Priest Colander, stand on my left and see that no one testifies falsely in this matter."

As these two officials took their places, Dorothy asked: "Why is the colander the High Priest?"

"He's the holiest thing we have in the kingdom," replied King Kleaver.

"Except me," said a sieve. "I'm the whole thing when it comes to holes."

"I demand they be killed several times, until they are dead!" shouted a pepper box, hopping around very excitedly.

"Compose yourself, Mr. Paprika," advised the King. "Your remarks are piquant and highly seasoned, but you need a smattering of common sense. It is only necessary to kill a person once to make him dead; but I do not see that it is necessary to kill this little girl at all."

"I don't either," said Dorothy.

"Pardon me, but you are not expected to advise me in this matter," replied King Kleaver.

"Why not?" asked Dorothy.

"You might be prejudiced in your own favor, and so mislead us," he said. "Now then, good subjects, who speaks next?"

"I'd like to smooth this thing over, in some way," said a flatiron. "We are supposed to be useful to mankind, you know."

"But the girl isn't mankind! She's womankind!" yelled a corkscrew.

"What do you know about it?" inquired the King.

"I'm a lawyer," said the corkscrew proudly. "I'm accustomed to appear at the bar."

"But you're crooked," retorted the King, "and that debars you. You may be a corking good lawyer, Mr. Pop, but I must ask you to withdraw your remarks."

"Very well," said the corkscrew sadly; "I see I haven't any pull at this court."

"I'd like to hear from Prince Karver," said the King. At this a stately carving knife stepped forward and bowed.

"The Captain was wrong to bring this girl here, and she was wrong to come," he said. "But now that the foolish deed is done, let us all prove our mettle and have a slashing good time."

"That's it! That's it!" screamed a fat chopping knife. "We'll make mincemeat of the girl and hash of the chicken and sausage of the dog!"

There was a shout of approval at this, and the King had to rap again for order.

"Gentlemen, gentlemen!" he said, "your remarks are somewhat cutting and rather disjointed, as might be expected from such as you. But you give no reasons for your demands."

"See here, Kleaver; you make me tired," exclaimed a saucepan, strutting before the King very impudently. "You are about the worst King that ever reigned in Utensia, and that's saying a good deal. Why don't you run things yourself, instead of asking everybody's advice, like the big, clumsy idiot you are?"

The King sighed. "I wish there wasn't a saucepan in my kingdom," he said. "You fellows are always stewing over something, and every once in a while you slop over and make a mess of it. Go hang yourself, sir — by the handle — and don't let me hear from you again."

Dorothy was much shocked by the dreadful language the utensils employed, and she thought they must have had very little proper training. So she said, addressing the King, who seemed very unfit to rule his turbulent subjects: "I wish you'd decide my fate right away. I can't stay here all day, trying to find out what you're going to do with me."

"What I'd like to know," said a can opener, in a shrill voice, "is why the girl came to our forest anyhow, and why she intruded upon Captain Dipp — who ought to be called Dippy — and who she is, and where she came from, and where she is going, and why and wherefore and therefore and when."

"I'm sorry to see, Sir Jabber," remarked the King to the can opener, "that you have such a prying disposition. As a matter of fact, all the things you mention are none of our business."

At this, a big kitchen fork pricked up its ears and said in a tiny voice: "Let's hear from Judge Sifter."

"That's proper," returned the king. So Judge Sifter turned around slowly several times and then said: "We have nothing against the girl except the stove-hearth upon which she sits. Therefore I order her instantly discharged."

"Discharged!" cried Dorothy. "Why, I never was discharged in my life, and I don't intend to be. If it's all the same to you, I'll resign."

"It's all the same," declared the King. "You are free — you and your companions — may go wherever you like."

THE LEGEND OF THE ROUND TABLE
from The Story of King Arthur and His Knights *by Howard Pyle*
retold by Michael Lamb

LONG AGO, the great King Arthur ruled the land of Britain. Those were the glorious days of the great castle at Camelot and the brave Knights of the Round Table. When first he saw Camelot, Arthur was amazed at its beauty. The walls were covered gold and painted with wonderful figures of the angels and saints. In the middle of the castle's great golden hall was a round table made of solid oak and it was so large that fifty men could sit around it. At each place on the table, there was a gold cup filled with choice wine and a golden dish with the finest pure white bread on it.

As Arthur entered the room, the wise old magician Merlin took hold of Arthur's hand and led him toward the great table. He looked deep into Arthur's eyes and declared "Lo, this is the Round Table and upon it shall you, Arthur, rule and bring peace to the troubled land."

Then King Arthur said, "Merlin, that which I see here is wonderful beyond all telling."

Merlin raised his arm and pointed to a high seat at the middle of the table. It was beautifully carved and gilded with gold. "Behold Lord King," said Merlin, "here is the Seat Royal, your seat Arthur." As Merlin spoke, suddenly there appeared letters of gold on the back of the seat that read: Arthur King. "Lord, this seat may well be called the center seat for in truth you are the very center of all that is most worthy of true knighthood." Then Merlin pointed to the seat that stood opposite to the King's. "That seat," said Merlin, "is called the Seat Perilous, for no man but one may sit there and he has yet to be born. If any other man shall dare to sit there, he will instantly suffer death as a punishment for his boldness. That is why it is called Seat Perilous."

Then the King said, "I beseech you Merlin, to find now the brave knights who will fill all the seats at the Round Table."

Merlin smiled, but not in a cheerful way, and replied, "Lord, what is your hurry? Do you not know that when all the seats are filled, your days of glory will soon end?"

King Arthur then looked very steadfastly into Merlin's face, "Old man" he said, "your work brings both wonders and wisdom. I wish only to serve God. I am in his hands. I do not wish for my own glory, but I do desire His good will to be accomplished even if my own days in Camelot must end."

"Lord Arthur," said the old magician, "you speak like a true king with a large and noble heart. Yet I cannot fill the Round Table now, for it is fifty seats, and in Britain now there are only thirty-two knights good enough to sit here."

"Then bring those thirty-two here," said Arthur.

"So will I do Lord King," replied Merlin.

Then he cast his eyes on Sir Pellimore, who was with them in the great hall. Merlin took Pellimore by the hand. "Behold King Arthur, here is the knight who next to thyself is most worthy to sit at the Round Table." To the left of the Royal seat, the name Pellimore suddenly appeared in letters of gold.

Then Arthur asked, "And who, old friend, will sit here on my right?"

Merlin said, "Lord, the man who will fill the seat will soon come to us, and he shall be the greatest knight in all the world."

It was Sir Lancelot who would come to fill the seat on Arthur's right. His heroic deeds would be praised throughout the land and he would become the King's closest friend. Many years later, Lancelot's son, Galahad, would occupy Seat Perilous, the last seat to be filled at the Round Table. He would go out upon the greatest adventure in the history of Camelot: the search for the Holy Grail. In completing the quest for the Grail, Sir Galahad accomplished the noblest task in all the great age of chivalry, bringing great glory to himself, King Arthur, and the Knights of Round Table.

Where one sits at the table has been a part of good manners for hundreds of years. The seat at the "head" of a rectangular table, or the center seats of a round table, are usually where parents sit. These seats are also often reserved for guests. Your parents are at the center of your life, and guests should be the center of attention when they visit, just as King Arthur was at the center of the Round Table.

When you are a guest, always wait for your host to seat you. Also, remember that when you have a friend over for a meal, that friend will want to sit next to you in the same way that Sir Lancelot sat next to his best friend, King Arthur.

CHAPTER FOUR

Washing and Dressing

1.
Washing

GRUNGY GRACE
by Jack Prelutsky

I am extremely devious,
my name is Grungy Grace.
I hardly ever brush my teeth
or wash my hands and face.
"It's time to wash," my father says,
but since I'm not a dope,
I simply turn the water on
and wet the towel and soap.
"Brush your teeth," my mother says,
I never even blink.
I squeeze out gobs of toothpaste,
and I brush the bathroom sink.
I'm very good at fooling them,
my brain's extremely keen,
but I've got lots of rashes,
and my teeth are turning green.

COMBING AND CURLING
by Gelett Burgess

When your mother combs your hair, here's a rhyme to say:
If you try it, I declare, it will take the snarls away!

In the ocean of my hair,
Many little waves are there;

Make the comb, a little boat,
Over all the billows float;
Sail the rough and tangled tide
Till it's smooth on every side,
Till, like other little girls,
I've a sea of wavy curls!

It's important to wash your face and hands, brush your teeth, comb your hair, and keep your nails neatly trimmed. These are healthy habits that make you more pleasing to yourself and those around you.

WASHING AND DRESSING
by Ann Taylor

Ah! Why will my dear little girl be so cross,
    And cry, and look sulky, and pout?
To lose her sweet smile is a terrible loss,
    I can't even kiss her without.

You say you don't like to be washed and be dressed,
    But would you be dirty and foul?
Come, drive that long sob from your dear little breast,
    And clear your sweet face from its scowl.

If the water is cold, and the comb hurts your head,
    And the soap has got into your eye,
Will the water grow warmer for all that you've said,
    And what good will it do you to cry?

It is not to tease you and hurt you, my sweet.
    But only for kindness and care,
That I wash you, and dress you, and make you look neat,
    And comb out your tanglesome hair.

I don't mind the trouble, if you would not cry,
    But pay me for all with a kiss;
That's right, — take the towel and wipe your wet eye,
    I thought you'd be good after this.

DIRTY JACK
by Ann and Jane Taylor

There was one little Jack,
Not very long back,
    And it's said to his lasting disgrace,
That he never was seen
With his hands at all clean,
    Nor yet ever clean was his face.

His friends were much hurt
To see so much dirt,
    And often and well did they scour;
But all was in vain,
He was dirty again
    Before they had done it an hour.

When to wash he was sent,
He reluctantly went,
    With water to splash himself o'er,
But he left the black streaks
All over his cheeks,
    And made them look worse than before.

The pigs in the dirt
Could not be more expert
    Than he was, at grubbing about;
And people have thought,

This gentleman ought,
　　To be made with four legs and a snout.

The idle and bad
May, like to this lad,
　　Be dirty and black, to be sure;
But good boys are seen
To be decent and clean,
　　Altho' they are ever so poor.

"Bid them wash their faces, and keep their teeth clean," wrote William Shakespeare. Keeping clean is polite because it gives the message to others that you respect yourself and them.

There are times when getting dirty is all right, such as when you're playing outside or helping your parents clean the house, wash the car, or weed the garden. These acts of love are far more important than looking nice.

Afterwards, try not to complain when your parents ask you to bathe, because that's part of their job in caring for you. Instead, think of all the fun you can have in the tub. You can play with your favorite bathtub toys and shape your hair into all sorts of fun styles with the lather from the shampoo. And you can pretend to be a shark or a deep-sea diver.

LEONIDAS IS SHAMPOOING HIS HAIR! — *or* — HOW THE GREEKS DEFEATED THE PERSIAN KING
by Karen Santorum

A LONG TIME AGO, in 480 B.C., there lived a very brave man named Leonidas, which means "like a lion." He was the King of Sparta, a city in Greece. Spartans were taught to be the bravest and most faithful of soldiers; and Leonidas proved this to be true. When the cities of Greece received word that King Xerxes from Persia was coming to conquer them, they grew fearful. King Xerxes had a tough reputation and an enormous army, and he had won many battles. In addition, the Greeks needed more time to prepare their defense.

Now Leonidas, being the most faithful servant of Greece and its bravest soldier, sent word that he and his army of men would guard the narrow pass of Thermopylae in order to delay Xerxes' army. Thermopylae was so named because there were hot springs there, and the meaning of the word Thermopylae is "hot gates."

This narrow passageway, in a great mountain, was the only way that Xerxes and his troops would be able to pass through to get to the cities of Greece. For two days Leonidas and his army of just a few thousand (including three hundred Spartans) held off King Xerxes' whole army, although they were vastly outnumbered.

Before the final battle, King Xerxes, who was perched on his throne, asked a spy to figure out what Leonidas and his troops were up to. When the spy returned, he said, "Leonidas is shampooing his hair."

King Xerxes and his troops laughed so hard that many of them were rolling in the grass. They thought it was hilarious that soldiers would be bathing and shampooing their hair at a time like this.

And, in fact, Leonidas and his men *were* bathing in the hot springs and grooming themselves. Leonidas was not just a brave man; he was also very wise. Bathing and grooming was part of his army's discipline and attention to detail. It was a sign of respect, both to their fellow soldiers and to their country, to be clean going into battle. It helped them to fight with all their might.

King Xerxes grew angry that his huge army was unable to defeat such a small one. So, the next day, he sent ten thousand men to fight for the passageway. Leonidas and his army fought long and hard to the bitter end. They all died except for one, who lived to tell the story of the brave soldiers and the honor they gave their country.

But because Leonidas was able to hold the pass for several days, the Greeks were given more time to prepare for the Persian invasion. Knowing Xerxes would conquer Athens, the people fled onto huge wooden ships. They were able to outsmart the Persians in a battle at sea.

The boastful King Xerxes left Greece humbled and never returned. Today, a large statue of Leonidas continues to guard the pass at Thermopylae.

What a feat that so few soldiers could hold off such a large, aggressive army! Was it because Leonidas and his men were well groomed? No one can say for sure, but in today's military, soldiers are required to be clean and well groomed, and their uniforms are always washed and pressed.

2.
Dressing

MY TEACHER WORE PAJAMAS
by Karen Santorum

Last night before I went to bed,
My mom told me to wear a suit
For tomorrow's Sunday service.
I must look like mister cute.

Starched shirts and ties, or blue jeans and sweats,
Do you think anyone really cares?
Please let me wear my jeans and sneaks,
You know this is extremely unfair.

My mom tucked me in and said goodnight;
I lay in my bed and pouted.
I complained of how my suit would feel;
"It's scratchy and tight," I shouted.

I tossed and turned, then fell asleep,
And had the funniest dream —
Of big wigs, silly shoes, and costumes.
It was absurd to the extreme!

I went to school to find my teacher
Dressed in pink polka-dot pajamas.
But that's not all, there's even more —
His fluffy slippers looked like llamas!

Oh, I could not pay attention
To a word or thing he taught.
It's not that it wasn't important;
He just looked so silly, I thought.

Before I knew it, at my school play,
My parents came dressed as clowns.
Big wigs, red noses, and long striped shoes,
They came over near me to sit down.

As I snuck away I turned to see,
My parents strumming ukuleles.
What could they possibly be thinking —
That my school name was "Barnum & Bailey"?

I was feeling rather dizzy,
So I went to see the school nurse,
She was dressed like a witch with long green nails.
Hard to believe, but things got even worse!

I tried to leave, I tried to run,
I said, "Please, don't you get close!"
She said, "I need to check your temp."
Oh no, Goodbye, *Adios!*

When I went to tell the principal,
He was in jeans and a tie-dyed tee.
And sitting on his left shoulder
Was his furry brown Chimpanzee!

I held my belly and laughed out loud,
The scene was so hilarious.
To think this man was my principal,
His authority precarious.

Suddenly, I'm on the baseball field,
Desperately trying to perform,
But my coach is in a ballet tutu —
Talk about out of uniform!

Thank goodness my alarm clock rang
And ended all of this nonsense.
Here's my pillow, my bear, and my trucks,
I'm so happy there's no more suspense.

I jumped out of bed and cheerfully
Put on my best suit and tie.
I looked in the mirror, tugged my jacket, and said,
"You are quite a handsome young guy!"

Different occasions call for different outfits. When you go to school, you need to dress well, and you may even have to wear a uniform. When playing sports, you wear the uniform of the team. If you're going shopping, to the movies, or out to play, you can wear casual clothes. When we go to church services, synagogue, weddings, funerals, or graduations, we wear formal clothes.

The way we dress makes a statement about how we feel about the particular events we attend. If you attended a wedding in sneakers and sweat pants, you would demonstrate that you didn't care about the service. When you dress nicely, it communicates respect.

IF ONLY I HAD A GREEN NOSE
by Max Lucado

LUCIA AND PUNCHINELLO looked out the window of Eli's work shop. Like other Wemmicks, they were wooden people. But unlike the other Wemmicks, they weren't standing in line in the village below.

"Look at them all!" Punchinello exclaimed.

"I don't understand it," Lucia wondered. "Why would anyone want to paint his nose green?"

"Because everyone else is," Eli responded without looking up from his workbench.

Punchinello didn't understand. "What do you mean?"

"Everyone wants to look like everyone else. Sometimes it's square hats. Sometimes it's tall shoes. Why, last year the big thing was yellow ears. Now it's green noses. Everyone wants a green nose."

"Does a green nose make them smarter?" Punchinello asked.

"No."

"Does a green nose make them stronger?"

"No."

"Does it make them faster?"

"No."

"Then what does a green nose make them?"

Eli looked up and smiled. "Greener."

But his smile left as he looked out the window at the long line of Wemmicks. "They think they'll be happier if they look like everyone else. But I made them different on purpose. Freckles, long noses, bright eyes, dark eyes . . . these were my ideas. Now they all want to look the same."

"Not me," said Lucia. "I'm happy just the way you made me."

"Me too," agreed Punchinello. "I don't need a green nose to feel special." Then he paused and looked at the village. "But I would like to see how a green nose looks up close. Want to go?"

Eli smiled as the two stood to leave.

"Just remember, I made you different on purpose," he told them.

From street level the line looked even longer and the noses even greener. Lucia and Punchinello worked their way to the front of the crowd and watched as one Wemmick after another stepped into the nose-coloring store and came out painted.

"It's the latest thing," barked a Wemmick on the sidewalk. "Don't be the only Wemmick with a plain nose."

"Who is that?" asked Punchinello.

Lucia shrugged. "I don't know."

"Why, that's Mr. Willy Withit," volunteered a Wemmick from behind them.

"Does he run the nose-painting store?" asked Punchinello.

"More than that," the Wemmick explained. "Painted noses were his idea. So were the square hats and the tall shoes and the yellow ears. New things are his thing. He decides what is 'withit.' Isn't he the best?"

Lucia and Punchinello took a good look at this tall Wemmick with the deep voice, big smile, tall hat, and green bow tie that matched his oh-so-great green nose. Both were thinking the same question. Lucia asked it. "Who made him the new-thing picker?"

The Wemmick looked puzzled, like he'd never been asked that question. "Well, I don't know. He always has." Then his eyes brightened. "Wait, look, here comes a new nose!"

"Oooh," said the Wemmicks.

"Ahhh," admired some of the others.

The just-painted Wemmick didn't stop to speak — he just kept his nose in the air and walked past. All the green-nosed Wemmicks did this. After all, how could your nose be seen if it wasn't in the air?

Walking around high-nosed, however, was risky. Wemmicks walked into walls, doors, even each other. Lucia and Punchinello had to be very careful. One Wemmick took up the whole street.

"Step back, step back," he announced. It was the mayor. "Make way, every Wemmick. My wife is coming in for a touch-up." With one hand he waved back the citizens. With the other he guided her through the crowd.

"Horrible, just horrible," she cried, covering her nose with both hands. "I chipped some paint when I bumped into a tree. Now the real me is showing. Horrible, just horrible."

As the crowd passed, Lucia shook her head. "Such a fuss over a green nose."

"Yeah," agreed Punchinello. "You'll never catch me in the nose-coloring store."

> Man looks at the outward appearance, but the LORD looks at the heart.
>
>
>
> 1 SAMUEL 16:7

"Aw, Punch, I was hoping you'd go."

Punchinello recognized the voice immediately. "Twiggy?" He turned and looked at the wide-eyed, sweet-smiling Wemmick. His ears began to turn red. They always did when he saw her. He reached up and covered them.

"Why don't you paint your nose, Punch? I painted mine. Everyone else is painting theirs. Besides, you'd look good in green." Twiggy reached up and touched the tip of his nose. "Yours is so cute." With that she turned and walked away. "Bye-bye." She waved.

Punchinello moved one hand from his ear to his nose. He turned and looked at his reflection in a store window.

Lucia had to grab his hand to get his attention. "Come on, Punchinello. Let's go."

As he walked past the store, he noticed Willy Withit examining his nose in a handheld mirror. Later at home, he did the same. "I never noticed before, but my nose sure looks pale."

The next morning, Punchinello walked down the street with his friends Splint and Woody.

"Are you really thinking about it?" Woody asked.

"Sort of," Punchinello answered.

"They say the paint stings your nose," Woody volunteered.

"And it stinks," Splint added.

"The brush could get in your eyes," Woody continued.

"And it only comes off with sandpaper." Splint nodded.

"Shhh." Punchinello put a finger to his lips and pointed at a large crowd of green-nosed Wemmicks standing in the square. "Something's going on."

The mayor was standing on a platform. His wife (nose freshly painted) and Willy Withit were on either side of him. "Welcome, one and all, to the first meeting of the Nosey Wemmicks Club," he announced. "Your glistening green sets you apart as a 'Withit Wemmick.'" As if on cue, Wemmicks began stroking their noses. "You are classy. You are keen. You are awesome. You are green!"

Proud of his poetry, the mayor smiled, and the Wemmicks applauded. "We owe it all to Willy Withit," he shouted over the noise, "the pioneer of the painted snout!" Everyone applauded even louder.

"People love me because of you!" one shouted.

"I have more friends!" cried another.

"With a green nose, I am a better Wemmick!" exclaimed a third.

The mayor hung a medal around the neck of Willy Withit. "You have changed the face of Wemmicksville. We salute your brilliance. Without you we'd all look like . . ."

> Why do you worry about clothes? See how the lilies of the field grow. They do not labor or spin. Yet I tell you that not even Solomon in all his splendor was dressed like one of these.
>
>
> MATTHEW 2:28–29

The mayor paused, looking for the right word. Then he saw Punchinello and his friends. Pointing in their direction, he declared with a scornful laugh, ". . . them!"

Everyone else laughed too. Punchinello and his two friends lowered their heads and covered their noses.

"Let's hear it for Willy Withit," shouted the mayor, "the Wemmick who discovered the cure for the common nose!"

As the townspeople shouted and applauded, Woody, Splint, and Punchinello quickly turned and walked away. They didn't stop until they stood in front of the nose-coloring shop. Within a matter of minutes all three were painted and walking down Wemmick Lane.

"Hey, Punchinello," asked Splint, pushing his nose upward, "am I doing it right?"

Punchinello didn't look, "I can't see you, Splint. If I turn, my nose won't be in the air."

"Whew, this is tough work," Woody added. "Not only do you have to get painted, but you have to walk weird."

"Yeah, but doesn't it feel great to be withit?" Punchinello asked.

And for a few days it did. They hung out with other green-noses and made weekly visits to the nose-a-curist for a nose-polish. They bought nose-gloves for cold days and nose-brellas for rainy ones. All three read

Willy Withit's new book, *Winner by a Nose*. Most of all, they enjoyed looking down their noses at the unpainted Wemmicks.

One day when they were feeling especially smug, Splint said to Punchinello, "I just can't imagine who wouldn't have a green nose."

Punchinello agreed, "Anyone without a green nose is so . . ."

"So what?" a voice interrupted. It was Lucia.

Punchinello was embarrassed. "I haven't seen you in a while," he said.

"You haven't seen anyone in a long time," she replied, "except yourself."

He started to speak, but didn't. He was bothered by what she said.

And he was even more bothered by what he saw. He saw it the next morning as the three were walking into Wemmicksville. Standing on the other side of the road was a Wemmick with a red nose.

"He needs to get with it," they said to each other.

But then they saw another Wemmick, also with a red nose. Then a third and a fourth. By the time they were in the village, they were surrounded by red-nosed Wemmicks. And those whose noses weren't red were in line to have them painted.

"Step right up," shouted Willy Withit from the steps of his store. "Green noses are out, and red noses are in!"

"But we just got our noses painted green!" they told him.

"No problem," he replied. "Our red will cover the green. Step right up and get in style."

The three friends looked at each other sadly. "We thought we were in style," Woody moaned. What could they do but stand in line and have their noses painted red? For a few days they fit in, until one morning they saw a blue-nosed Wemmick.

"Oh, no," they said to each other, "not again." So they changed colors.

But it was only a short time until blue noses were out, and pink noses were in.

Then pink was out, and yellow was in.

Then yellow was out, and orange was in.

Soon Punchinello and his buddies had so many layers of paint on their noses that they couldn't remember what they really looked like.

"This has to be the final color," they said the day they walked out with orange noses.

But once again they were wrong. "I'm so tired of this," Woody moaned when he saw a purple-painted Wemmick. "I wish my nose was common again."

The three sat on a rock and hung their heads. "Me, too," agreed

Punchinello. "I should have listened to Eli."

"You think he would help us?"

"Why don't you ask him?"

All three turned at the sound of the familiar voice. "Lucia," they said.

"He asks about you every day," she told them.

"Is he mad?" Punchinello wondered.

"Sad, but not mad."

Punchinello looked up toward Eli's house on the hill.

"He told me to tell you to come." Lucia spoke again.

"Could I take my friends?"

"Of course."

"Would you go with me?"

"Certainly."

And so the four began the long walk up the hill to Eli's house. When they reached the top of the hill, Eli stepped out of the workshop and began walking toward them. He met them in the yard. One by one he examined their noses.

"Been trying to fit in, eh?"

Punchinello nodded.

"Did you succeed?"

"Not really. Every time we got close, someone changed the rules."

"That's the way it is."

"And my neck hurt from sticking my nose in the air," Woody added.

"You weren't built to walk that way."

"We just want to be ourselves again," Splint said.

"I'm glad to hear that."

"Can we?" they asked.

"Of course you can," Eli replied. "I'll always help you be who I made you to be." Then he reached in his pocket and pulled out a piece of sandpaper. "But it's going to take some time."

And so Punchinello and his friends followed their maker into his workshop where he spent the rest of the day removing the paint. It hurt to be sanded, but it was worth it to be normal again.

We are all made in the image of God, and the clothes we wear should reflect our respect for Him. Just because "everyone else" is wearing something doesn't mean we have to. Designer clothes may be too expensive for your family, or they may not be appropriate for your age, your figure, or the occasion. The world would be boring if everyone dressed the same. Just be yourself, and let God's image shine through you.

Dress Quickly!
by Gelett Burgess

All your life you'll have to dress,
Every single day (unless
You should happen to be sick),
Why not learn to do it quick?
Hang your clothes the proper way,
So you'll find them fresh next day;
Treat them with a little care,
Fold them neatly on a chair;
So, without a bit of worry,
You can dress in quite a hurry.
Think of the slovenly Goops, before
You strew your clothing on the floor!

Anne of Green Gables
by Lucy Maud Montgomery

We return once again to Anne of Green Gables. In the first selection below, Marilla has made Anne some dresses for Sunday school. In the second, Anne is in "the depths of despair" over her hair.

Chapter 11

"WELL, HOW DO YOU LIKE THEM?" said Marilla. Anne was standing in the gable room, looking solemnly at three new dresses spread out on the bed. One was of snuffy colored gingham which Marilla had been tempted to buy from a peddler the preceding summer because it looked so serviceable; one was of black-and-white checked sateen which she had picked up at a bargain counter in the winter; and one was a stiff print of an ugly blue shade which she had purchased that week at a Carmody store.

She had made them up herself, and they were all made alike — plain skirts pulled tightly to plain waists, with sleeves as plain as waist and skirt and tight as sleeves could be.

"I'll imagine that I like them," said Anne soberly.

"I don't want you to imagine it," said Marilla, offended. "Oh, I can see you don't like the dresses! What is the matter with them? Aren't they neat and clean and new?"

"Yes."

"Then why don't you like them?"

"They're — they're not — pretty," said Anne reluctantly.

"Pretty!" Marilla sniffed. "I didn't trouble my head about getting pretty dresses for you. I don't believe in pampering vanity, Anne, I'll tell you that right off. Those dresses are good, sensible, serviceable dresses, without any frills or furbelows about them, and they're all you'll get this summer. The brown gingham and the blue print will do you for school when you begin to go. The sateen is for church and Sunday school. I'll expect you to keep them neat and clean and not to tear them. I should think you'd be grateful to get most anything after those skimpy wincey things you've been wearing."

"Oh, I am grateful," protested Anne. "But I'd be ever so much gratefuller if — if you'd made just one of them with puffed sleeves. Puffed sleeves are so fashionable now. It would give me such a thrill, Marilla, just to wear a dress with puffed sleeves."

"Well, you'll have to do without your thrill. I hadn't any material to waste on puffed sleeves. I think they are ridiculous-looking things anyhow. I prefer the plain, sensible ones."

"But I'd rather look ridiculous when everybody else does than plain and sensible all by myself," persisted Anne mournfully.

"Trust you for that! Well, hang those dresses carefully up in your closet, and then sit down and learn the Sunday school lesson. I got a quarterly from Mr. Bell for you and you'll go to Sunday school tomorrow," said Marilla, disappearing downstairs in high dudgeon.

Anne clasped her hands and looked at the dresses.

"I did hope there would be a white one with puffed sleeves," she whispered disconsolately. "I prayed for one, but I didn't much expect it on that account. I didn't suppose God would have time to bother about a little orphan girl's dress. I knew I'd just have to depend on Marilla for it.

Well, fortunately I can imagine that one of them is of snow-white muslin with lovely lace frills and three-puffed sleeves."

CHAPTER 27

ARILLA, WALKING HOME one late April evening from an Aid meeting, realized that the winter was over and gone with the thrill of delight that spring never fails to bring to the oldest and saddest as well as to the youngest and merriest. Marilla was not given to subjective analysis of her thoughts and feelings. She probably imagined that she was thinking about the Aids and their missionary box and the new carpet for the vestry room, but under these reflections was a harmonious conscious-ness of red fields smoking into pale purply mists in the declining sun, of long, sharp-pointed fir shadows falling over the meadow beyond the brook, of still, crimson-budded maples around a mirror-like wood-pool, of a wakening in the world and a stir of hidden pulses under the gray sod. The spring was abroad in the land and Marilla's sober, middle-aged step was lighter and swifter because of its deep, primal gladness.

Her eyes dwelt affectionately on Green Gables, peering through its network of trees and reflecting the sunlight back from its windows in several little coruscations of glory. Marilla, as she picked her steps along the damp lane, thought that it was really a satisfaction to know that she was going home to a briskly snapping wood fire and a table nicely spread for tea, instead of to the cold comfort of old Aid meeting evenings before Anne had come to Green Gables.

Consequently, when Marilla entered her kitchen and found the fire black out, with no sign of Anne anywhere, she felt justly disappointed and irritated. She had told Anne to be sure and have tea ready at five o'clock, but now she must hurry to take off her second-best dress and prepare the meal herself against Matthew's return from plowing.

"I'll settle Miss Anne when she comes home," said Marilla grimly, as she shaved up kindlings with a carving knife and more vim than was strictly necessary. Matthew had come in and was waiting patiently for his tea in his corner. "She's gadding off somewhere with Diana, writing stories or practicing dialogues or some such tomfoolery, and never thinking once about the time or her duties. She's just got to be pulled up short and sudden on this sort of thing. I don't care if Mrs. Allan does say she's the brightest and sweetest child she ever knew. She may be bright and sweet enough, but her head is full of nonsense and there's never any knowing what shape it'll break out in next. Just as soon as she grows out of one freak she takes up with another. But there! Here I am saying the very thing I was so riled with Rachel Lynde for saying at the Aid today. I was real glad when Mrs. Allan spoke up for Anne, for if she hadn't I know I'd have said something too sharp to Rachel before everybody. Anne's got plenty of faults, goodness knows, and far be it from me to deny it. But I'm bringing her up and not Rachel Lynde, who'd pick faults in the Angel Gabriel himself if he lived in Avonlea. Just the same, Anne has no business to leave the house like this when I told her she was to stay home this afternoon and look after things. I must say, with all her faults, I never found her disobedient or untrustworthy before and I'm real sorry to find her so now."

"Well now, I dunno," said Matthew, who, being patient and wise and, above all, hungry, had deemed it best to let Marilla talk her wrath out unhindered, having learned by experience that she got through with whatever work was on hand much quicker if not delayed by untimely argument. "Perhaps you're judging her too hasty, Marilla. Don't call her untrustworthy until you're sure she has disobeyed you. Maybe it can all be explained — Anne's a great hand at explaining."

"She's not here when I told her to stay," retorted Marilla. "I reckon she'll find it hard to explain that to my satisfaction. Of course I knew you'd take her part, Matthew. But I'm bringing her up, not you."

It was dark when supper was ready, and still no sign of Anne, coming hurriedly over the log bridge or up Lovers' Lane, breathless and repentant with a sense of neglected duties. Marilla washed and put away the dishes grimly. Then, wanting a candle to light her down cellar, she went up to the east gable for the one that generally stood on Anne's table. Lighting it, she turned around to see Anne herself lying on the bed, face downward among the pillows.

"Mercy on us," said astonished Marilla, "have you been asleep, Anne?"

"No," was the muffled reply.

"Are you sick then?" demanded Marilla anxiously going over to the bed.

Anne cowered deeper into her pillows as if desirous of hiding herself forever from mortal eyes.

"No. But please, Marilla, go away and don't look at me. *I'm in the depths of despair* and I don't care who gets head in class or writes the best composition or sings in the Sunday school choir anymore. Little things like that are of no importance now because I don't suppose I'll ever be able to go anywhere again. My career is closed. Please, Marilla, go away and don't look at me."

"Did any one ever hear the like?" the mystified Marilla wanted to know. "Anne Shirley, whatever is the matter with you? What have you done? Get right here this minute and tell me. This minute, I say. There now what is it?"

Anne had slid to the floor in despairing obedience.

"Look at my hair, Marilla," she whispered.

Accordingly, Marilla lifted her candle and looked scrutinizingly at Anne's hair, flowing in heavy masses down her back. It certainly had a very strange appearance.

"Anne Shirley, what have you done to your hair? Why, it's green!"

Green it might be called, if it were any earthly color — a queer, dull, bronzy green, with streaks here and there of the original red to heighten the ghastly effect. Never in all her life had Marilla seen anything so grotesque as Anne's hair at that moment.

"Yes, it's green," moaned Anne. "I thought nothing could be as bad as red hair. But now I know it's ten times worse to have green hair. Oh, Marilla, you little know how utterly wretched I am."

"I little know how you got into this fix, but I mean to find out," said Marilla. "Come right down to the kitchen — it's too cold up here — and tell me just what you've done. I've been expecting something queer for some time. You haven't got into any scrape for over two months, and I was sure another one was due. Now, then, what did you do to your hair?"

"I dyed it."

"Dyed it! Dyed your hair! Anne Shirley, didn't you know it was a wicked thing to do?"

"Yes, I knew it was a little wicked," admitted Anne. "But I thought it was worthwhile to be a little wicked to get rid of red hair. I counted the cost, Marilla. Besides, I meant to be extra good in other ways to make up for it."

"Well," said Marilla sarcastically, "if I'd decided it was worthwhile to dye my hair I'd have dyed it a decent color at least. I wouldn't have dyed it green."

"But I didn't mean to dye it green, Marilla," protested Anne dejectedly. "If I was wicked I meant to be wicked to some purpose. He said it would turn my hair a beautiful raven black — he positively assured me that it would. How could I doubt his word, Marilla? I know what it feels like to have your word doubted. And Mrs. Allan says we should never suspect any one of not telling us the truth unless we have proof that they're not. I have proof now — green hair is proof enough for anybody. But I hadn't then and I believed every word he said *implicitly*."

"Who said? Who are you talking about?"

"The peddler that was here this afternoon. I bought the dye from him."

"Anne Shirley, how often have I told you never to let one of those peddlers in the house! I don't believe in encouraging them to come around at all."

"Oh, I didn't let him in the house. I remembered what you told me, and I went out, carefully shut the door, and looked at his things on the step. He had a big box full of very interesting things and he told me he was working hard to make enough money to bring his wife and children out from Germany. He spoke so feelingly about them that it touched my heart. I wanted to buy something from him to help him in such a worthy object. Then all at once I saw the bottle of hair dye. The peddler said it was warranted to dye any hair a beautiful raven black and wouldn't wash off. In a trice I saw myself with beautiful raven black hair and the temptation was irresistible. But the price of the bottle was seventy-five cents and I had only fifty cents left out of my chicken money. I think the peddler had a very kind heart, for he said that seeing it was me, he'd sell it for fifty cents and that was just giving it away. So I bought it, and as soon as he had gone I came up here and applied it with an old hairbrush as the directions said. I used up the whole bottle, and oh, Marilla, when I saw the dreadful color it turned my hair I repented of being wicked, I can tell you. And I've been repenting ever since."

"Well, I hope you'll repent to good purpose," said Marilla severely, "and that you've got your eyes opened to where your vanity has led you, Anne. Goodness knows what's to be done. I suppose the first thing is to give your hair a good washing and see if that will do any good."

Accordingly, Anne washed her hair, scrubbing it vigorously with soap and water, but for all the difference it made she might as well have been scouring its original red. The peddler had certainly spoken the truth when he declared that the dye wouldn't wash off, however his veracity might be impeached in other respects.

Being neatly and nicely dressed is a noble thing. However, we can become too preoccupied with our hair and the clothes we wear.

King Louis XIV of France was called the Grand Monarch because he was a vain show-off. He wore expensive and colorful clothes, big powdered wigs, and bright red shoes that had high heels in order to make himself look tall and handsome. He strutted about like a proud peacock, always looking at himself in the huge mirrors that hung on the walls of his grand palace at

Versailles. He thought that his fine clothes and jewels made him important and grand. His extravagant spending helped lead to the monarchy's downfall in the French Revolution.

But George Washington had a different perspective: "Do not conceive that fine clothes make fine men any more than fine feathers make fine birds. A plain genteel dress is more admired, and obtains more credit than lace and embroidery, in the eyes of the judicious and sensible." (Letter to Bushrod Washington, January 15, 1783)

Kindness looks beyond clothing and sees into the heart.

CHAPTER FIVE

Appreciating People with Disabilities

Appreciating People with Disabilities

We all have friends, relatives, or classmates with disabilities. When you see a person in a wheelchair, a person making their way with a seeing-eye dog, or a person using sign language — or if you know a person who has any other condition that limits their daily activities — always treat them with respect and dignity. See beyond the wheelchair or seeing-eye dog. Look deeply at the person. People with disabilities are the same in God's eyes as you are. They have hopes and dreams, just like you. And, perhaps even more than you, they need love and attention.

You Are Special
by Max Lucado

The Wemmicks

THE WEMMICKS were small wooden people carved by a woodworker named Eli. His workshop sat on a hill overlooking their village.

Each Wemmick was different. Some had big noses, others had large eyes. Some were tall and others were short. Some wore hats, others wore coats. But all were made by the same carver, and all lived in the village.

And all day, every day, the Wemmicks did the same thing: They gave each other stickers. Each Wemmick had a box of golden star stickers and a box of gray dot stickers. Up and down the streets all over the city, people spent their days sticking stars or dots on one another.

The pretty ones, those with smooth wood and fine paint, always got stars. But if the wood was rough or the paint chipped, the Wemmicks gave dots.

The talented ones got stars, too. Some could lift big sticks high above their heads or jump over tall boxes. Still others knew big words or could sing pretty songs. Everyone gave them stars.

Some Wemmicks had stars all over them! Every time they got a star, it made them feel so good! It made them want to do something else and get another star.

Others, though, could do little. They got dots.

Punchinello was one of these. He tried to jump high like the others, but he always fell. And when he fell, the others would gather around and give him dots.

Sometimes when he fell, his wood got scratched, so the people would give him more dots.

Then when he would try to explain why he fell, he would say something silly, and the Wemmicks would give him more dots.

After a while he had so many dots that he didn't want to go outside. He was afraid he would do something dumb such as forget his hat or step in the water, and then people would give him another dot. In fact, he had so many gray dots that some people would come up and give him one for no reason at all.

"He deserves lots of dots," the wooden people would agree with one another.

"He's not a good wooden person."

After a while Punchinello believed them. "I'm not a good Wemmick," he would say.

The few times he went outside, he hung around other Wemmicks who had a lot of dots. He felt better around them.

Lucia

O NE DAY Punchinello met a Wemmick who was unlike any he'd ever met. She had no dots or stars. She was just wooden. Her name was Lucia.

It wasn't that people didn't try to give her stickers; it's just that the stickers didn't stick. Some of the Wemmicks admired Lucia for having no dots, so they would run up and give her a star. But it would fall off.

Others would look down on her for having no stars, so they would give her a dot. But it wouldn't stay either.

That's the way I want to be, thought Punchinello.

I don't want anyone's marks.

So he asked the stickerless Wemmick how she did it.

"It's easy," Lucia replied. "Every day I go see Eli."

"Eli?"

"Yes, Eli. The woodcarver. I sit in the workshop with him."

"Why?"

"Why don't you find out for yourself? Go up the hill. He's there." And with that the Wemmick who had no stickers turned and skipped away.

"But will he want to see me?" Punchinello cried out. Lucia didn't hear.

So Punchinello went home. He sat near a window and watched the wooden people as they scurried around giving each other stars and dots.

"It's not right," he muttered to himself. And he decided to go see Eli.

The Woodcarver

P UNCHINELLO walked up the narrow path to the top of the hill and stepped into the big shop. His wooden eyes widened at the size of everything. The stool was as tall as he was. He had to stretch on his tiptoes to see the top of the workbench. A hammer was as long as his arm. Punchinello swallowed hard. "I'm not staying here!" And he turned to leave.

Then he heard his name.

"Punchinello?" The voice was deep and strong.

Punchinello stopped.

"Punchinello! How good to see you. Come and let me have a look at you."

Punchinello turned slowly and looked at the large bearded craftsman. "You know my name?" the little Wemmick asked.

"Of course I do. I made you."

Eli stooped down and picked him up and set him on the bench. "Hmm," the maker spoke thoughtfully as he looked at the gray dots. "Looks like you've been given some bad marks."

"I didn't mean to, Eli. I really tried hard."

"Oh, you don't have to defend yourself to me, child. I don't care what the other Wemmicks think."

"You don't?"

"No, and you shouldn't either. Who are they to give stars or dots? They're Wemmicks just like you. What they think doesn't matter, Punchinello. All that matters is what I think. And I think you are pretty special."

> I praise you because
> I am fearfully and
> wonderfully made; your
> works are wonderful,
> I know that full well.
>
>
>
> PSALM 139:14

Punchinello laughed. "Me, special? Why? I can't walk fast. I can't jump. My paint is peeling. Why do I matter to you?"

Eli looked at Punchinello, put his hands on those small wooden shoulders, and spoke very slowly. "Because you're mine. That's why you matter to me."

Punchinello had never had anyone look at him like this — much less his maker. He didn't know what to say.

"Every day I've been hoping you'd come," Eli explained.

"I came because I met someone who had no marks," said Punchinello.

"I know. She told me about you."

"Why don't the stickers stay on her?"

The maker spoke softly. "Because she has decided that what I think is more important than what they think. The stickers only stick if you let them."

"What?"

"The stickers only stick if they matter to you. The more you trust my love, the less you care about their stickers."

"I'm not sure I understand."

Eli smiled. "You will, but it will take time. You've got a lot of marks. For now, just come to see me every day and let me remind you how much I care."

Eli lifted Punchinello off the bench and set him on the floor.

"Remember," Eli said as the Wemmick walked out the door, "you are special because I made you. And I don't make mistakes."

Punchinello didn't stop, but in his heart he thought, *I think he really means it.*

And when he did, a dot fell to the ground.

All too often, the world cares only about what's on the outside — how a person looks, or how talented he or she is. But the most important thing is what's on the inside. Punchinello was a good boy who, like many good boys and girls, was wrongly judged and labelled. In your neighborhood, there may be a child who is teased. Name-calling is hurtful and wrong. According to the Book of Genesis, each person is made in the image of God. How we treat others shows what we think of God and his creation.

Punchinello could not walk fast, nor could he jump, and his paint was peeling, but he meant everything to Eli because Eli was his maker. God is the maker of the world, and every one of us is priceless to Him.

"The Queen of Hearts"
by Karen Santorum

HELEN BROOKE TAUSSIG was born on May 24, 1898, in Cambridge, Massachusetts. She was born into an academic family for whom learning and success in school came with ease. Both of her parents had been well educated at the finest schools in America, so it seemed that any child of theirs would follow in their footsteps. However, for little Helen, this was not so.

She would sit at the kitchen table for hours, trying to figure out the printed words in books. Her frustration would mount as she stared at them, because the words kept changing. Helen had a learning disability, called "dyslexia," which makes reading and writing difficult.

Helen loved learning but had to work much harder than other children. Strengthened by her parents' encouragement, she worked on her reading for several hours each day.

When Helen was only eleven years old, she lost her mother to tuberculosis. Her close relationship with her father helped her cope with the pain. Her father also continued to help her in her daily struggle with dyslexia.

Through her dedication to her studies, especially reading, she was able to graduate from high school. She went on to attend college, and after she studied medicine at Boston University. She was an extraordinary success. Despite her continued struggles with dyslexia, she became one of the finest doctors of her day.

In 1930, she became the head of the Johns Hopkins pediatric heart clinic. Soon after taking the position, she began to lose her hearing. The thought of not being able to hear horrified her. When she examined the babies, she needed to listen to their hearts and lungs. But Dr. Taussig was a strong woman who was prepared to deal with adversity, thanks to her struggles with dyslexia. She was not going to allow hearing loss to interfere with the care of her partients. Eventually, she learned to examine her tiny patients with her hands.

Dr. Taussig made many valuable contributions in the field of medicine, but the most famous was the special shunt, or passageway, she developed to help cyanotic or "blue" babies. She changed the field of cardiology with her contributions towards the care of the heart. Dr. Taussig worked tirelessly, devoting her life to the care of infants, and for this she received many prestigious awards, including the medal of freedom from President Lyndon Johnson.

But her greatest achievement was the knowledge that through her efforts, many babies were able to grow into happy and productive adults.

Some people have disabilities that you can see; others have hidden disabilities. Learning disabilities like dyslexia can be painful to live with, not just because of the challenges they present, but because of the rude comments people can make about those who suffer from them. Helen Brooke Taussig overcame challenges and made remarkable contributions in the field of medicine. She once said, "Whatever field you choose, just work quietly and steadily to make this world a better place to live, and your life will be worthwhile."

THE PRESIDENT IN THE WHEELCHAIR
by Michael Lamb

THINGS COULD NOT have been going better. The handsome young lawyer from New York was having a wonderfully successful career. First, he won the election to the New York State Legislature. Then, just four years later, he was made the Assistant Secretary of the Navy. Within another six years, this rising political star was nominated to be the Democratic candidate for Vice President. It was 1920, he was only thirty-eight years old, and although he lost the election for Vice President, young Franklin Delano Roosevelt seemed to have a limitless future. He did not know then that his life would soon be permanently changed.

It was the summer of 1921. The illness began in a simple way. Roosevelt felt achy all over and he had a fever. It really did not seem like anything more than a bad cold. Then he began to feel steadily weaker. Things continued to worsen. He couldn't move his legs. Franklin Delano Roosevelt, the man who seemed to have everything, had been stricken with a disease called polio. The handsome politician, the son of one of America's richest families, the fellow who had appeared to have such a bright future, was now paralyzed.

Franklin Delano Roosevelt was one of thousands of Americans that were crippled by polio that summer. There was no cure for the disease at that time, but there was therapy that might help. Roosevelt started a vigorous therapy program. For months he couldn't walk. But he undertook a program of swimming in the pool at Warm Springs, Georgia. Slowly, he regained some strength in his legs. He needed to wear heavy leg braces, but he could stand for a short while. Eventually, he would even be able to walk a few steps. Roosevelt did not get much better than that. He would need a wheelchair for the rest of his life.

Although he never walked normally again, Roosevelt was determined to succeed in spite of his disability. He also became dedicated to helping others who had been disabled by polio. Roosevelt used his wealth to set up the Warm Springs Foundation, which helped poor children suffering from polio. In 1924, Roosevelt reentered politics and was elected governor of New York. The illness may have weakened Franklin Roosevelt's legs, but it strengthened his spirit. He was a strong leader and a more sensitive man than he had been before his illness. The whole terrible ordeal had made him a better person.

Not long after that, Franklin Delano Roosevelt was elected president of the United States. During the important years of his presidency, Roosevelt needed a wheelchair to get from place to place. He was only able to stand for short periods of time, so the majority of his work was done sitting down. Most of the photographs of Roosevelt during this time showed him seated. He did not permit reporters to photograph him in his wheelchair. His aides were instructed to keep the wheelchair out of sight as much as possible. He wore long baggy pants to cover the leg braces he sometimes wore. In those days disabilities were viewed by many as a weakness. Roosevelt wanted to look normal and strong in public. He wondered if the country would accept him as a leader if they really knew how paralyzed he was.

Franklin Roosevelt accomplished a great deal during his years as president. He was a great friend to farmers and industrial workers. His programs built highways, parks, and dams throughout the country. He guided the nation through the "Great Depression" and led the United States to victory over Nazi Germany and Japan in World War II. During that war, Nazi Germany was ruled by Adolf Hitler, a cruel dictator. Hitler believed that only the strong should survive. In Germany, people with mental and physical disabilities were viewed as weaklings and were often put to death. When America entered World War II, Hitler laughed. He told his people that the Americans would never win the war, for they were led by a weakling president who was crippled. How wrong he was! Franklin Delano Roosevelt was a tremendous leader. Some historians even think that he was the greatest president in the history of the United States.

What we can do is more important than what we can't do. The great composer Ludwig van Beethoven became deaf, but he still "heard" symphonies in his mind. Louis Braille was blind, but he could "see" how to create a reading system for people who were visually impaired. Franklin Roosevelt couldn't walk, yet he led the nation through some of the most difficult times in its history.

We never know what life has in store for us. When Franklin Roosevelt became paralyzed, it made him more sensitive and aware of the difficulties that people with disabilities sometimes encounter. If you were in a wheelchair, or in any way disabled, you wouldn't want people to stare at you or call you names. Put yourself in the place of others, and you will behave gently towards them.

TALKING WITHOUT WORDS
by Marie Hall

"GIVE ME SOME of your peanuts," says Bear, but he doesn't say it in words. He just opens his mouth and holds up his paw.

"I want to see *them* without their seeing *me*," says Sister, but not in words. She just hides behind the house and peeks.

"I love the smell of flowers!" says Little Brother, but he doesn't say it in words. He just runs and smells the flowers whenever he sees some.

"Come here. I have something nice for you," says Mother to Little Brother, but not in words. She just motions to him.

When I'm too hot, I take off my coat. When Sister's too cold, she hugs herself and shivers. We don't need to use words to say so.

"Throw it to me, too!" says Little Brother when Big Brother and Sister are playing ball. He just says it with his hands.

"I don't want to hear!" says Little Brother when Mother starts scolding. He doesn't say it in words. He just covers his ears.

"Don't wake the baby," says Mother, but without using words. She just motions by putting a finger on her lips and Little Brother understands.

"Good-bye!" I wave as you go away. You are too far for words, so I only hope you'll turn around and wave good-bye to me.

Talking with our mouths is only one way of speaking. We also can talk with our hands, our facial expressions, and our movements. When you are with someone who can't hear or understand spoken words, be creative and think of other ways to talk with them.

MY FRIEND LESLIE
by Maxine B. Rosenberg

*L*ESLIE AND I have been friends for a long time. My name is Karin, but she calls me "Froggie." Leslie likes to tell jokes to make me laugh.

This year Leslie and I are in the same kindergarten, and we ride to school together. Since Leslie is so little, her mommy boosts her onto the bus.

"Where are you sitting?" Leslie calls to me loudly. Out goes my hand, and she finds me.

Leslie has trouble with her eyes and doesn't see clearly unless things are up close. That's just the way she was born. Sometimes, when we're talking, she leans so near to look at me that her face touches mine. Then we both begin to giggle and we clunk heads.

Leslie was also born with a hearing problem. She couldn't understand anyone who didn't speak in a loud voice. So now she wears two hearing aids, one in each ear. They are attached to the ends of a headband and work like microphones, making sounds louder.

When I talk to Leslie now, I never have to yell anymore for her to hear me. But if I whisper, she says my voice is too soft. So we go behind the bookshelves, where nobody can hear us, and I speak a little louder. Then she tells me a secret, too, in her deep voice.

I remember the first day of school. Everyone in the class stared at Leslie. They wondered about those things in her ears and why she moved closer whenever someone talked.

Ms. Klein, our teacher, explained about Leslie's eyes and ears. She said that sometimes Leslie has trouble moving, too, and she might need our help. So we started bringing Leslie her paper and crayons, and we even carried her around.

Then Ms. Klein said that Leslie didn't need that much help. She was right. Even though Leslie is handicapped, she can do almost everything for herself. It just takes her a little longer than some people.

When we paint together, Leslie puts on her own smock. But I button it for her, because she can't move her fingers and hands easily. She was born with stiff muscles that don't stretch like rubber bands, as most people's do.

It's also hard for Leslie to turn the faucet on and off when she changes the paint water. That doesn't stop her, though. She goes back and forth to the sink, emptying and filling the cups. She likes her brushes to be clean. So do I.

Red and green. Those are Leslie's favorite colors. She puts her face up to the cans to find out which is which. Then she usually paints a flower, bigger than anyone else's.

Sometimes Leslie moves so close to see her picture that a red smudge lands on her nose. If I tell her she looks like a circus clown, she takes her brush and tries to make me her twin.

When Ms. Klein calls, "Music time," we sit on a special rug and learn a new song. Ms. Klein plays the piano softly and sings to us in a low voice.

If Leslie is too far away, she jumps up and stamps her feet. "Louder, louder," she shouts. "I can't hear." I'm always afraid she might cry.

Then our teacher says, "Come up closer, Leslie." Standing next to Ms. Klein, Leslie watches the teacher's mouth carefully and lip-reads the words. She puts her hands on the piano, too, and smiles. She says the sound vibrations tickle. When Leslie starts swaying to the rhythm of the music, everyone else starts swaying with her.

Sometimes our class makes soup or stew. Leslie and I work together and share a vegetable peeler. But first Leslie likes to feel the onions, carrots, and potatoes. Then she guesses what they are by their smell. I think she has a nose like a rabbit!

Peeling the onions always makes us cry. We run to the water fountain and wash away the sting.

In our class, we take turns doing many jobs. Everyone wants to be "Child of the Week." That means you can walk down the hallway alone, bringing messages to other classrooms.

When it's Leslie's turn, I get to go with her because she needs someone to show her the way. It's fun to go through the school by ourselves. Some days we peek into the library or ask the art teacher for extra clay.

One time we had a message for Leslie's brother's fourth grade teacher. When Leslie saw her brother, she shouted, "Hi, Greg!"

I told her, "Be quiet," but she didn't listen.

Even more than being "Child of the Week," Leslie likes to read. And no wonder! She is the best reader in the class. I can read a few words, but she can read a whole story. Her favorite is "Little Red Riding Hood," and Ms. Klein lets her read it aloud to us.

Leslie holds the book close. She could wear her glasses to make the words look bigger. But she says they bother her and that she sees better with her face near the page.

Leslie acts out the different parts of the story. First she speaks in a deep voice so we think she's the wolf. Then she pretends she is Little Red Riding Hood and talks in a high, squeaky voice. We try to be quiet, but Leslie is so funny we can't help laughing.

When she is finished, everyone claps. Leslie takes a bow, almost touching her toes.

Leslie is good at touching her toes. In gym, she can do it ten times in a row. She is also good at twirling around like an airplane and growing tall like a flower.

But if we climb the ropes, Leslie needs help. Her stiff muscles make it hard for her to cling to the rope with her hands and feet. So Mrs. Kramer, our gym teacher, boosts Leslie to a big knot. She holds on to her while Leslie swings.

On sunny days we go outside. Leslie and I love the merry-go-round best. She sits in the middle so she won't topple off. We both scream when it goes fast.

One day our class took a trip to a nature center. At first Leslie was unhappy and wanted to go home. The prairie dogs and porcupines were too far back in their cages for her to see. She couldn't find the gray snake that was lying near the rock, either. Finally, she sat down on the ground and wouldn't take another step.

I didn't know what to do. Then Ms. Klein said, "Lunchtime," and Leslie jumped up to be the first in line. We ate our picnic lunch under a tall tree. During dessert, Leslie stuck the watermelon pits on her cheeks and said she had chicken pox.

After lunch we went wading in the nearby brook. The water was so cold!

Leslie splashed me with her toes, and I laughed so much my stomach hurt.

By the time we rode the bus home, my shorts and shirt were dripping wet, but I didn't care.

"It was a great trip," Leslie said to me, yawning. Before I could agree, her head was on my shoulder.

I thought Leslie must like having a good friend like me. I know how lucky I am to have a good friend like Leslie.

When you're in school, or playing with your friends in your neighborhood, always be attentive to any special needs a person may have.

The Lion and the Mouse
by Aesop

A Lion, who was hot and tired from hunting, lay down under a big shady oak tree. When he fell asleep a company of little mice played around and over him. The Lion woke with a start and slapped his big paw down on one of them and held him fast.

"Please don't kill me, Lion," squeaked the Mouse. "I didn't mean any harm and if you will let me go I'll help you out sometime."

"Haw! haw!" laughed the Lion, "a little smidge like you help me! That is funny." But the Lion wasn't really mean and he felt quite happy, so he let the Mouse go.

Not long after that the Lion ran into a big net that some hunters had set to catch him. He let out a roar that shook the forest all around. The Mouse heard him and thought he recognized the voice of his friend, so he went over to see what had happened.

There was the Lion all tangled up in the rope net, just about ready to give up and wait for the hunters to come and kill him.

"Well, Lion, even you are in a fix this time," said the Mouse, and with his sharp little teeth he gnawed the net apart until the Lion could crawl out and run free.

The lion thought the mouse would never be of any help since he was so small. But everyone has their own unique talents.

Some of the greatest contributions to society have come from people who were once called "handicapped." Everyone has disadvantages, and it's how one copes with them that makes all the difference.

Thomas Edison was one of our most brilliant inventors. He created the electric light bulb, the phonograph, and the movie projector. He could not hear, and some people believe he had attention deficit disorder.

Harriet Tubman fought hard to lead hundreds of slaves to freedom and established schools where they could learn to read and write. She suffered from epilepsy.

Wilma Rudolph suffered from polio and was unable to walk at the age of four. At the age of eight, after years of physical therapy, she was able to walk with the aid of a brace and orthotic shoe. She went on to become one of the world's fastest runners, winning three gold medals in the 1960 Olympics.

Senator Robert Dole endured severe injuries in World War II and was told he would never walk again. He also lost most of the use of his right shoulder, arm, and hand. Senator Dole never gave up. After years of rehabilitation, he was able to walk again and use his right hand. Senator Dole became the longest serving Republican leader in the history of the U.S. senate, and was nominated for vice president and president of the United States.

Stevie Wonder was born prematurely and in order to save his life doctors had to give him large amounts of oxygen. The oxygen did save him, but it left him blind. Stevie is one of our most talented musicians, and he continues to delight audiences all over the world.

Chris Burke has made millions of people realize that having Down's Syndrome is certainly not a tragedy. He is a talented actor who has had many successful television and movie roles. Most importantly, he is a person filled with joy and compassion.

Jim Abbott was born without a right hand, but he saw his disability as a challenge instead of a handicap. He went on to become a distinguished major league baseball player. Like most people with disabilities, Jim wishes to be seen as an ordinary person. He once said, "I don't think of myself as being handicapped — I mean, my hand has not kept me from doing anything that I wanted to do. However, it's something that's always going to be part of my story. I understand that, and I'm not going to run away from it. Ideally, though, I'd prefer to be recognized for pitching well and nothing else."

A CHILD'S PRAYER
by M. Betham-Edwards

God, make my life a little light
    Within the world to glow;
A little flame that burneth bright
    Wherever I may go.

God, make my life a little flower
    That giveth joy to all,
Content to bloom in native bower,
    Although the place be small.

God, make my life a little song
    That comforteth the sad,
That helpeth others to be strong
    And makes the singer glad.

God, make my life a little staff
    Whereon the weak may rest,
And so what health and strength I have
    May serve my neighbors best.

God, make my life a little hymn
    Of tenderness and praise;
Of faith, that never waxeth dim,
    In all His wondrous ways.

CHAPTER SIX

Caring for the Elderly and Sick

1.
Befriending the Elderly

CONSIDERATION
by Gelett Burgess

When you're old, and get to be,
Thirty-four or forty-three,
Don't you hope that you will see
Children all respect you?

Will they, without being told,
Wait on you, when you are old,
Or be heedless, selfish, cold?
I *hope* they'll not neglect you!

An elderly person might seem frail and gray, but they were once young like you. And now that they've lived a long time, they can be full of wisdom.

To show love and respect for the elderly, offer to help when you visit. When you are with an elderly person who cannot hear well, be sure to speak loudly and clearly. You may need to repeat yourself. It's also polite to keep the television off and the background noise to a minimum.

If a person has a hard time seeing, or is blind, offer to take his arm and help him. Let him know what pieces of furniture he needs to navigate around. If you are outside, let him know if there is a step or a dip in the yard.

THE WILLOW MAN
by Juliana Horatia Ewing

There once was a Willow, and he was very old,
And all his leaves fell off from him, and left him in the cold;
But ere the rude winter could buffet him with snow,
There grew upon his hoary head a crop of mistletoe.

All wrinkled and furrowed was this old Willow's skin,
His taper fingers trembled, and his arms were very thin;
Two round eyes and hollow, that stared but did not see,
And sprawling feet that never walked, had this most ancient tree.

A dame who dwelt near was the only one who knew
That every year upon his head the Christmas berries grew;
And when the dame cut them, she said — it was her whim —
"A merry Christmas to you, sir!" *and left a bit for him.*

"Oh, Granny dear, tell us," the children cried, "where we
May find shining mistletoe that grows upon a tree?"
At length the dame told them, but cautioned them to mind
To greet the Willow civilly, *and leave a bit behind.*

"Who cares," said the children, "for this old Willow-man?
We'll take the mistletoe, and he may catch us if he can."
With rage the ancient Willow shakes in every limb,
For they have taken all, and *have not left a bit for him!*

Then bright gleamed the holly, the Christmas berries shone,
But in the wintry wind without the Willow-man did moan:
"Ungrateful, and wasteful! the mystic mistletoe
A hundred years hath grown on me, but never more shall grow."

A year soon passed by, and the children came once more,
But not a sprig of mistletoe the aged Willow bore.
Each slender spray pointed; he mocked them in his glee,
And chuckled in his wooden heart, that ancient Willow tree.

LEWIS CARROLL
author unknown

"You are wise, Mr. Dodgson," the young child said,
"And your forehead is getting a wrinkle;
And yet you've so twinkling an eye in your head —
I'm wondering what makes it twinkle?"
"In my youth," Mr. Dodgson replied to the child,
"I acquired mathematical habits
To keep my odd thoughts from becoming as wild
As March Hares, and as frequent as Rabbits."
"You are wise, Lewis Carroll," the child said again,
"And the College you live in is hoary;
But if you've such numbers of thoughts in your brain —
Do you think you could tell me a story?"
"In my youth, if you must know the truth," whispered he,
"I kept those same thoughts very supple
By letting my stories run quite fancy-free —
Allow me to tell you a couple!"

Some older people are quite good storytellers. You may be surprised at how much you can enjoy and learn from your grandparents' stories.

HALF A BLANKET
a German fable

In France an old king, weak with age, gave his kingdom and all his lands to his son. In return, the son promised to personally care for him. Soon afterward the son took himself a wife, who did not like his father.

Spitefully, she said, "The old man is always coughing at the table until it takes away all my pleasure in eating."

So to please her, the son gave his father a place to lie beneath the stairs. For many years he lay there on a bed of hay and straw, like one they would make for the dogs.

The queen gave birth to a son, who grew into a proud and virtuous lad. Concerned by the situation, he brought whatever food and drink he could find to his grandfather. One day the grandfather asked for an old horse blanket to protect him from the cold, and the virtuous youth ran off to fulfill his wish.

In the stall he found a good horse blanket. He took it from the horse and ripped it in two. Seeing him, his father asked him what he was doing with the horse blanket.

"I am taking half of it for your father's bed," he said. "The other half I'll save for you when you are sleeping there where you now have your father locked in."

POMONA AND THE OLD WOMAN
adapted by Michael Lamb

POMONA was a beautiful but quiet girl who cared for the fruit trees in a great orchard. She loved working among her pear trees, apple trees, plum trees, and grapevines. Her work was never tiresome. She pruned and tended her trees from dawn until dark. She watered their roots and trimmed off the excess shoots.

Pomona trained the grapevines to climb up along the trunks of trees, so that their branches appeared to have large clusters of beautiful deep purple grapes hanging from them. She became famous for her wonderful fruit. Although many boys were interested in Pomona and sought to be her lover, she seemed to care only for her fruit orchard. Many young men tried to entice her and all were promptly sent away.

The country people who lived nearby had gardens and orchards of their own. They were a source of great trouble to Pomona. Often they came to steal her fruit and cut the branches off her trees to graft onto their own. Pomona would many times give away her fruit to strangers and neighbors who came by, but she could not tolerate people who stole from her and damaged her trees. So she built a high wall around her garden and allowed no suitors or country folk to enter through her little gate. Soon people left her alone. They spread stories that she was coldhearted and selfish. The young men no longer seemed interested, except one who loved her best of all.

His name was Vertumnus and he was the god of changing seasons. He possessed the power of taking any form he wished. He couldn't believe that this lovely girl was coldhearted, mean, and selfish. So he decided to see for himself if it was true. He would test her by changing into an ugly old woman and wearing a dark cloak with a dark hood. Vertumnus knew that truly good and kind people always respect their elders and treat them courteously.

Rise in the presence of the aged, show respect for the elderly and revere your God.

LEVITICUS 19:32

182

The old woman came to the garden gate and asked Pomona for permission to enter and see the luscious fruits. Pomona smiled and swung the gate wide open. She spoke very kindly to the old lady, led her to a grassy bank, and helped her to seat herself in the shade of a large tree. She then gathered her reddest apples and her largest plums and offered them to her visitor.

"Do you tend this orchard by yourself?" asked the woman. "Do you mean to live by yourself in solitude forever?" Pomona said she had never met a young man who she could love more than her garden.

Then the old woman pointed to an elm tree on which Pomona had trained her grapes. "If this vine did not twine around the elm tree it would fall to the ground. Its grapes would never feel the sun's warmth and would not grow. You are like the vine and need someone like the elm," said the old stranger.

As she spoke her dark cloak fell away from her, her wrinkles vanished, and her bent shoulders straightened. It was a handsome young man, Vertumnus himself, who now stood before Pomona. He knew that Pomona was good and unselfish. He loved her very much. When he spoke again to her it was in a voice very different from that of the old woman. Pomona thought it more beautiful than any voice she had ever heard. As she led him through the garden, Pomona looked upon his kind and beautiful face, saying, "You are indeed like the elm tree and I am glad to be like the vine."

THE GREAT GRANDFATHER
by Charles and Mary Lamb

My father's grandfather lives still.
His age is fourscore years and ten;
He looks a monument of time,
The agedest of aged men.

Though years lie on him like a load,
A happier man you will not see

Than he, whenever he can get
His great-grandchildren on his knee.

When we our parents have displeased,
He stands between us as a screen;
By him our good deeds in the sun,
Our bad ones in the shade are seen.

His love's a line that's long drawn out,
Yet lasteth firm unto the end;
His heart is oak, yet unto us
It like the gentlest reed can bend.

A fighting soldier he has been
Yet by his manners you would guess,
That he his whole long life had spent
In scenes of country quietness.

His talk is all of things long past,
For modern facts no pleasure yield
Of the far-famed year of forty-five,
Of William, and Culloden's field.

The deeds of this eventful age,
Which princes from their thrones have hurled,
Can no more interest wake in him
Than stories of another world.
When I his length of days revoke,
How like a strong tree he hath stood,
It brings into my mind almost
Those patriarchs old before the Flood.

Sometimes older people are unable to get out of their homes. Sending cards and little thoughtful gifts means a great deal to them, because it helps them feel less alone. Visit often, bringing meals and offering to help around the house. Ask how they are, and tell them about your life. Your thoughtfulness can lift their spirits.

SOMEBODY'S MOTHER
by Mary Dow Brine

The woman was old and ragged and gray
And bent with the chill of the Winter's day.

The street was wet with a recent snow
And the woman's feet were aged and slow.

She stood at the crossing and waited long,
Alone, uncared for, amid the throng

Of human beings who passed her by
Nor heeded the glance of her anxious eye.

Down the street, with laughter and shout,
Glad in the freedom of "school let out,"

Came the boys like a flock of sheep,
Hailing the snow piled white and deep.

Past the woman so old and gray
Hastened the children on their way.

Nor offered a helping hand to her
So meek, so timid, afraid to stir

Lest the carriage wheels or the horses' feet
Should crowd her down in the slippery street.

At last came one of the merry troop,
The gayest laddie of all the group;

He paused beside her and whispered low,
"I'll help you cross, if you wish to go."

Her aged hand on his strong young arm
She placed, and so, without hurt or harm,

He guided the trembling feet along,
Proud that his own were firm and strong.

Then back again to his friends he went,
His young heart happy and well content.

"She's somebody's mother, boys, you know,
For all she's aged and poor and slow,

"And I hope some fellow will lend a hand
To help my mother, you understand,

"If ever she's poor and old and gray,
When her own dear boy is far away."

And "somebody's mother" bowed low her head
In her home that night, and the prayer she said

Was, "God be kind to the noble boy,
Who is somebody's son, and pride and joy!"

2.
Caring for the Sick

MISS TIZZY
by Libba Moore Gray

MISS TIZZY always wore a purple hat with a white flower in it and high-top green tennis shoes. The neighbors thought her peculiar. But the children loved her.

Miss Tizzy's house was pink and sat like a fat blossom in the middle of a street with white houses, white fences, and very neat flower gardens. Miss Tizzy had no fence at all but she had flowers that grew everywhere and spilled over onto the sidewalk.

Miss Tizzy let the children pick the flowers. Then she gave them clean glass jelly jars to put them in. And the children loved it.

Miss Tizzy's big, yellow cat, Hiram, slept in a window box in the middle of some red geraniums. Sometimes he climbed on her shoulders and hung there like a tired old fur piece.

On Mondays, Miss Tizzy baked cookies. She let the neighborhood children put in the raisins, and then lick the bowl while the cookies were baking. The children loved it.

On Tuesdays, Miss Tizzy made puppets out of old socks. She made a puppet for each boy and girl. They made up their own stories and put on shows for Miss Tizzy. She laughed and clapped every time. And the children loved it.

On Wednesdays, Miss Tizzy played her bagpipes. She gave the children spoons and pans and let them pretend they were playing real drums. Each Wednesday, one child got to be special and play, a silver penny whistle. Every child got a turn. They marched up and down the street with Miss Tizzy and her bagpipes leading the parade. Hiram sometimes marched along, and the children loved it.

On Thursdays, Miss Tizzy gave the children clean, white paper and crayons. They drew pictures of sunshine and butterflies. They put them in Miss Tizzy's red wagon and delivered them all over town to people who had stopped smiling, and had grown too tired to come out of their houses anymore. Hiram rode in the front of the wagon with a red ribbon around his neck. And the children loved it.

On Fridays, Miss Tizzy opened her trunk and they all played dress up. There were hats with feathers and hats with bows. There were baseball caps and straw hats with bright, red bands. Everyone wore a hat. Miss Tizzy put on a lace shawl and served pink lemonade in her best china cups. The children loved it.

On Saturdays, Miss Tizzy put roller skates on her green tennis shoes and went up and down the sidewalks. The children came out of the white houses and joined her. They made a roller-skate train holding on to Miss Tizzy's long skirt. Hiram was usually the caboose. The children made train sounds and Miss Tizzy was the engineer. She never scolded the children for being too loud, and the children loved it.

On Sundays, when the day was over, the children stretched out on bright quilts in Miss Tizzy's backyard and looked up at the stars. The tree frogs croaked their summer sounds as Miss Tizzy sang songs about the moon, slightly off-key. The children didn't care. They loved it.

One day Miss Tizzy took off her purple hat with the white flower and laid it on the window seat. Then she took off her high-top green tennis shoes and placed them under her high white bed. Miss Tizzy lay down on her feather mattress. She was very sick. Hiram left his window box and curled up at her feet. He did not purr anymore. The doctor came and went. He shook his head and looked very serious.

The children were sad. They didn't know what to do. They missed their grown-up friend. Finally . . . they had an idea.

On Monday, they baked cookies with raisins and brought them to the pink house.

On Tuesday, they stood in the yard and held up puppets to the window. They put on a puppet show just for Miss Tizzy.

On Wednesday, they brought pans and spoons and played a soft little drumming sound just outside the door.

On Thursday, they drew pictures with orange and red crayons and put them in Miss Tizzy's mailbox.

On Friday, they put on funny hats and left a tea tray at the front door. They left Hiram a bowl of cool milk.

On Saturday, they put a brand new pair of skates in a big box with a purple ribbon on top and took them to Miss Tizzy.

On Sunday, when the sun went away, the children stood underneath Miss Tizzy's window. They sang all the moon songs she had taught them.

Miss Tizzy's hat glowed in the moonlight. She was having a peaceful dream. She heard the children singing, and she loved it.

The children knew all of Miss Tizzy's favorite things, and demonstrated their love for her when she was sick. When your parents are sick, spend time with them and give them lots of hugs and kisses. If your mother loves flowers and tea, arrange a few hand-picked flowers in a vase and bring them to her with a cup of tea in her favorite mug. If your grandfather is sick and you know he loves model cars, maybe you could keep him company as the two of you build a model car. If your best friend is in bed with a broken leg and you know she loves chocolate chip cookies, bake some for her!

DON'T YOU FEEL WELL, SAM?
by Amy Hest

IT WAS A COLD, cold night on Plum Street. In the little white house, Mrs. Bear was putting Sam to bed. She closed their favorite book, and they both blew out the candle.

"Kiss me good night, Sam," Mrs. Bear said.

And she wrapped him all cozy in the blanket that was red. But suddenly she heard a cough — *Hck, hck!* And there sat Sam, curled up and small and caughing in his bed.

Mrs. Bear put her arms around Sam.

"Don't you feel well, Sam?"

Sam shook his head. *Hck, hck!*

"Poor Sam." Mrs. Bear hugged him harder and kissed his warm cheek.

"You have a cough," she said.

And she dashed down the stairs — and up again — with syrup.

"Open wide, Sam!" Mrs. Bear said.

Sam shook his head. "Tastes *bad*," he said.

"Yes," said his mama. "You need to be brave."

Sam put the blanket on his head.

"I *don't* have a cough!" *Hck, hck!*

"Try again, Sam," said his mama.

Sam shook the blanket off his head. He opened up, then closed his mouth tight. The spoon was too big.

"Too big," said Sam. *Hck, hck!*

"You can do it," Mrs. Bear said. "I *know* you can, Sam!"

Sam opened up, then closed his mouth tight.

Too much syrup on a too-big spoon.

"Too much," said Sam. *Hck, hck!*

Mrs. Bear rubbed frost off the window and peeked outside, "Soon it will snow," she said. "Open wide, Sam, and afterward we'll go downstairs and wait for snow."

Snow!

Sam opened wide. Then very wide. He sputtered and snorted and made a big face, and the syrup went down.

"Brave Sam," he said.

Mrs. Bear and Sam held hands on the stairs. Sam wore his robe that was blue, and his slippers were, too.

They lit a little fire in the kitchen, then made a pot of tea. Mrs. Bear put extra honey in the tea, and it was nice sliding down.

After tea, they sat in the big purple chair near the window and waited for snow. Mrs. Bear told a story about a bear called Sam. Sam liked the story, so she told it again.

Hck, hck! went the cough, every now and then.

Sam leaned back on his mama's soft belly, and it wriggled while she talked. The little fire glowed and the kitchen was warm.

All through the night, Mrs. Bear and Sam sat in the big purple chair and waited.

And finally it snowed.

When a family member or friend is in the hospital, cheer him up by sending a card or paying a visit. A homemade card is special because it takes time and care to create. If you do visit someone at the hospital, bring flowers to brighten up the room and think of some pleasant things to talk about — like what's happening at home or school. Try to keep your visit brief, since people in hospitals need rest in order to recover. Your thoughtfulness will be appreciated. Love and care is the best medicine.

PINOCCHIO
by Carlo Collodi

This next story comes from the last two chapters of Pinocchio. *At this point, Pinocchio has been through quite a lot. He ran away from home, refused to go to school, and led a vagabond life. He turned into a donkey and was forced to dance and jump through hoops. Later, a man bought him with the intention of turning his skin into a drum, and then tried to drown him. Fortunately for Pinocchio, the blue Fairy sent a shoal of fish to release him as he sank into the sea. Pinocchio swam away — only to be eaten up, along with a talking fish named Tunny, by the gigantic Dogfish.*

CHAPTER 35

*P*INOCCHIO, having taken leave of his friend the Tunny, began to grope his way in the dark through the body of the Dogfish, taking a step at a time in the direction of the light that he saw shining dimly at a great distance.

The farther he advanced, the brighter became the light; and he walked and walked until at last he reached it; and when he reached it . . . what did he find? I will give you a thousand guesses. He found a little table spread out, and on it a lighted candle stuck into a green glass bottle, and seated at the table was a little old man. He was eating some live fish, and they were so very much alive that while he was eating them they sometimes even jumped out of his mouth.

At this sight Pinocchio was filled with such great and unexpected joy that he became almost delirious. He wanted to laugh, he wanted to cry, he wanted to say a thousand things, and instead he could only stammer out a few confused and broken words. At last he succeeded in uttering a cry of joy, and opening his arms he threw them around the little old man's neck, and began to shout:

"Oh, my dear papa! I have found you at last! I will never leave you more, never more, never more!"

"Then my eyes tell me true?" said the little old man, rubbing his eyes. "Then you are really my dear Pinocchio?"

"Yes, yes, I am Pinocchio, really Pinocchio! And you have quite forgiven me, have you not? Oh, my dear papa, how good you are . . . and to think that I, on the contrary . . . Oh, but if you only knew what misfortunes have been poured on my head, and all that has befallen me! Only imagine, the day that you, poor dear papa, sold your coat to buy me a spelling book that I might go to school, I escaped to see the puppet show, and the showman wanted to put me on the fire that I might roast his mutton, and it was he who afterwards gave me five gold pieces to take them to you, but I met the Fox and the Cat, who took me to the inn of the Red Crawfish, where they ate like wolves, and I left by myself in the middle of the night, and I encountered assassins who ran after me, and I ran away, and they followed, and I ran, and they always followed me, and I ran, until they hung me to a branch of a Big Oak, and the beautiful Child with blue hair sent a little carriage to fetch me, and the doctors when they had seen me said immediately: 'If he is not dead, it is proof that he is still alive' — and then by chance I told a lie, and my nose began to grow until I could no longer get through the door of the room, for which reason I went with the Fox and the Cat to bury the four gold pieces, for one I had spent at the inn, and the Parrot began to laugh, and instead of two thousand gold pieces I found none left, for which reason the judge when he heard that I had been robbed had me immediately put in prison to content the robbers, and then when I was coming away I saw a beautiful bunch of grapes in a field, and I was caught in a trap, and the peasant, who was quite right, put a dog collar round my neck that I might guard the poultry yard, and acknowledging my innocence let me go, and the Serpent with the smoking tail began to laugh and broke a blood vessel in his chest, and so I returned to the house of the beautiful Child who was dead, and the Pigeon, seeing that I was crying, said to me, 'I have seen your father who was building a little boat to go in search of you,' and I said to him, 'Oh, if I also had wings!' and he said to me, 'Do you want to go to your father?' and I said, 'Without doubt! But who will take me to him?' and he said to me, 'I will take you,' and I said to him, 'How?' and he said to me, 'Get on my back,' and so we flew all night, and then in the morning all the fishermen who were looking out to sea said to me, 'There is a poor man in a boat who is on the point of being drowned,' and I recognized you at once, even at that distance, for my heart told me, and I made signs to you to return to land . . ."

"I also recognized you," said Geppetto, "and I would willingly have returned to the shore: but what was I to do? The sea was tremendous, and a great wave upset my boat. Then a horrible Dogfish who was near, as soon as he saw me in the water, came toward me, and putting out his tongue took hold of me, and swallowed me as if I had been a little Bologna tart."

"And how long have you been shut up here?" asked Pinocchio.

"Since that day — it must be nearly two years ago: two years, my dear Pinocchio, that have seemed like two centuries!"

"And how have you managed to live? And where did you get the candle? And the matches to light it? Who gave them to you?"

"Stop, and I will tell you everything. You must know then, that in the same storm in which my boat was upset, a merchant vessel foundered. The sailors were all saved, but the vessel went to the bottom, and the Dogfish, who had that day an excellent appetite, after he had swallowed me, swallowed also the vessel . . ."

"How?"

"He swallowed it in one mouthful, and the only thing that he spat out was the mainmast, that had stuck between his teeth like a fishbone. Fortunately for me the vessel was laden with preserved meat in tins, biscuits, bottles of wine, dried raisins, cheese, coffee, sugar, candles, and boxes of wax matches. With this providential supply I have been able to live for two years. But I have arrived at the end of my resources; there is nothing left in the larder, and this candle that you see burning is the last that remains . . ."

"And after that?"

"After that, dear boy, we shall both remain in the dark."

"Then, dear little papa," said Pinocchio, "there is no time to lose. We must think of escaping."

"Of escaping? . . . And how?"

"We must escape through the mouth of the Dogfish, throw ourselves into the sea and swim away."

"You talk well: but, dear Pinocchio, I don't know how to swim."

"What does that matter? I am a good swimmer, and you can get on my shoulders and I will carry you safely to shore."

"All illusions, my boy!" replied Geppetto, shaking his head, with a melancholy smile. "Do you suppose it possible that a puppet like you, scarcely a meter high, could have the strength to swim with me on his shoulders!"

"Try it and you will see!"

Without another word Pinocchio took the candle in his hand, and going in front to light the way, he said to his father:

"Follow me, and don't be afraid."

And they walked for some time and traversed the body and the stomach of the Dogfish. But when they arrived at the point where the monster's big throat began, they thought it better to stop to give a good look around and to choose the best moment for escaping.

Now I must tell you that the Dogfish, being very old, and suffering from asthma and palpitation of the heart, was obliged to sleep with his mouth open. Pinocchio, therefore, having approached the entrance to his throat and, looking up, could see beyond the enormous gaping mouth a large piece of starry sky and beautiful moonlight.

"This is the moment to escape," he whispered, turning to his father. "The Dogfish is sleeping like a dormouse, the sea is calm, and it is as light as day. Follow me, dear papa, and in a short time we shall be in safety."

They immediately climbed up the throat of the sea monster, and having reached his immense mouth, they began to walk on tiptoe down his tongue.

Before taking the final leap the puppet said to his father:

"Get on my shoulders and put your arms tight around my neck. I will take care of the rest."

As soon as Geppetto was firmly settled on his son's shoulders, Pinocchio, feeling sure of himself, threw himself into the water and began to swim. The sea was as smooth as oil, the moon shone brilliantly, and the Dogfish was sleeping so profoundly that even a cannonade would have failed to wake him.

CHAPTER 36

WHILE PINOCCHIO was swimming quickly toward the shore he discovered that his father, who was on his shoulders with his legs in the water, was trembling as violently as if the poor man had got an attack of ague fever.

Was he trembling from cold or from fear? Perhaps a little from both the one and the other. But Pinocchio, thinking that it was from fear, said to comfort him.

"Courage Papa! In a few minutes we shall be safely on shore."

"But where is this blessed shore?" asked the little old man, becoming still more frightened, and screwing up his eyes as tailors do when they wish to thread a needle. "I have been looking in every direction and I see nothing but the sky and the sea."

"But I see the shore as well," said the puppet. "You must know that I am like a cat: I see better by night than by day."

Poor Pinocchio was making a pretense of being in good spirits, but in reality . . . in reality he was beginning to feel discouraged; his strength was failing, he was gasping and panting for breath . . . he could do no more, and the shore was still far off.

He swam until he had no breath left; then he turned his head to Geppetto and said in broken words:

"Papa . . . help me . . . I am dying!"

The father and son were on the point of drowning when they heard a voice like a guitar out of tune saying:

"Who is it that is dying?"

"It is I, and my poor father!"

"I know that voice! You are Pinocchio!"

"Precisely; and you?"

"I am the Tunny, your prison companion in the body of the Dogfish."

"And how did you manage to escape?"

"I followed your example. You showed me the road, and I escaped after you."

"Tunny, you have arrived at the right moment! I implore you to help us, or we are lost."

Share with God's people who are in need. Practice hospitality.

ROMANS 12:13

"Willingly and with all my heart. You must, both of you, take hold of my tail and allow me to guide you. I will take you on shore in four minutes."

Geppetto and Pinocchio, as I need not tell you, accepted the offer at once; but instead of holding on by his tail they thought it would be more comfortable to get on the Tunny's back.

Having reached the shore, Pinocchio sprang first on land that he might help his father to do the same. He then turned to the Tunny, and said to him in a voice full of emotion:

"My friend, you have saved my papa's life. I can find no words with which to thank you properly. Permit me at least to give you a kiss as a sign of my eternal gratitude!"

The Tunny put his head out of the water, and Pinocchio, kneeling on the ground, kissed him tenderly on the mouth. At this spontaneous proof of warm affection, the poor Tunny, who was not accustomed to it, felt extremely touched, and ashamed to let himself be seen crying like a child, he plunged under the water and disappeared.

By this time the day had dawned. Pinocchio, then offering his arm to Geppetto, who had scarcely breath to stand, said to him:

"Lean on my arm, dear papa, and let us go. We will walk very slowly, like the ants, and when we are tired we can rest by the wayside."

"And where shall we go?" asked Geppetto.

"In search of some house or cottage, where they will give us for charity a mouthful of bread, and a little straw to serve as a bed."

They had not gone a hundred yards when they saw by the roadside two villainous-looking individuals begging.

They were the Cat and the Fox, but they were scarcely recognizable. Fancy! The Cat had so long feigned blindness that she had become blind in reality; and the Fox, old, mangy, and with one side paralyzed, had not even his tail left. That sneaking thief, having fallen into the most squalid misery, one fine day had found himself obliged to sell his beautiful tail to a traveling peddler, who bought it to drive away flies.

"Oh, Pinocchio!" cried the Fox. "Give a little in charity to two poor infirm people."

"Infirm people," repeated the Cat.

"Begone, impostors!" answered the puppet. "You took me in once, but you will never catch me again."

"Believe me, Pinocchio, we are now poor and unfortunate indeed!"

"If you are poor, you deserve it. Recollect the proverb: 'Stolen money never fructifies.' Begone, impostors!"

And thus saying, Pinocchio and Geppetto went their way in peace. When they had gone another hundred yards they saw, at the end of a path in the middle of the fields, a nice little straw hut with a roof of tiles and bricks.

"That hut must be inhabited by someone," said Pinocchio. "Let us go and knock at the door."

They went and knocked.

"Who is there?" said a little voice from within.

"We are a poor father and son without bread and without a roof," answered the puppet.

"Turn the key and the door will open," said the same little voice.

Pinocchio turned the key and the door opened. They went in and looked here, there, and everywhere, but could see no one.

"Oh, where is the master of the house?" said Pinocchio, much surprised.

"Here I am up here!"

The father and son looked immediately up to the ceiling, and there on a beam they saw the Talking Cricket.

"Oh, my dear little Cricket!" said Pinocchio, bowing politely to him.

"Ah! Now you call me your 'dear little Cricket.' But do you remember the time when you threw the handle of a hammer at me, to drive me from your house?"

"You are right, Cricket! Drive me away also . . . throw the handle of a hammer at me; but have pity on my poor papa . . ."

"I will have pity on both father and son, but I wished to remind you of the ill treatment I received from you, to teach you that in this world, when it is possible, we should show courtesy to everybody, if we wish it to be extended to us in our hour of need."

"You are right, Cricket, you are right, and I will bear in mind the lesson you have given me. But tell me how you managed to buy this beautiful hut."

"This hut was given to me yesterday by a goat whose wool was of a beautiful blue color."

"And where has the goat gone?" asked Pinocchio, with lively curiosity.

"I do not know."

"And when will it come back?"

"It will never come back. It went away yesterday in great grief and, bleating, it seemed to say: 'Poor Pinocchio . . . I shall never see him more . . . by this time the Dogfish must have devoured him!'"

"Did it really say that? . . . Then it was she! . . . It was she! . . . It was my dear little Fairy!" exclaimed Pinocchio, crying and sobbing.

When he had cried for some time he dried his eyes, and prepared a comfortable bed of straw for Geppetto to lie down upon. Then he asked the Cricket:

"Tell me, little Cricket, where can I find a tumbler of milk for my poor papa?"

"Three fields off from here there lives a gardener called Giangio who keeps cows. Go to him and you will get the milk you are in want of."

Pinocchio ran all the way to Giangio's house; and gardener asked him:

"How much milk do you want?"

"I want a tumblerful."

"A tumbler of milk costs a halfpenny. Begin by giving the halfpenny."

"I have not even a farthing," replied Pinocchio, grieving and mortified.

"That is bad, Puppet," answered the gardener. "If you have not even a farthing, I have not even a drop of milk."

"I must have patience!" said Pinocchio, and he turned to go.

"Wait a little," said Giangio. "We can come to an arrangement together. Will you undertake to turn the pumping machine?"

"What is the pumping machine?"

"It is a wooden pole which serves to draw up the water from the cistern to water the vegetables."

"You can try me . . ."

"Well, then, if you will draw a hundred buckets of water. I will give you in compensation a tumbler of milk."

"It is a bargain."

Giangio then led Pinocchio to the kitchen garden and taught him how to turn the pumping machine. Pinocchio immediately began to work; but before he had drawn up the hundred buckets of water the perspiration was pouring from his head to his feet. Never before had he undergone such fatigue.

"Up till now," said the gardener, "the labor turning the pumping machine was performed by my little donkey, but the poor animal is dying."

"Will you take me to see him?" said Pinocchio.

"Willingly."

When Pinocchio went into the stable he saw a beautiful little donkey stretched on the straw, worn out from hunger and overwork. After looking at him earnestly, he said to himself, much troubled:

"I am sure I know this little donkey! His face is not new to me."

And bending over him, he asked him in asinine language:

"Who are you?"

At this question the little donkey opened his dying eyes, and answered in broken words in the same language:

"I am . . . Can . . . dle . . . wick . . ."

And, having again closed his eyes, he expired.

"Oh, poor Candlewick!" said Pinocchio in a low voice; and taking a handful of straw, he dried a tear that was rolling down his face.

"Do you grieve for a donkey that cost you nothing?" said the gardener. "What must it be to me who bought him for ready money?"

"I must tell you . . . he was my friend!"

"Your friend?"

"One of my schoolfellows!"

"How?" shouted Giangio, laughing loudly. "How? Had you donkeys for schoolfellows? . . . I can imagine what wonderful studies you must have made!"

The puppet, who felt much mortified at these words, did not answer; but taking his tumbler of milk, still quite warm, he returned to the hut.

And from that day for more than five months he continued to get up at daybreak every morning to go and turn the pumping machine, to earn the tumbler of milk that was of such benefit to his father in his bad state of health. Nor was he satisfied with this; for, during the time that he had left over, he learned to make hampers and baskets of rushes, and with the money he obtained by selling them, he was able with great economy to provide for all the daily expenses. Among other things he constructed an elegant little wheelchair, in which he would take his father out on fine days to breathe a mouthful of fresh air.

By his industry, ingenuity, and his anxiety to work and to overcome difficulties, he not only succeeded in maintaining his father, who continued infirm, in comfort, but he also contrived to put aside forty pence to buy himself a new coat.

One morning he said to his father.

"I am going to the neighboring market to buy myself a jacket, a cap, and a pair of shoes. When I return," he added, laughing, "I shall be so well dressed that you will take me for a fine gentleman."

And leaving the house, he began to run merrily and happily along. All at once he heard himself called by name, and turning around he saw a big Snail crawling out from the hedge.

"Do you not know me?" asked the Snail.

"It seems to me . . . and yet I am not sure . . ."

"Do you not remember the Snail who was lady's maid to the Fairy with blue hair? Do you not remember the time when I came downstairs to let you in, and you were caught by your foot which you had stuck through the house door?"

"I remember it all!" shouted Pinocchio. "Tell me quickly, my beautiful little Snail, where have you left my good Fairy? What is she doing? Has she forgiven me? Does she still remember me? Does she still wish me well? Is she far from here? Can I go and see her?"

To all these rapid, breathless questions the Snail replied in her usual phlegmatic manner:

"My dear Pinocchio, the poor Fairy is lying in bed at the hospital!"

"At the hospital?"

"It is only too true. Overtaken by a thousand misfortunes, she has fallen seriously ill, and she has not even enough to buy herself a mouthful of bread."

"Is it really so? Oh, what sorrow you have given me! Oh, poor Fairy, poor Fairy, poor Fairy! . . . If I had a million I would run and carry it to her . . . but I have only forty pence . . . Here they are: I was going to buy a new coat. Take them, Snail, and carry them at once to my good Fairy."

"And your new coat?"

"What matters my new coat? I would sell even these rags that I have got on to be able to help her. Go, Snail, and be quick, and in two days return to this place, for I hope I shall then be able to give you some more

> A good example is the best sermon.
>
>
>
> BENJAMIN FRANKLIN
> *Poor Richard's Almanac*

money. Up to this time I have worked to maintain my papa; from today I will work five hours more that I may also maintain my good mamma. Good-by, Snail, I shall expect you in two days."

The Snail, contrary to her usual habits, began to run like a lizard in a hot August sun.

That evening Pinocchio, instead of going to bed at ten o'clock, sat up till midnight had struck; and instead of making eight baskets of rushes he made sixteen.

Then he went to bed and fell asleep. And while he slept he thought that he saw the Fairy smiling and beautiful, who after having kissed him, said to him:

"Well done, Pinocchio! To reward you for your good heart I will forgive you for all that is past. Boys who minister tenderly to their parents, and assist them in their misery and infirmities, are deserving of great praise and affection, even if they cannot be cited as examples of obedience and good behavior. Try and do better in the future and you will be happy."

At this moment his dream ended, and Pinocchio opened his eyes and awoke.

But imagine his astonishment when upon awakening he discovered that he was no longer a wooden puppet, but that he had become instead a boy, like all other boys. He gave a glance round and saw that the straw walls of the hut had disappeared, and that he was in a pretty little room furnished and arranged with a simplicity that was almost elegance. Jumping out of bed, he found a new suit of clothes ready for him, a new cap, and a pair of new leather boots that fitted him beautifully.

He was hardly dressed when he naturally put his hands in his pockets, and pulled out a little ivory purse on which these words were written: "The Fairy with blue hair returns the forty pence to her dear Pinocchio, and thanks him for his good heart." He opened the purse, and instead of forty copper pennies he saw forty shining gold pieces fresh from the mint.

He then went and looked at himself in the glass, and he thought he was someone else. For he no longer saw the usual reflection of a wooden puppet; he was greeted instead by the image of a bright, intelligent boy with chestnut hair, blue eyes, and looking as happy and joyful as if it were the Easter holidays.

In the midst of all these wonders succeeding each other Pinocchio felt quite bewildered, and he could not tell if he was really awake or if he was dreaming with his eyes open.

"Where can my papa be!" he exclaimed suddenly, and going into the next room, he found old Geppetto quite well, lively, and in good humor, just as he had been formerly. He had already resumed his trade of wood carving, and he was designing a rich and beautiful frame of leaves, flowers, and the heads of animals.

"Satisfy my curiosity, dear papa," said Pinocchio throwing his arms around his neck and covering him with kisses. "How can this sudden change be accounted for?"

"This sudden change in our home is all your doing," answered Geppetto.

"How my doing?"

"Because when boys who have behaved badly turn over a new leaf and become good, they have the power of bringing contentment and happiness to their families."

"And where has the old wooden Pinocchio hidden himself?"

"There he is," answered Geppetto, and he pointed to a big puppet, leaning against a chair, with its head on one side, its arms dangling, and its legs so crossed and bent that it was really a miracle that it remained standing.

Pinocchio turned and looked at it; and after he had looked at it for a short time, he said to himself with great complacency.

"How ridiculous I was when I was a puppet! And how glad I am that I have become a well-behaved little boy!"

Because he faced death in the belly of the Dogfish, Pinocchio finally grew up and learned to care for others. The Cricket left him with a valuable lesson: "in this world, when it is possible, we should show courtesy to everybody, if we wish it to be extended to us in our hour of need." Pinocchio is a good example of how we can all ease the suffering of the sick.

The Secret Garden
by Frances Hodgson Burnett

In this next story, you will meet two ten-year-old children, Mary and Colin. Mary is a spoiled girl who used to live in India in a beautiful mansion. She had everything she could ever dream of — even her own personal servant. But she becomes very bitter when she has to move in with her uncle in England after losing her parents to the plague. Soon after arriving at her new home, *she meets her sickly cousin Colin, who has been in bed since birth. Despite their difficult personalities, Mary and Colin become friends. Mary tells Colin about her secret garden, which was a favorite place of Colin's deceased mother, and is now a favorite place for Mary.*

Chapter 16

"*I* won't!" said Mary. They found a great deal to do that morning and Mary was late in returning to the house and was also in such a hurry to get back to her work that she quite forgot Colin until the last moment.

"Tell Colin that I can't come and see him yet," she said to Martha. "I'm very busy in the garden."

Martha looked rather frightened.

"Eh! Miss Mary," she said, "it may put him all out of humor when I tell him that."

But Mary was not as afraid of him as other people were and she was not a self-sacrificing person.

"I can't stay," she answered. "Dickon's waiting for me"; and she ran away.

The afternoon was even lovelier and busier than the morning had been. Already nearly all the weeds were cleared out of the garden and most of the roses and trees had been pruned or dug about. Dickon had brought a spade of his own and he had taught Mary to use all her tools, so that by this time it was plain that though the lovely wild place was not likely to become a "gardener's garden" it would be a wilderness of growing things before the springtime was over.

"There'll be apple blossoms an' cherry blossoms overhead," Dickon said, working away with all his might. "An' there'll be peach an' plum trees in bloom against th' walls, an' th' grass'll be a carpet o' flowers."

The little fox and the rook were as happy and busy as they were, and the robin and his mate flew backward and forward like tiny streaks of lightning. Sometimes the rook flapped his black wings and soared away over the tree-tops in the park. Each time he came back and perched near Dickon and cawed several times as if he were relating his adventures, and Dickon talked to him just as he had talked to the robin. Once when Dickon was so busy that he did not answer him at first, soot flew on to his shoulders and gently tweaked his ear with his large beak. When Mary wanted to rest a little Dickon sat down with her under a tree and once he took his pipe out of his pocket and played the soft strange little notes and two squirrels appeared on the wall and looked and listened.

"Tha's a good bit stronger than tha' was," Dickon said, looking at her as she was digging. "Tha's beginning to look different, for sure."

Mary was glowing with exercise and good spirits.

"I'm getting fatter and fatter every day," she said quite exultantly. "Mrs. Medlock will have to get me some bigger dresses. Martha says my hair is growing thicker. It isn't so flat and stringy."

The sun was beginning to set and sending deep gold-colored rays slanting under the trees when they parted.

"It'll be fine tomorrow," said Dickon. "I'll be at work by sunrise."

"So will I," said Mary.

She ran back to the house as quickly as her feet would carry her. She wanted to tell Colin about Dickon's fox cub and the rook and about what the springtime had been doing. She felt sure he would like to hear. So it was not very pleasant when she opened the door of her room, to see Martha standing waiting for her with a doleful face.

"What is the matter?" she asked. "What did Colin say when you told him I couldn't come?"

"Eh!" said Martha, "I wish tha'd gone. He was nigh goin' into one o' his tantrums. There's been a nice to do all afternoon to keep him quiet. He would watch the clock all th' time."

Mary's lips pinched themselves together. She was no more used to considering other people than Colin was and she saw no reason why an ill-tempered boy should interfere with the thing she liked best. She knew nothing about the pitifulness of people who had been ill and nervous and who did not know that they could control their tempers and need not make other people ill and nervous, too. When she had had a headache in India she had done her best to see that everybody else also had a headache or something quite as bad. And she felt she was quite right; but of course now she felt that Colin was quite wrong.

He was not on his sofa when she went into his room. He was lying flat on his back in bed and he did not turn his head toward her as she came in. This was a bad beginning and Mary marched up to him with her stiff manner.

"Why didn't you get up?" she said.

"I did get up this morning when I thought you were coming," he answered, without looking at her. "I made them put me back in bed this afternoon. My back ached and my head ached and I was tired. Why didn't you come?"

"I was working in the garden with Dickon," said Mary.

Colin frowned and condescended to look at her.

"I won't let that boy come here if you go and stay with him instead of coming to talk to me," he said.

Mary flew into a fine passion. She could fly into a passion without making a noise. She just grew sour and obstinate and did not care what happened.

"If you send Dickon away, I'll never come into this room again!" she retorted.

"You'll have to if I want you," said Colin.

"I won't!" said Mary.

"I'll make you," said Colin. "They shall drag you in."

"Shall they, Mr. Rajah!" said Mary fiercely. "They may drag me in but they can't make me talk when they get me here. I'll sit and clench my teeth and never tell you one thing. I won't even look at you. I'll stare at the floor!"

They were a nice agreeable pair as they glared at each other. If they had been two little street boys they would have sprung at each other and had a rough-and-rumble fight. As it was, they did the next thing to it.

"You are a selfish thing!" cried Colin.

"What are you?" said Mary. "Selfish people always say that. Anyone is selfish who doesn't do what they want. You're more selfish than I am. You're the most selfish boy I ever saw."

"I'm not!" snapped Colin. "I'm not as selfish as your fine Dickon is! He keeps you playing in the dirt when he knows I am all by myself. He's selfish, if you like!"

Mary's eyes flashed fire.

"He's nicer than any other boy that ever lived!" she said. "He's — he's like an angel!" It might sound rather silly to say that but she did not care.

"A nice angel!" Colin sneered ferociously. "He's a common cottage boy off the moor!"

"He's better than a common Rajah!" retorted Mary. "He's a thousand times better!"

Because she was the stronger of the two she was beginning to get the better of him. The truth was that he had never had a fight with any one like himself in his life and, upon the whole, it was rather good for him, though neither he nor Mary knew anything about that. He turned his head on his pillow and shut his eyes and a big tear was squeezed out and ran down his cheek. He was beginning to feel pathetic and sorry for himself — not for any one else.

"I'm not as selfish as you, because I'm always ill, and I'm sure there is a lump coming on my back," he said. "And I am going to die besides."

"You're not!" contradicted Mary unsympathetically.

He opened his eyes quite wide with indignation. He had never heard such a thing said before. He was at once furious and slightly pleased, if a person could be both at one time.

"I'm not?" he cried. "I am! You know I am! Everybody says so."

"I don't believe it!" said Mary sourly. "You just say that to make people sorry. I believe you're proud of it. I don't believe it! If you were a nice boy it might be true — but you're too nasty!"

In spite of his invalid back Colin sat up in bed in quite a healthy rage.

"Get out of the room!" he shouted and he caught hold of his pillow and threw it at her. He was not strong enough to throw it far and it only fell at her feet, but Mary's face looked as pinched as a nutcracker.

"I'm going," she said. "And I won't come back!"

She walked to the door and when she reached it she turned round and spoke again.

"I was going to tell you all sorts of nice things," she said. "Dickon brought his fox and his rook and I was going to tell you all about them. Now I won't tell you a single thing!"

She marched out of the door and closed it behind her, and there to her great astonishment she found the trained nurse standing as if she had been listening and, more amazing still — she was laughing. She was a big handsome young woman who ought not to have been a trained nurse at all, as she could not bear invalids and she was always making excuses to leave Colin to Martha or any one else who would take her place. Mary had never liked her, and she simply stood and gazed up at her as she stood giggling into her handkerchief.

"What are you laughing at?" she asked her.

"At you two young ones," said the nurse. "It's the best thing that could happen to the sickly pampered thing to have some one to stand up to him that's as spoiled as himself"; and she laughed into her handkerchief again. "If he'd had a young vixen of a sister to fight with it would have been the saving of him."

"Is he going to die?"

"I don't know and I don't care," said the nurse. "Hysterics and temper are half what ails him."

"What are hysterics?" asked Mary.

"You'll find out if you work him into a tantrum after this — but at any rate you've given him something to have hysterics about, and I'm glad of it."

Mary went back to her room not feeling at all as she had felt when she had come in from the garden. She was cross and disappointed but not at all sorry for Colin. She had looked forward to telling him a great many things and she had meant to try to make up her mind whether it would be safe to trust him with the great secret. She had been beginning to think it would be, but now she had changed her mind entirely. She would never tell him and he could stay in his room and never get any fresh air and die if he liked! It would serve him right. She felt so sour and unrelenting that for a few minutes she almost forgot about Dickon and the green veil creeping over the world and the soft wind blowing down from the moor.

Martha was waiting for her and the trouble in her face had been temporarily replaced by interest and curiosity. There was a wooden box on the table and its cover had been removed and revealed that it was full of neat packages.

"Mr. Craven sent it to you," said Martha. "It looks as if it had picture-books in it."

Mary remembered what he had asked her the day she had gone to his room. "Do you want anything — dolls — toys — books?" She opened the package wondering if he had sent a doll, and also wondering what she should do with it if he had. But he had not sent one. There were several beautiful books such as Colin had, and two of them were about gardens and were full of pictures. There were two or three games and there was a beautiful little writing-case with a gold monogram on it and a gold pen and inkstand.

Everything was so nice that her pleasure began to crowd her anger out of her mind. She had not expected him to remember her at all and her hard little heart grew quite warm.

"I can write better than I can print," she said, "And the first thing I shall write with that pen will be a letter to tell him I am much obliged."

If she had been friends with Colin she would have run to show him her presents at once, and they would have looked at the pictures and read some of the gardening books and perhaps tried playing the games, and he would have enjoyed himself so much he would never once have thought he was going to die or have put his hand on his spine to see if there was a lump coming. He had a way of doing that which she could not bear. It gave her an uncomfortable frightened feeling because he always looked so frightened himself. He said that if he felt even quite a little lump some day he should know his hunch had begun to grow. Some thing he had heard Mrs. Medlock whispering to the nurse had given him the idea and he had thought over it in secret until it was quite firmly fixed in his mind.

Mrs. Medlock had said his father's back had begun to show its crooked-ness in that way when he was a child. He had never told any one but Mary that most of his "tantrums" as they called them grew out of his hysterical hidden fear. Mary had been sorry for him when he had told her.

"He always began to think about it when he was cross or tired," she said to herself. "And he has been cross today. Perhaps — perhaps he has been thinking about it all afternoon."

She stood still, looking down at the carpet and thinking.

"I said I would never go back again — " she hesitated, knitting her brows — "but perhaps, just perhaps, I will go and see — if he wants me — in the morning. Perhaps he'll try to throw his pillow at me again, but — I think — I'll go."

Sometimes sickness makes people very grumpy. We don't have to tolerate unreasonable demands, but it's good to care for the sick, even when they're unpleasant.

CHAPTER SEVEN

Out and About: Getting Along with Others

1.
Visiting Other People's Homes

BLOCK CITY
by Robert Louis Stevenson

What are you able to build with your blocks?
Castles and palaces, temples and docks.
Rain may keep raining, and others go roam,
But I can be happy and building at home,

Let the sofa be mountains, the carpet be sea,
There I'll establish a city for me:
A church and a mill and a palace beside,
And a harbor as well where my vessels may ride.

Great is the palace with pillar and wall,
A sort of a tower on the top of it all,
And steps coming down in an orderly way
To where my toy vessels lie safe in the bay.

This one is sailing and that one is moored:
Hark to the song of the sailors on board!
And see, on the steps of my palace, the kings
Coming and going with presents and things!

Now I have done with it, down let it go!
All in a moment the town is laid low.
Block upon block lying scattered and free,
What is there left of my town by the sea?

Yet as I saw it, I see it again,
The church and the palace, the ships and the men,
And as long as I live and where'er I may be,
I'll always remember my town by the sea.

When playing at a friend's house, it's impolite to say, "I'm bored." This poem shows us just how creative we can be. So when you're with your friends and you think there's nothing to do, just think of this little poem and go sailing on the sea, build castles, and climb mountains.

THE TALE OF TWO BAD MICE
by Beatrix Potter

ONCE UPON A TIME there was a very beautiful doll's house; it was red brick with white windows, and it had real muslin curtains and a front door and a chimney.

It belonged to two dolls called Lucinda and Jane, at least it belonged to Lucinda, but she never ordered meals.

Jane was the Cook; but she never did any cooking, because the dinner had been bought ready-made, in a box full of shavings.

There were two red lobsters and a ham, a fish, a pudding, and some pears and oranges.

They would not come off the plates, but they were extremely beautiful.

One morning Lucinda and Jane had gone out for a drive in the doll's perambulator. There was no one in the nursery, and it was very quiet. Presently there was a little scuffling, scratching noise in a corner near the fire-place, where there was a hole under the skirting-board.

Tom Thumb put out his head for a moment, and then popped it in again.

Tom Thumb was a mouse.

A minute afterwards, Hunca Munca, his wife, put her head out, too; and when she saw that there was no one in the nursery, she ventured out on the oilcloth under the coalbox.

The doll's house stood at the other side of the fireplace. Tom Thumb and Hunca Munca went cautiously across the hearthrug. They pushed the front door — it was not fast.

Tom Thumb and Hunca Munca went upstairs and peeped into the dining room. Then they squeaked with joy!

Such a lovely dinner was laid out upon the table! There were tin spoons, and lead knives and forks, and two dolly-chairs — all so convenient!

Tom Thumb set to work at once to carve the ham. It was a beautiful shiny yellow, streaked with red.

The knife crumpled up and hurt him; he put his finger in his mouth.

"It is not boiled enough; it is hard. You have a try, Hunca Munca."

Hunca Munca stood up in her chair, and chopped at the ham with another lead knife.

"It's as hard as the hams at the cheesemonger's," said Hunca Munca.

The ham broke off the plate with a jerk, and rolled under the table.

"Let it alone," said Tom Thumb; "give me some fish, Hunca Munca!"

Hunca Munca tried every tin spoon in turn; the fish was glued to the dish.

Then Tom Thumb lost his temper. He put the ham on the middle of the floor, and hit it with the tongs and with the shovel — bang, bang, smash, smash!

The ham flew all into pieces, for underneath the shiny paint it was made of nothing but plaster!

> He that cannot bear with other people's passions cannot govern his own.
>
>
>
> BENJAMIN FRANKLIN
> *Poor Richard's Almanac*

Then there was no end to the rage and disappointment of Tom Thumb and Hunca Munca. They broke up the pudding, the lobsters, the pears, and the oranges.

As the fish would not come off the plate, they put it into the red-hot crinkly paper fire in the kitchen; but it would not burn either.

Tom Thumb went up the kitchen chimney and looked out at the top — there was no soot.

While Tom Thumb was up the chimney, Hunca Munca had another disappointment. She found some tiny canisters upon the dresser, labeled — Rice — Coffee — Sugar — but when she turned them upside down, there was nothing inside except red and blue beads.

Then those mice set to work to do all the mischief they could — especially Tom Thumb! He took Jane's clothes out of the chest of drawers in her bedroom, and he threw them out of the top floor window.

But Hunca Munca had a frugal mind. After pulling half the feathers out of Lucinda's bolster, she remembered that she herself was in want of a feather bed.

With Tom Thumb's assistance she carried the bolster downstairs, and across the hearthrug. It was difficult to squeeze the bolster into the mouse-hole; but they managed it somehow.

Then Hunca Munca went back and fetched a chair, a book-case and the bird-cage and several small odds and ends. The book-case and the bird-cage refused to go into the mouse-hole.

Hunca Munca left them behind the coalbox, and went to fetch a cradle.

Hunca Munca was just returning with another chair, when suddenly there was a noise of talking outside upon the landing. The mice rushed back to their hole, and the dolls came into the nursery.

What a sight met the eyes of Jane and Lucinda! Lucinda sat upon the upset kitchen stove and stared; and Jane leant against the kitchen dresser and smiled — but neither of them made any remark.

The book-case and the bird-cage were rescued from under the coal-box — but Hunca Munca has got the cradle, and some of Lucinda's clothes.

She also has some useful pots and pans, and several other things.

The little girl that the doll's-house belonged to, said, — "I will get a doll dressed like a policeman!"

But the nurse said, — "I will set a mouse-trap!"

So that is the story of the two Bad Mice, — but they were not so very naughty after all, because Tom Thumb paid for everything he broke.

He found a crooked sixpence under the hearthrug; and upon Christmas Eve, he and Hunca Munca stuffed it into one of the stockings of Lucinda and Jane.

And very early every morning — before anybody is awake — Hunca Munca comes with her dust-pan and her broom to sweep the Dollies' house!

Remember the Golden Rule: treat others as you would want to be treated. Tom Thumb and Hunca Munca went uninvited into another's home, made a mess of it, and even stole some things. A polite mouse would have treated another's belongings with respect. When visiting another person's home, or a place like a museum or store, remember this famous saying: "Look, don't touch."

HOSPITALITY
by Gelett Burgess

When a person visits you, remember he's your guest,
Receive him very kindly, and be sure he has the best;
Make him very comfortable and show him all your toys,
And only play the games you're very sure that he enjoys.

When you pay a visit, never grumble or complain,
Try to be so affable they'll want you there again;
Don't forget the older ones, your hostess least of all,
When you're leaving tell her you have had a pleasant call!

When you go to a friend's home, make sure to play only in the rooms that the parents approve of for play. It's not polite to run all over the house, or to take food out of the kitchen or dining area. Help pick up the toys you play with, and be a pleasant visitor.

A Prince Meets a Pauper
from The Prince and the Pauper *by Mark Twain*
adapted by Michael Lamb

TOM CANTY GOT UP HUNGRY, played hungry, and went to bed hungry. People would push and shove the poor ragged boy and speak harshly to him. This didn't stop the boy from dreaming. In fact, Tom loved to dream. He especially enjoyed sweet thoughts of lords and ladies, princes, kings, and castles.

He had never seen a real castle so he was surprised when his wanderings took him just outside a great stone building, the biggest building he had ever seen. Tom's eyes were as big as saucers. He stood there outside the palace of the king, utterly filled with wonder and delight. The ragged little fellow had but one desire: to get close to the prince and have a good devouring look at him. Before he knew it, he had his face against the bars of the palace gate. The next instant one of the soldiers snatched him rudely away, and sent him spinning among the gaping crowd of country gawks and London idlers. The soldier said, "Mind your manners, you young beggar!" The crowd jeered and laughed; but the young prince sprang to the gate with his face flushed, and his eyes flashing with indignation, and cried out: "How dare you use a poor lad like that! How dare you use even the lowest subject of my father the king so rudely. Open the gates, and let him in!"

You should have seen that fickle crowd snatch off their hats then. You should have heard them cheer and shout "Long live the Prince of Wales!" The soldiers presented arms with their halberds, opened the gates, and presented again as the little Prince of Poverty passed through, in his fluttering rags, to join hands with the Prince of Limitless Plenty. "You look tired and hungry" said the prince. "You've been treated badly, come with me my lad." Half a dozen attendants sprang forward to — I don't know what; interfere, no doubt. But they were waved aside with a right royal gesture, and they stopped stock still where they were like so many statues. The Prince took Tom to a rich apartment in the palace, which he called his cabinet. By his command a meal was brought such as Tom had never encountered before except in books. The prince, with princely delicacy and breeding, sent away the servants, so that his humble guest might not be embarrassed by their critical presence; then he sat near by, and asked questions while Tom ate. Oh, did he eat. He ate white bread, roasted meats, fine cheeses, cakes, puddings, and savory pies. It was the best food he had ever tasted.

The English are famous for their good manners. In this story, England's Prince of Wales shows his guards and subjects that we must treat all people kindly. When Tom came to the young prince's house, he was treated well. Whether a person is a king or a ragged pauper, he should be treated with respect and kindness.

The Lost Princess
by George MacDonald

In this next story, we meet a spoiled princess named Rosamond, who was introduced to you in the first chapter of this book. As the story continues, the princess is kidnapped by a wise old woman who is going to try to help her learn right from wrong. The wise woman takes Rosamond to her cottage in the woods, where she will begin instructing the child about good behavior.

Chapter 1

THERE WAS A CERTAIN COUNTRY where things used to go rather oddly. You could never tell whether it was going to rain or hail, or whether the milk was going to turn sour. It was impossible to say whether the next baby would be a boy or a girl, or even, after the baby was a week old, whether he or she would wake sweet-tempered or cross.

In strict accordance with the peculiar nature of this country of uncertainties, it came to pass one day that a shower of rain fell that might well be called golden, for the sun shone through the drops as they fell, and every drop was good for a grain of golden corn or a buttercup or a dandelion. While this splendid rain was falling with a musical patter upon the great leaves of the horse chestnuts, and on the leaves of the sycamores, and on a multitude of flowers, of which some stood up and boldly held out their cups to catch their share . . . While this lovely rain was washing all the air clean, while it fell, splashing and sparkling, with a hum, and a rush, and a soft clashing . . . While the rain was thus falling, and the leaves and the flowers and the sheep and the cattle and the hedgehog were all busily receiving the golden drops, something happened. It was not a great battle nor an earthquake nor a coronation, but something more important than all those put together.

A baby girl was born.

Her father was a king, her mother was a queen, and she had uncles and aunts who were princes and princesses. So the little girl was Somebody. And yet, for all of that, strange to say, the first thing she did was to cry. I told you it was a strange country.

As she grew up, everybody about her did his best to convince her that she was Somebody, and the girl herself was so easily persuaded of it that she quite forgot that anybody had even told her so. That she was Somebody she took for a fundamental, primary, first-born, self-evident idea and principle. And far be it from me to deny it. I will even go so far as to assert that in this odd country there was a huge number of Somebodies. Indeed, it was one of its oddities that every boy and girl in this country was rather too ready to think he or she was Somebody. And the worst of it was that the princess never thought of there being more than one Somebody — and that was herself.

Far away to the north in the same country, on the side of a bleak hill, where a horse chestnut or a sycamore was never seen, where there were no meadows rich with buttercups, only steep, rough, breezy slopes covered with dry prickly furze with its few blossoms of red gold . . . There (would you believe it?) while the same cloud that was dropping down golden rain all about the queen's new baby was dashing huge, fierce handfuls of hail upon the hills with such force that they flew spinning off the rocks and stones, went burrowing in the sheep's wool, stung the cheeks and chin of the shepherd with their sharp, spiteful little blows, and made his dog wink and whine as they bounded off his hard wise head and long, sagacious nose . . .

There, among the hailstones and the heather and the cold mountain air, another little girl was born.

Her father was a shepherd, her mother was a shepherdess, and she had uncles and aunts who were shepherds and dairymaids. And yet (would you believe it?) she too cried the very first thing. It was an odd country. And, what is still more surprising, the shepherd and the shepherdess and the common aunts and uncles were not a bit wiser than the king and the queen and the royal aunts and uncles. For they too, one and all, so constantly taught the little child that she was Somebody that she also forgot that there were a great many more Somebodies besides herself in the world.

It was indeed a peculiar country, very different from ours — so different that my reader must not be too much surprised when I add the amazing fact that most of its inhabitants, instead of enjoying the things they had, were always wanting the things they had not, often even the things it was least likely they ever could have.

The grown men and women being like this, it is not surprising that the Princess Rosamond — the name her parents gave her because it means "Rose of the World" — should grow up like them, wanting everything she could and everything she could not have. The things she could have were a great many too many, for her foolish parents always gave her what they could. But still there remained a few things they couldn't give her, for they were only a common king and queen. They could and did give her a lighted candle when she cried for it, and managed by much care that she should not burn her fingers or set her frock on fire. But when she cried for the moon, that they could not give her. Instead, however, they did the worst thing possible, for they pretended to do what they could not. They got her a thin disc of brilliantly polished silver, as near the size of the moon as they could agree upon; and for a time she was delighted.

But, unfortunately, one evening she made the discovery that her moon was a little peculiar — it could not shine in the dark. Her nurse happened to snuff out the candles as she was playing with it, and instantly came a shriek of rage, for her moon had vanished. Presently, through the opening of the curtains, she caught sight of the real moon far away in the sky and shining quite calmly, as if it had been there all the time; and her rage increased to such a degree that if it had not passed off in a fit, I do not know what might have come of it.

As she grew up it was still the same, with this difference: not only must she have everything, but she got tired of everything almost as soon as she had it. There was an accumulation of things in her nursery and schoolroom and bedroom that was perfectly appalling. Her mother's wardrobes were almost useless to her, so packed were they with things of which she never took any notice.

When she was five years old, they gave her a splendid gold watch so close set with diamonds and rubies that the back was just one crust of gems. In one of her little tempers, as they called her hideously ugly rages, she dashed it against the back of the chimney, after which it never gave a single tick; and some of the diamonds went to the ash-pit.

As she grew older still, she became fond of animals, but not in a way that brought them much pleasure or herself much satisfaction. When she was angry, she would beat them and try to pull them to pieces, and as soon as she became a little used to them, she would neglect them altogether. Then, if they could, they would run away, and she would be furious. Some white mice, which she had ceased feeding altogether, did so, and soon the palace was swarming with them. Their red eyes might be seen glowing and their white skins gleaming in every dark corner. But when it came to the king's finding a nest of them in his second-best crown, he was angry and ordered them to be drowned. The princess heard of it, however, and raised such a clamor that there they were left until they should run away on their own, and the poor king had to wear his best crown every day till then. Nothing that was the princess's property, whether she cared for it or not, was to be meddled with.

Of course, as she grew, she grew worse, for she never tried to grow better. She became more and more ill-tempered every day — dissatisfied not only with what she had but with all that was around her. She was constantly wishing things in general to be different. She found fault with everything and everybody and all that happened, and grew more and more disagreeable to everyone who had to do with her.

At last, when she had tormented all of her animals, and had nearly killed her nurse, and was miserable from morning to night, her parents thought it time to do something.

CHAPTER 5

*T*HE WISE WOMAN lifted the princess tenderly and washed and dressed her far more carefully than even her nurse. Then she set the princess down by the fire and prepared her breakfast. The princess was very hungry, and the bread and milk were as good as they could be, so she thought she had never in her life eaten anything nicer. Nevertheless, as soon as she began to have enough, she said to herself, "Ha! I see how it is! The old woman wants to fatten me! That is why she gives me such nice creamy milk. She doesn't kill me now because she's going to kill me then! She is an ogress after all!"

Thereupon the princess laid down her spoon and would not eat another mouthful. She only followed the basin with longing looks as the wise woman carried it away.

When she stopped eating, her hostess knew exactly what she was thinking. But it was one thing to understand the princess and quite another to make the princess understand her; that would require time. For the present she took no notice, but went about the affairs of the house, sweeping the floor, brushing down the cobwebs, cleaning the hearth, dusting the table and chairs, and watering the bed of heather to keep it fresh and alive — for she never had more than one guest at a time, and she never would allow that guest to go to sleep upon anything that had no life in it.

> Do not seek revenge or bear a grudge against one of your people, but love your neighbor as yourself.
>
>
>
> LEVITICUS 19:18

All the time the wise woman was thus busied she spoke not a word to the princess — which, for the princess, served to confirm her notion of the wise woman's purposes. But whatever the wise woman might have said would only have been perverted by the princess into yet stronger proof of her evil designs, for a fancy in the princess's own head would outweigh any multitude of facts in another's. The princess kept staring at the fire and never looked around to see what the wise woman might be doing.

By and by the wise woman came up close to the back of the princess's chair and said, "Rosamond!"

But the princess had fallen into one of her sulky moods and had shut herself up with her own ugly Somebody, so she never looked around or even answered the wise woman.

"Rosamond," she repeated, "I am going out. If you are a good girl — that is, if you do as I tell you — I will carry you back to your father and mother the moment I return."

The princess did not take the least notice.

"Look at me, Rosamond," said the wise woman.

But Rosamond never moved, never even shrugged her shoulders — perhaps because they were already up to her ears and could go no farther.

"I want to help you to do what I tell you," said the wise woman. "Look at me."

Still Rosamond was motionless and silent, saying only to herself, "I know what she's after! She wants to show me her horrid teeth. But I won't look. I'm not going to be frightened out of my senses to please her."

"You had better look, Rosamond. Have you forgotten how you kissed me this morning?"

But Rosamond now regarded that little throb of affection as a momentary weakness into which the deceitful ogress had betrayed her, and she almost despised herself for it. She was one of those people who are the more disagreeable the more they are coaxed. For such behavior the wise woman had an awful punishment, but she remembered that the princess had been very badly brought up and therefore wished to try her with all gentleness first.

She stood silent for a moment to see what effect her words might have. But Rosamond only said to herself, "She wants to fatten and eat me."

And it was such a little while since she had looked into the wise woman's loving eyes, thrown her arms around her neck, and kissed her!

"Well," said the wise woman gently, after pausing as long as it seemed possible she might be considering something, "I must tell you then without your attention: whoever listens with her back turned listens but half and gets but half the help."

"She wants to fatten me," said the princess.

"You must keep the cottage tidy while I am out. When I come back, I must see the fire bright, the hearth swept, and the kettle boiling; no dust on the table or chairs, the windows clear, the floor clean, and the heather in blossom — which last comes of sprinkling it with water three times a day. When you are hungry, put your hand into that hole in the wall, and you will find a meal."

"She wants to fatten me," muttered the princess.

"But on no account leave the house till I come back," continued the wise woman, "or you will grievously repent it. Remember what you have already gone through to reach it. Dangers lie all around this cottage of mine, but inside it is the safest place — in fact, the only quite safe place in all the country."

"She means to eat me," said the princess to herself, "and therefore wants to frighten me from running away."

The princess heard the voice no more. Then, suddenly startled at the thought of being alone, she looked hastily over her shoulder. The cottage was indeed empty of all visible life. It was soundless, too: there was not even a ticking clock or a flapping flame. The fire burned still, smoldering, but it was all the company she had, and she turned again to stare into it.

Soon she began to grow weary of having nothing to do. Then she remembered that the old woman, as she called her, had told her to keep the house tidy.

"This miserable little pigsty!" she said. "Where's the use of keeping such a hovel clean?"

But in truth she would have been glad of the employment; it was only because she had been told to do it that she was unwilling. For there are people — however unlikely it may seem — who object to doing a thing for no other reason than that it is required of them.

"I am a princess," she said, "and it is very improper to ask me to do such a thing."

She might have judged it quite as suitable for a princess to sweep away the dust as to sit in the center of a world of dirt. But just because she ought, she wouldn't. Perhaps she feared that if she gave in to doing her duty once, she might have to do it always — which was true enough, for that was the very thing for which she had been specially born.

Unable, however, to feel quite comfortable in the resolve to neglect it, she said to herself, "I'm sure there's time enough for such a nasty job as that!" and sat on, watching the fire as it burned away, the glowing red casting off white flakes, and sinking lower and lower on the hearth.

By and by, merely for want of something to do, the princess went to see what the old woman had left for her in the hole in the wall. But when she put in her hand, she found nothing there except the dust which she ought by this time to have wiped away. Never reflecting that the wise woman had told her she would find food there *when she was hungry*, she flew into one of her furies, calling the wise woman a cheat, a thief, a liar, an ugly old witch, an ogress, and I do not know how many other wicked names besides. She raged until she was quite exhausted and then fell fast asleep on her chair. When she awoke, the fire was out.

By this time she was hungry. But without looking in the hole she began again to storm at the wise woman, in which labor she would no doubt have once more exhausted herself had not something white caught her eye: it was the corner of a napkin hanging from the hole in the wall. She bounded to it, and there was a dinner for her of something strangely good — one of her favorite dishes, only better than she had ever tasted it before. This might surely have at least changed her mood towards the wise woman, but she only grumbled to herself that it was as it ought to be, ate up the food, and lay down on the bed, never thinking of dusting or building up the fire or watering the heather.

The wind began to moan about the cottage, and it grew louder and louder till a great gust came down the chimney and again scattered the white ashes all over the place. But the princess was by this time fast asleep and never woke till the wind had sunk to silence. One of the consequences of sleeping when one ought to be awake, however, is waking when one ought to be asleep, and the princess awoke in the black midnight and found enough to keep her awake.

For although the wind had fallen, there was a far more terrible howling than that of the wildest wind all about the cottage. Nor was the howling all. The air was full of strange cries, and everywhere she heard the noise of claws scratching against the house, which seemed all doors and windows, so crowded were the sounds, and coming from so many directions. All the night long she lay half swooning yet listening to the hideous noises. But with the first glimmer of morning they ceased.

Then she said to herself, "How fortunate it was that I woke! They would have eaten me up if I had been asleep." The miserable little wretch actually talked as if she had kept the beasts out! If she had done her work in the day, she would have slept through the terrors of the darkness and awaked fearless; whereas now she had in the storehouse of her heart a whole harvest of agonies reaped from the dark fields of the night!

They were not wolves which had caused her such dismay, but creatures of the air, more frightful still. As soon as the smoke of the burning pine wood ceased to spread itself abroad, and the sun was a sufficient distance down the sky, and the lone, cold woman was out, they came flying and howling about the cottage, trying to get in at every door and window. Down the chimney they would have got, except that at the heart of the fire there always lay a certain pine cone which looked like red-hot solid gold, and which, although it might easily get covered up with ashes so as to be quite invisible, was continually in a glow fit to kindle all the pine cones in the world. This it was which had kept the horrible birds — some say they have a claw at the tip of every wing feather — from tearing the poor naughty princess to pieces and gobbling her up.

When she rose and looked about her, she was dismayed to see what a state the cottage was in. The fire was out, and the windows were all dim from the wings and claws of the dirty birds, while the bed from which she had just risen was brown and withered, and half its purple bells had fallen. But she consoled herself that she could set all to rights in a few minutes — only she must breakfast first. And, sure enough, there was a

> Neglect mending a small fault and it will soon be a great one.
>
>
>
> BENJAMIN FRANKLIN
> *Poor Richard's Almanac*

basin of the delicious bread and milk ready for her in the hole in the wall!

After she had eaten it, she felt comfortable, and she sat for a long time building castles in the air — till she was actually hungry again, without having done an atom of work. She ate again, and was idle again, and ate again. Then it grew dark, and she went trembling to bed, for now she remembered the horrors of the last night. This time she never slept at all but spent the long hours in grievous terror, for the noises were worse than before. She vowed she would not pass another night in such a hateful, haunted old shed for all the ugly women, witches, and ogresses in the wide world. In the morning, however, she fell asleep, and she slept late.

Breakfast was of course her first thought, after which she could not avoid that of work. It made her very miserable, but she feared the consequences of being found with it undone. A few minutes before noon, she actually got up, took her pinafore for a duster, and proceeded to dust the table. But the wood ashes flew about so that it seemed useless to attempt getting rid of them, and she sat down again to think what was to be done. But there is very little indeed to be done when we will not do that which we have to do.

Her first thought now was to run away at once while the sun was high and get through the forest before night came on. She fancied she could easily go back the way she had come and get home to her father's palace. But not even the most experienced traveler in the world can ever go back the way the wise woman has brought him.

She got up and went to the door. It was locked! What could the old woman have meant by telling her not to leave the cottage? She was indignant.

The wise woman had meant to make it difficult but not impossible. Before the princess could find the way out, however, she heard a hand at the door and darted in terror behind it. The wise woman opened it and, leaving it open, walked straight to the hearth. Rosamond immediately slid out, ran a little way, and then laid herself down in the long heather.

If you visit your friend's home and leave it looking like a hurricane passed through, you may not be invited back. Here are a few suggestions: place your shoes neatly by the door when you enter; leave the bathroom clean and dry; hang the towel after you wash your hands; return games and toys to their shelves; don't open the refrigerator or kitchen cabinets without asking first; bring your plate, cup, and utensils to the sink after a meal; and wipe spills from the floor. These are just a few ideas to get you started!

2.
Seeing the Good in People

POLLYANNA
by Eleanor H. Porter

You probably know someone who is always bright and cheerful, someone who seems to spread these happy feelings wherever they go. You also might know someone who always looks sad and unhappy. They're gloomy and complain a lot, like Eeyore in the Winnie the Pooh stories.

This story involves a charming girl named Pollyanna. She moves in with her very strict aunt, who is unmarried and has never raised a child. The people in the town where Pollyanna is now living are cold and unpleasant.

Pollyanna breathes new life into the town with her "glad game." She touches many souls with her cheerful disposition, leaving them all a little happier and their lives a little brighter.

CHAPTER 5

"POOR LITTLE LAMB!" said Nancy. "And you must be hungry, too. I — I'm afraid you'll have ter have bread and milk in kitchen with me. Yer aunt didn't like it — because you didn't come down ter supper, ye know."

"But I couldn't. I was up here," Pollyanna replied.

"Yes; but — she didn't know that, you see," observed Nancy, dryly, stifling a chuckle. "I'm sorry about the bread and milk; I am, I am."

"Oh, I'm not. I'm glad," said Pollyanna.

"Glad! Why?"

"Why, I like bread and milk, and I'd like to eat with you. I don't see any trouble about being glad about that."

"You don't seem ter see any trouble bein' glad about everything," retorted Nancy, choking a little over her remembrance of Pollyanna's brave attempts to like the bare little attic room.

Pollyanna laughed softly.

"Well, that's the game, you know, anyway."

"The — *game*?"

"Yes — the 'just being glad' game."

"Whatever in the world are you talkin' about?"

"Why, it's a game. Father told it to me, and it's lovely," rejoined Pollyanna. "We've played it always, ever since I was a little, little girl. I told the Ladies' Aid, and they played it — some of them."

"What is it? I ain't much on games, though."

Pollyanna laughed again, but she sighed, too; and in the gathering twilight her face looked thin and wistful.

"Why, we began it on some crutches that came in a missionary barrel."

"*Crutches!*"

"Yes. You see, I'd wanted a doll, and Father had written them so; but when the barrel came the lady wrote that there hadn't any dolls come in, but the little crutches had. So she sent 'em along as they might come in handy for some child, some time. And that's when we began it."

"Well, I must say I can't see any game about that," declared Nancy, almost irritably.

"Oh, yes; the game was to just find something about everything to be glad about — no matter what 'twas," rejoined Pollyanna earnestly. "And we began right then — on the crutches."

"Well, goodness me! I can't see anythin' ter be glad about — gettin' a pair of crutches when you wanted a doll!"

Pollyanna clapped her hands.

"There is — there is," she crowed. "But *I* couldn't see it, either, Nancy, at first," she added, with quick honesty. "Father had to tell it to me."

"Well, then, suppose *you'll* tell me," almost snapped Nancy.

"Goosey! Why, just be glad because you *don't — need — 'em!*" exulted Pollyanna triumphantly. "You see it's just as easy — when you know how!"

"Well, of all the queer doin's!" breathed Nancy, regarding Pollyanna with almost fearful eyes.

"Oh, but it isn't queer — it's lovely," maintained Pollyanna enthusiastically. "And we've played it ever since. And the harder 'tis, the more fun 'tis to get 'em out; only — only — sometimes it's almost too hard — like

Hear no ill of a friend, nor speak any of an enemy.

BENJAMIN FRANKLIN
Poor Richard's Almanac

226

when your father goes to heaven, and there isn't anybody but a Ladies' Aid left."

"Yes, or when you're put in a snippy little room 'way at the top of the house with nothin' in it," growled Nancy.

Pollyanna sighed.

"That *was* a hard one, at first," she admitted, "specially when I was so kind of lonesome. I just didn't feel like playing the game, anyway, and I *had* been wanting pretty things, so! Then I happened to think how I hated to see freckles in the looking-glass, and I saw that lovely picture out the window too; so then I knew I'd found the things to be glad about. You see, when you're hunting for the glad things, you sort of forget the other kind — like the doll you wanted, you know."

"Humph!" choked Nancy, trying to swallow the lump in her throat.

"Most generally it doesn't take so long," sighed Pollyanna; "and lots of times now I just think of them without thinking, you know. I've got so used to playing it. It's a lovely game. F-Father and I used to like it so much," she faltered. "I suppose, though, it — it'll be a little harder now, as long as I haven't anybody to play it with. Maybe Aunt Polly will play it, though," she added, as an afterthought.

"My stars and stockings!" breathed Nancy, behind her teeth. Then, aloud, she said doggedly, "See here, Miss Pollyanna, I ain't sayin' that I'll play it very well, and I ain't sayin' that I know how, anyway; but I'll play it with ye, after a fashion – I just will, I will!"

"Oh, Nancy!" exulted Pollyanna, giving her a rapturous hug. "That'll be splendid! Won't we have fun?"

"Er — maybe," conceded Nancy, in open doubt. "But you mustn't count too much on me, ye know. I never was no case fur games, but I'm a'goin' ter make a most awful old try on this one. You're goin' ter have someone ter play it with, anyhow," she finished, as they entered the kitchen together to enjoy the bread and milk.

The little things make life brighter — like smiling and finding the good in people and situations. We are called to bring joy to others. The best way to do this is to be grateful and content ourselves.

MARGARET OF NEW ORLEANS
by Sara Cone Bryant

*I*F YOU EVER GO to the beautiful city of New Orleans, somebody will be sure to take you down into the old business part of the city, where there are banks and shops and hotels, and show you a statue which stands in a little square there. It is the statue of a woman, sitting in a low chair, with her arms around a child, who leans against her. The woman is not at all pretty: she wears thick, common shoes, a plain dress, with a little shawl, and a sun-bonnet; she is stout and short, and her face is a square-chinned Irish face; but her eyes look at you like your mother's.

Now there is something very surprising about this statue: it was the first one that was ever made in this country in honor of a woman. Even in old Europe there are not many monuments to women, and most of the few are to great queens or princesses, very beautiful and very richly dressed. You see, this statue in New Orleans is not quite like anything else.

It is the statue of a woman named Margaret. Her whole name was Margaret Haughery, but no one in New Orleans remembers her by it, any more than you think of your dearest sister by her full name; she is just Margaret. This is her story, and it tells why people made a monument for her.

When Margaret was a tiny baby, her father and mother died, and she was adopted by two young people as poor and as kind as her own parents. She lived with them until she grew up. Then she married, and had a little baby of her own. But very soon her husband died, and then the baby died, too, and Margaret was all alone in the world. She was poor, but she was strong, and knew how to work.

All day, from morning until evening, she ironed clothes in a laundry. And every day, as she worked by the window, she saw the little motherless children from the orphan asylum, near by, working and playing about. After a while, there came a great sickness upon the city, and so many mothers and fathers died that there were more orphans than the asylum could possibly take care of. They needed a good friend, now. You would hardly think, would you, that a poor woman who worked in a laundry could be much of a friend to them? But Margaret was. She went straight to the kind Sisters who had the asylum and told them she was going to give them part of her wages and was going to work for them, besides. Pretty soon she had worked so hard that she had some money saved from her wages. With this, she bought two cows and a little delivery cart. Then she carried her milk to her customers in the little cart every morning; and as she went, she begged the left-over food from the hotels and rich houses, and brought it back in the cart to the hungry children in the asylum. In the very hardest times, that was often all the food the children had.

A part of the money Margaret earned went every week to the asylum, and after a few years that was made very much larger and better. And Margaret was so careful and so good at business that, in spite of her giving, she bought more cows and earned more money. With this, she built a home for orphan babies; she called it her baby house.

After a time, Margaret had a chance to get a bakery, and then she became a bread-woman instead of a milk-woman. She carried the bread just as she had carried the milk, in her cart. And still she kept giving money to the asylum. Then the Great War came, our Civil War. In all the trouble and sickness and fear of that time, Margaret drove her cart of bread; and somehow she had always enough to give the starving soldiers, and for her babies, besides what she sold. And despite all this, she earned enough so that when the war was over she built a big steam factory for her bread. By this time everybody in the city knew her. The children all over the city loved her; the businessmen were proud of her; the poor people all came to her for advice. She used to sit at the open door of her office, in a calico gown and a little shawl, and give a good word to everybody, rich or poor.

Then, by and by, one day, Margaret died. And when it was time to read her will, the people found that, with all her giving, she had still saved a great deal of money, and that she had left every cent of it to the different orphan asylums of the city — each one of them was given something. Whether they were for white children or black, for Jews, Catholics, or Protestants, it made no difference; for Margaret always said, "They are all orphans alike." And that splendid, wise will was signed only with a cross, instead of a name, for Margaret had never learned to read or write!

When the people of New Orleans learned that Margaret was dead, they said, "She was a mother to the motherless; she was a friend to those who had no friends; she had wisdom greater than schools can teach; we will not let her memory go from us." So they made a statue of her, just as she used to look, sitting in her own office door, or driving in her own little cart. And there it stands today, in memory of the great love and the great power of plain Margaret Haughery, of New Orleans.

Margaret was a beautiful example of generosity. She understood that the more riches you give away, the more happiness you have. This is the grace of all graces, the sign of a well-ordered soul.

A Little Princess
by Frances Hodgson Burnett

In this story, we meet Sara, a little girl who, like Pollyanna, has a cheerful disposition. Her father always told her that she was a little princess. Unfortunately, her father was called to service in the war, and Sara was placed in a boarding school for girls. The school is under the rigid rule of Miss Minchin, who never smiles.

Sara has a vivid imagination and always tells beautiful stories to the girls at school. There is one girl in particular who delights in Sara's stories, Becky, a hard-working servant who lives in horrible conditions in the attic of the school. One day, while she is telling a story, Sara notices the servant girl putting coals on the fire especially slowly, so that she can catch bits of Sara's story. Sara askes her friend Mariette who the servant girl is and learns that Miss Minchin has forbidden them to talk or play with Becky. But Sara befriends her anyway — and, through her stories, teaches Becky that she is a little princess, too.

Chapter 5

"Who is that little girl who makes the fires?" she asked Mariette that night.

Mariette broke forth into a flow of description.

Ah, indeed, Mademoiselle Sara might well ask. She was a forlorn little thing who had just taken the place of scullery maid — though, as to being scullery maid, she was everything else besides. She blacked boots and grates, and carried heavy coal-scuttles up and down stairs, and scrubbed floors and cleaned windows, and was ordered about by everybody. She was fourteen years old, but was so stunted in growth that she looked about twelve. In truth, Mariette was sorry for her. She was so timid that if one chanced to speak to her it appeared as if her poor, frightened eyes would jump out of her head.

"What is her name?" asked Sara, who had sat by the table, with her chin on her hands, as she listened absorbedly to the recital.

Her name was Becky. Mariette heard everyone belowstairs calling, "Becky, do this," and "Becky, do that," every five minutes in the day.

Sara sat and looked into the fire, reflecting on Becky for some time after Mariette left her. She made up a story of which Becky was the ill-used heroine. She thought she looked as if she had never had quite enough to eat. Her very eyes were hungry. She hoped she should see her again, but though she caught sight of her carrying things up or down stairs on several occasions, she always seemed in such a hurry and so afraid of being seen that it was impossible to speak to her.

But a few weeks later, on another foggy afternoon, when she entered her sitting room she found herself confronting a rather pathetic picture. In her own special easy-chair before the bright fire, Becky — with a coal smudge on her nose and several on her apron, with her poor little cap sitting half off her head, and an empty coal box on the floor near her — sat fast asleep, tired out beyond even the endurance of her hard-working young body. She had been sent up to put the bedrooms in order for the evening. There were a great many of them, and she had been running about all day. Sara's room she had saved until the last. They were not like the other rooms, which were plain and bare. Ordinary pupils were expected to be satisfied with mere necessaries. Sara's comfortable sitting room seemed a bower of luxury to the scullery maid, though it was, in fact, merely a nice, bright little room. But there were pictures and books in it, and curious things from India; there was a sofa and low, soft chair; Emily [her doll] sat in a chair of her own, with the air of a presiding goddess, and there was always a glowing fire and a polished grate. Becky saved it until the end of her afternoon's work, because it rested her to go into it, and she always hoped to snatch a few minutes to sit down in the soft chair and look about her, and think about the wonderful good fortune of the child who owned such surroundings and who went out on the cold days in beautiful hats and coats one tried to catch a glimpse of through the area railing.

> Whatever is true, whatever is noble, whatever is right, whatever is pure, whatever is lovely, whatever is admirable — think about such things.
>
>
>
> PHILIPPIANS 4:8

On this afternoon, when she had sat down, the sensation of relief to her short, aching legs had been so wonderful and delightful that it had seemed to soothe her whole body, and the glow of warmth and comfort from the fire had crept over her like a spell, until, as she looked at the red coals, a tired, slow smile stole over her smudged face, her head nodded forward without her being aware of it, her eyes drooped, and she fell fast asleep. She had really been only about ten minutes in the room Sara entered, but she was in as deep a sleep as if she had been, like the Sleeping Beauty, slumbering for a hundred years. But she did not look — poor Becky — like a Sleeping Beauty at all. She looked only like an ugly, stunted, worn-out little scullery drudge.

Sara seemed as much unlike her as if she were a creature from another world.

On this particular afternoon she had been taking her dancing lesson, and the afternoon on which the dancing master appeared was rather a grand occasion at the seminary, though it occurred every week. The pupils were attired in their prettiest frocks, and as Sara danced particularly well, she was very much brought forward, and Mariette was requested to make her as diaphanous and fine as possible.

Today a frock the color of a rose had been put on her, and Mariette had bought some real buds and made her a wreath to wear on her black locks. She had been learning a new, delightful dance in which she had been skimming and flying about, like a large rose-colored butterfly, and the enjoyment and exercise had brought a brilliant, happy glow into her face.

When she entered the room, she floated in with a few of the butterfly steps — and there sat Becky, nodding her cap sideways off her head.

"Oh!" cried Sara, softly, when she saw her. "That poor thing!"

It did not occur to her to feel cross at finding her pet chair occupied by the small, dingy figure. To tell the truth, she was quite glad to find her there. When the ill-used heroine of her story wakened, she could talk to her. She crept toward her quietly, and stood looking at her. Becky gave a little snore.

"I wish she'd waken herself," Sara said. "I don't like to waken her. But Miss Minchin would be cross if she found out. I'll just wait a few minutes."

She took a seat on the edge of the table, and sat swinging her slim, rose-colored legs, and wondering what it would be best to do. Miss Amelia might come in at any moment, and if she did, Becky would be sure to be scolded.

"But she is so tired," she thought. "She is so tired!"

A piece of flaming coal ended her perplexity for her that very moment. It broke off from a large lump and fell on to the fender. Becky started, and opened her eyes with a frightened gasp. She did not know she had fallen asleep. She had only sat down for one moment and felt the beautiful glow — and here she found herself staring in wild alarm at the wonderful pupil, who sat perched quite near her, like a rose-colored fairy, with interested eyes.

She sprang up and clutched her cap. She felt it dangling over her ear, and tried wildly to put it straight. Oh, she had got herself into trouble now with a vengeance! To have impudently fallen asleep on such a young lady's chair! She would be turned out of doors without wages.

She made a sound like a big breathless sob.

"Oh, miss! Oh, miss!" she stuttered. "I arst yer pardon, miss! Oh, I do, miss!"

Sara jumped down, and came quite close to her.

"Don't be frightened," she said, quite as if she had been speaking to a little girl like herself. "It doesn't matter the least bit."

"I didn't go to do it, miss," protested Becky. "It was the warm fire — an' me bein' so tired. It — it *wasn't* imperence!"

Sara broke into a friendly little laugh, and put her hand on her shoulder.

"You were tired," she said; "you could not help it. You are not really awake yet."

How poor Becky stared at her! In fact, she had never heard such a nice, friendly, sound in anyone's voice before. She was used to being ordered about and scolded, and having her ears boxed. And this one — in her rose colored dancing afternoon splendor — was looking at her as if she were not a culprit at all — as if she had a right to be tired — even to fall asleep! The touch of the soft, slim little paw on her shoulder was the most amazing thing she had ever known.

"Ain't — ain't yer angry, miss?" she gasped. "Ain't yer goin' to tell the missus?"

"No," cried out Sara. "Of course I'm not."

> Search others for their virtues, thyself for thy vices.
>
> ༄
>
> BENJAMIN FRANKLIN
> *Poor Richard's Almanac*

The woeful fright in the coal-smutted face made her suddenly so sorry that she could scarcely bear it. One of her queer thoughts rushed into her mind. She put her hand against Becky's cheek.

"Why," she said, "we are just the same — I am only a little girl like you. It's just an accident that I am not you, and you are not me!"

Becky did not understand in the least. Her mind could not grasp such amazing thoughts, and "an accident" meant to her a calamity in which some one was run over or fell off a ladder and was carried to "the 'orspital."

"An accident, miss," she fluttered respectfully. "Is it?"

"Yes," Sara answered, and she looked at her dreamily for a moment. But the next she spoke in a different tone. She realized that Becky did not know what she meant.

"Have you done your work?" she asked. "Dare you stay here a few minutes?"

Becky lost her breath again.

"Here, miss? Me?"

Sara ran to the door, opened it, and looked out and listened.

"No one is anywhere about," she explained. "If your bedrooms are finished, perhaps you might stay a tiny while. I thought — perhaps — you might like a piece of cake."

The next ten minutes seemed to Becky like a sort of delirium. Sara opened a cupboard, and gave her a thick slice of cake. She seemed to rejoice when it was devoured in hungry bites. She talked and asked questions, and laughed until Becky's fears actually began to calm themselves, and she once or twice gathered boldness enough to ask a question or so herself, daring as she felt it be.

"Is that — " she ventured, looking longingly at the rose-colored frock. And she asked it almost in a whisper. "Is that there your best?"

"It is one of my dancing-frocks," answered Sara. "I like it, don't you?"

For a few seconds Becky was almost speechless with admiration. Then she said in an awed voice, "Once I seen a princess. I was standin' in the street with the crowd outside Covin' Gardens, watchin' the swells go inter the operer. An' there was one everyone stared at most. They ses to each other, 'That's the princess.' She was a growed-up young lady, but she was pink all over — gown an' cloak, an' flowers an' all. I called her to mind the minnit I see you, sittin' there on the table, miss. You looked like her."

"I've often thought," said Sara, in her reflecting voice, "that I should like to be a princess; I wonder what it feels like. I believe I will begin pretending I am one."

Becky stared at her admiringly, and, as before, did not understand in the least. She watched her with a sort of adoration. Very soon Sara left her reflections and turned to her with a new question.

"Becky," she said, "weren't you listening to that story?"

"Yes, miss," confessed Becky, a little alarmed again. "I knowed I hadn't orter, but it was that beautiful I — I couldn't help it."

"I like you to listen to it," said Sara. "If you tell stories, you like nothing so much as to tell them to people who want to listen. I don't know why it is. Would you like to hear the rest?"

Becky lost her breath again.

"Me hear it?" she cried. "Like as if I was a pupil, miss! All about the Prince — and the little white Merbabies swimming about laughing — with stars it their hair?"

Sara nodded.

"You haven't time to hear it now, I'm afraid," she said; "but if you will tell me just what time you come to do my rooms, I will try to be here and tell you a bit of it every day until it is finished. It's a lovely long one — and I'm always putting new bits to it."

"Then," breathed Becky, devoutly, "I wouldn't mind how heavy the coal boxes was — or what the cook done to me, if — if I might have that to think of."

"You may," said Sara. "I'll tell it *all* to you."

When Becky went downstairs, she was not the same Becky who had staggered up, loaded down by the weight of the coal scuttle. She had an extra piece of cake in her pocket, and she had been fed and warmed, but not only by cake and fire. Something else had warmed and fed her, and that something else was Sara.

When she was gone Sara sat on her favorite perch on the end of he table. Her feet were on a chair, her elbows on her knees, and her chin in her hands.

"If I was a princess — a real princess," she murmured, "I could scatter largess to the populace. But even if I am only a pretend princess, I can invent little things to do for people. Things like this. She was just as happy as if it was largess. I'll pretend that to do things people like is scattering largess. I've scattered largess."

The heart of good manners is unselfishness. Sara was a generous and warm-hearted girl. People like her, who are able to look beyond themselves, focus not on their own gratification, but seek to gratify others. Sara is a good example of how one person can bring much happiness into another's life.

The well-mannered person does not look for defects in others; rather, she notices and praises what is good.

GRACE
by Bono

Grace, she takes the blame
She covers the shame
Removes the stain
It could be her name

Grace, it's the name for a girl
It's also a thought that changed the world
And when she walks on the street
You can hear the strings
Grace finds goodness in everything

Grace, she's got the walk
Not on a ramp or on chalk
She's got the time to talk

She travels outside of karma
She travels outside of karma
When she goes to work
You can hear her strings
Grace finds beauty in everything

Grace, she carries a world on her hips
No champagne flute for her lips
No twirls or skips between her fingertips
She carries a pearl in perfect condition

What once was hurt
What once was friction
What left a mark
No longer stings
Because Grace makes beauty
Out of ugly things

Grace makes beauty out of ugly things

Grace is a word that radiates meaning — for us and for our world. In the beautiful words of Bono's poetic song, grace heals and redeems. God's grace is freely given. It transforms us, opening our eyes to beauty. If we act graciously toward others, looking beyond any shortcomings they may have, we'll help them become better people, too.

3.
Celebrating Your Friends' Successes

LITTLE WOMEN
by Louisa May Alcott

Do you recognize the name of the woman who wrote this story? You learned about her in "A True Story About a Girl," by Sara Cone Bryant, in the first chapter of this book.

Little Women, *which is based on the author's own life, is about four sisters — Jo, Meg, Beth, and Amy — and their parents, Mr. and Mrs. March. Jo has a passion for writing and has written a manuscript (what a book is called before it's published), which she has entered into a contest.*

CHAPTER 27

THE MANUSCRIPT was privately dispatched, accompanied by a note, modestly saying that if the tale didn't get the prize, which the writer hardly dared expect, she would be very glad to receive any sum it might be considered worth.

Six weeks is a long time to wait, and a still longer time for a girl to keep a secret; but Jo did both, and was just beginning to give up all hope of ever seeing her manuscript again, when a letter arrived which almost took her breath away; for on opening it, a check for a hundred dollars fell into her lap. For a minute she stared at it as if it had been a snake, then she read her letter and began to cry. If the amiable gentleman who wrote that kindly note could have known what intense happiness he was giving a fellow-creature, I think he would devote his leisure hours, if he has any, to that amusement; for Jo valued the letter more than the money, because it was encouraging; and after years of effort it was so pleasant to find that she had learned to do something, though it was only to write a sensation story.

A prouder young woman was seldom seen than she, when, having composed herself, she electrified the family by appearing before them with the letter in one hand, the check in the other, announcing that she had won the prize. Of course there was a great jubilee, and when the story came every one read and praised it; though after her father had told her that the language was good, the romance fresh and hearty, and the tragedy quite thrilling, he shook his head, and said in his unworldly way —

"You can do better than this, Jo. Aim at the highest, and never mind the money."

"*I* think the money is the best part of it. What *will* you do with such a fortune?" asked Amy, regarding the magic slip of paper with a reverential eye.

"Send Beth and mother to the seaside for a month or two," answered Jo promptly.

"Oh, how splendid! No, I can't do it, dear, it would be so selfish," cried Beth, who had clapped her thin hands, and taken a long breath, as if pining for fresh ocean-breezes; then stopped herself, and motioned away the check which her sister waved before her.

"Ah, but you shall go, I've set my heart on it; that's what I tried for, and that's why I succeeded. I never get on when I think of myself alone, so it will help me to work for you, don't you see? Besides, Marmee needs the change, and she won't leave you, so you must go. Won't it be fun to see you come home plump and rosy again? Hurrah for Dr. Jo, who always cures her patients!"

To the seaside they went, after much discussion; and though Beth didn't come home as plump and rosy as could be desired, she was much better, while Mrs. March declared she felt ten years younger; so Joe was satisfied with the investment of her prize money, and fell to work with a cheery spirit, bent on earning more of those delightful checks. She did earn several that year, and began to feel herself a power in the house; for by the magic of a pen, her "rubbish" turned into comforts for them all. "The Duke's Daughter" paid the butcher's bill, "A Phantom Hand" put down a new carpet, and the "Curse of the Coventrys" proved the blessing of the Marches in the way of the groceries and gowns.

Wealth is certainly a most desirable thing, but poverty has its sunny side, and one of the sweet uses of adversity is the genuine satisfaction which comes from hearty work of head or hand; and to the inspiration of necessity, we owe half the wise, beautiful, and useful blessing of the world.

Jo enjoyed a taste of this satisfaction and ceased to envy richer girls, taking great comfort in the knowledge that she could supply her own wants, and need ask no one for a penny.

Little notice was taken of her stories, but they found a market; and, encouraged by this fact, she resolved to make a bold stroke for fame and fortune. Having copied her novel for the fourth time, read it to all her confidential friends, and submitted it with fear and trembling to three publishers, she at last disposed of it, on condition that she would cut it down one third, and omit all the parts which she particularly admired.

"Now I must either bundle it back into my tin-kitchen to mould, pay for printing it myself, or chop it up to suit purchasers, and get what I can for it. Fame is a very good thing to have in the house, but cash is more convenient; so I wish to take the sense of the meeting on this important subject," said Jo, calling a family council.

> Success has ruined many a man.
>
>
>
> BENJAMIN FRANKLIN
> *Poor Richard's Almanac*

"Don't spoil your book, my girl, for there is more in it than you know, and the idea is well worked out. Let it wait and ripen," was her father's advice; and he practiced as he preached, having waited patiently thirty years for fruit of his own to ripen, and being in no haste to gather it, even now, it was sweet and mellow.

"It seems to me that Jo will profit more by making the trial than by waiting," said Mrs. March. "Criticism is the best test of such work, for it will show her both unsuspected merits and faults, and help her to do better next time. We are too partial; but the praise and blame of outsiders will prove useful, even if she gets but little money."

"Yes," said Joe, knitting her brows, "that's just it; I've been fussing over the thing so long, I really don't know whether it's good, bad, or indifferent. It will be a great help to have cool, impartial persons take a look at it, and tell me what they think of it."

"I wouldn't leave out a word of it; you'll spoil it if you do, for the interest of the story is more in the minds than in the actions of the people, and it will be all a muddle if you don't explain as you do early on," said Meg, who firmly believed that this book was the most remarkable novel ever written.

"But Mr. Allen says, 'Leave out the explanations, make it brief and dramatic, and let the characters tell the story,'" interrupted Jo, turning to the publisher's note.

"Do as he tells you; he knows what will sell, and we don't. Make a good popular book, and get as much money as you can. By and by, when you've got a name, you can afford to digress, and have philosophical and metaphysical people in your novel," said Amy, who took a strictly practical view of the subject.

"Well," said Jo, laughing, "if my people are 'philosophical and metaphysical,' it isn't my fault, for I know nothing about such things, except what I hear father say, sometimes. If I've got some of his wise ideas jumbled up with my romance, so much the better for me. Now, Beth, what do you say?"

"I should so like to see it printed *soon*," was all Beth said, and smiled in saying it; but there was an unconscious emphasis on the last word, and a wistful look in the eyes that never lost their childlike candor, which chilled Jo's heart, for a minute, with a foreboding fear, and decided here to make her little venture "soon."

Jo did earn money for her manuscript. But her sisters didn't envy her. They celebrated her success as if it were their own. This is how family and friends should treat each other. Jo, in turn, did not focus attention on herself; instead, she immediately wanted to spend her money on her family.

The Secret Garden
by Frances Hodgson Burnett

In the secret graden that Mary discovered, Colin — who has been unable to walk all his life — takes his first steps. And with Mary and Dickon, Colin even finds the strength to till the garden.

Chapter 22

WHEN HIS HEAD was out of sight Colin turned to Mary. "Go and meet him," he said; and Mary flew across the grass to the door under the ivy.

Dickon was watching him with sharp eyes. There were scarlet spots on his cheeks and he looked amazing, but he showed no signs of falling.

"I can stand," he said, and his head was still held up and he said it quite grandly.

"I told thee tha' could as soon as tha' stopped bein' afraid," answered Dickon. "An' tha's stopped."

"Yes, I've stopped," said Colin.

Then suddenly he remembered something Mary had said.

"Are you making Magic?" he asked sharply.

Dickon's curly mouth spread in a cheerful grin.

"Tha's doin' Magic thysel'," he said. "It's same Magic as made these 'ere work out o' th' earth," and he touched with his thick boot a clump of crocuses in the grass.

Colin looked down at them.

"Aye," he said slowly, "there couldna' be bigger Magic than that there — there couldna' be."

He drew himself up straighter than ever.

"I'm going to walk to that tree," he said, pointing to one a few feet away from him. "I'm going to be standing when Weatherstaff [the gardener] comes here. I can rest against the tree if I like. When I want to sit down I will sit down, but not before. Bring a run from the chair."

He walked to the tree and though Dickon held his arm he was wonderfully steady. When he stood against the tree trunk it was not too plain that he supported himself against it, and he still held himself so straight that he looked tall.

When Ben Weatherstaff came through the door in the wall he saw him standing there and he heard Mary muttering something under breath.

"What art sayin'?" he asked rather testily because he did not want his attention distracted from the long thin straight boy figure and proud face.

But she did not tell him. What she was saying was this:

"You can do it! You can do it! I told you could! You can do it! You can do it! You can!"

She was saying it to Colin because she wanted to make Magic and keep him on his feet looking like that. She could not bear that he should give in before Ben Weatherstaff. He did not give in. She was uplifted by a sudden feeling that he looked quite beautiful in spite of his thinness. He fixed his eyes on Ben Weatherstaff in his funny imperious way.

"Look at me!" he commanded. "Look at me all over! Am I a hunchback? Have I got crooked legs?"

Ben Weatherstaff had not quite got over his emotion, but he had recovered a little and answered almost in his usual way.

"Not tha'," he said. "Nowt o' th' sort. What's tha' been doin' with thysel' — hidin' out o' sight an' lettin' folk think tha' was cripple an' half-witted?"

"Half-witted!" said Colin angrily. "Who thought that?"

"Lots o' fools," said Ben. "Th' world's full o' jackasses brayin' an' they never bray nowt but lies. What did tha' shut thysel' up for?"

"Everyone thought I was going to die," said Colin shortly. "I'm not!"

And he said it with such decision Ben Weatherstaff looked him over, up and down, down and up.

"Tha' die!" he said with dry exultation. "Nowt o' th' sort! Tha's got too much pluck in thee. When I see thee put tha' legs on th' ground in such a hurry I knowed tha' was all right. Sit thee down on th' rug a bit yonder Mester an' give me thy orders."

There was a queer mixture of crabbed tenderness and shrewd understanding in his manner. Mary had poured out speech as rapidly as she could as they had come down the Long Walk. The chief thing to be remembered, she had told him, was that Colin was getting well — getting well. The garden was doing it. No one must let him remember about having humps and dying.

The Rajah condescended to seat himself on a rug under the tree.

"What work do you do in the gardens, Weatherstaff?" he inquired.

"Anythin' I'm told to do," answered old Ben. "I'm kep' on by favor — because she liked me."

"She?" said Colin.

"Tha' mother," answered Ben Weatherstaff.

"My mother?" said Colin, and he looked about him quietly. "This was her garden, wasn't it?"

"Aye, it was that!" and Ben Weatherstaff looked about him too. "She were main fond of it."

"It is my garden now. I am fond of it. I shall come here every day," announced Colin. "But it is to be a secret. My orders are that no one is to know that we come here. Dickon and my cousin have worked and made it come alive. I shall send for you sometimes to help — but you must come when no one can see you."

Ben Weatherstaff's face twisted itself in a dry old smile.

"I've come here before when no one saw me," he said.

"What!" exclaimed Colin. "When?"

"Th' last time I was here," rubbing his chin and looking round, "was about two year' ago."

"But no one has been in it for ten years!" cried Colin. "There was no door!"

"I'm no one," said old Ben dryly. "An' I didn't come through th' door. I come over th' wall. Th' rheumatics held me back th' last two year'."

"Tha' come an' did a bit o' prunin'!" cried Dickon. "I couldn't make out how it had been done."

"She was so fond of it — she was!" said Ben Weatherstaff slowly. "An' she was such a pretty young thing. She says to me once, 'Ben,' says she laughin', 'if ever I'm ill or if I go away you must take care of my roses.' When she did go away th' orders was no one was ever to come nigh. But I come. Over th' wall I come — until th' rheumatics stopped me — an' I did a bid o' work once a year. She'd gave her order first."

"It wouldn't have been as wick as it is if tha' hadn't done it," said Dickon. "I did wonder."

"I'm glad you did it, Weatherstaff," said Colin. "You'll know how to keep the secret."

"Aye, I'll know, sire," answered Ben. "An' it'll be easier for a man wi' rheumatics to come in at th' door."

On the grass near the tree Mary had dropped her trowel. Colin stretched out his hand and took it up. An odd expression came into his face as he began to scratch at the earth. His thin hand was weak enough but presently as they watched him — Mary with quite breathless interest — he drove the end of the trowel into the soil and turned some over.

"You can do it! You can do it!" said Mary to herself. "I tell you, you can!"

Dickon's round eyes were full of eager curiousness but he said not a word. Ben Weatherstaff looked on with an interested face.

Colin persevered. After he had turned a few trowelfuls of soil he spoke exultantly to Dickon in his best Yorkshire.

"Tha' said as tha'd have me walking' about here same as other folk — an' tha' said tha'd have me diggin'. I thowt tha' was just leein' to please me. This is only th' first day an' I've walked — an' here I am diggin'."

Ben Weatherstaff's mouth fell open again when he heard him, but he ended by chuckling.

"Eh!" he said, "that sounds as if tha'd got wits enow. Tha'rt a Yorkshire lad for sure. An' tha'rt diggin', too. How'd tha' like to plant a bit o' somethin'? I can get thee a rose in a pot."

"Go an get it!" said Colin, digging excitedly. "Quick! Quick!"

It was done quickly enough indeed. Ben Weatherstaff went his way forgetting rheumatics. Dickon took his spade and dug the hole deeper and wider than a new digger with thin white hands could make it. Mary slipped out to run and bring back a watering-can. When Dickon had deepened the hole Colin went on turning the soft earth over and over. He looked up at the sky, flushed and glowing with the strangely new exercise, slight as it was.

Blessed is he that expects nothing for he shall never be disappointed.

BENJAMIN FRANKLIN
Poor Richard's Almanac

"I want to do it before the sun goes quite — quite down," he said.

Mary thought that perhaps the sun held back a few minutes just on purpose. Ben Weatherstaff brought the rose in its pot from the greenhouse. He hobbled over the grass as fast as he could. He had begun to be excited, too. He knelt down by the hole and broke the pot from the mould.

"Here, lad," he said, handing the plant to Colin. "Set it in the earth thysel' same as th' king does when he goes to a new place."

The thin white hands shook a little and Colin's flush grew deeper as he set the rose in the mould and held it while old Ben made firm the earth. It was filled in and pressed down and made steady. Mary was leaning forward on her hands and knees. Soot had flown down and marched forward to see what was being done. Nut and Shell chattered about it from a cherry-tree.

"It's planted!" said Colin at last. "And the sun is only slipping over the edge. Help me up, Dickon. I want to be standing when it goes. That's part of the Magic."

And Dickon helped him, and the Magic — or whatever it was — so gave him strength that when the sun did slip over the edge and end the strange lovely afternoon for them there he actually stood on his two feet — laughing.

In The Secret Garden, *we see how friends can help each other grow. Mary and Colin matured and learned to look beyond themselves. And because of the encouragement of his friends, Colin did more than he ever thought he could. Mary and Dickon celebrated Colin's success and praised him for his efforts. Great things can happen when you tell your friends, "You can do it!"*

A Friend's Greeting
by Edgar A. Guest

I'd like to be the sort of friend that you have been to me;
I'd like to be the help that you've been always glad to be;
I'd like to mean as much to you each minute of the day
As you have meant, old friend of mine, to me along the way.

I'd like to do the big things and the splendid things for you,
To brush the gray from out your skies and leave them
    only blue;

I'd like to say the kindly things that I so oft have heard,
And feel that I could rouse your soul the way that mine
  you've stirred.

I'd like to give you back the joy that you have given me,
Yet that were wishing you a need I hope, will never be;
I'd like to make you feel as rich as I, who travel on
Undaunted in the darkest hours with you to lean upon.

I'm wishing at this Christmas time that I could but repay
A portion of the gladness that you've strewn along my way;
And could I have one wish this year, this only would it be:
I'd like to be the sort of friend that you have been to me.

4.
Helping Each Other

SQUANTO, THE PILGRIMS' FRIEND
by Michael Lamb

THE SHIP SEEMED VERY SMALL even though its captain claimed it was quite seaworthy. The vessel was named the Mayflower, and on September 16, 1620, 102 Pilgrims crowded onto its deck. These men, their wives, and their children were leaving England in search of freedom in the New World, the land we now call America. The voyage was long and hard. For many days the boat was tossed to and fro over the turbulent gray-green waters of the Atlantic Ocean. More than three months later, they finally landed at a site they would name Plymouth. This was the beginning of the Plymouth Colony.

By December 21, 1620, the cold winter winds were in full force, and the Pilgrims had little food. They were not prepared for the winter and would not have survived if not for the Indians who lived nearby.

Especially helpful was Squanto, an American Indian who years before had been kidnapped by an English captain and then sold as a slave to the Spanish. As a captive he learned to speak English and Spanish. After much hardship Squanto returned to his native land. It was then that he met the Pilgrims.

Because he understood English, Squanto was a great help to the Plymouth Colony. He showed the new settlers where the best fishing spots were and how to hunt for deer and turkey. Squanto also helped the Pilgrims find huge oyster beds, edible wild fruits, and delicious berries. He introduced them to other Indians, including Samoset, Hobomack and the great chief Massasoit. And, most importantly, he showed them the Indian method of planting corn and beans. By planting these crops, the Pilgrims were able to store enough food each fall to enable them to survive the cold New England winter. Because of the hospitality of Squanto, the Pilgrims and the Indians became friends. The two groups celebrated the first Thanksgiving together in 1621. That same year the leaders of the Plymouth Colony signed a pact of friendship with Chief Massasoit that allowed the Pilgrims and Indians to live in peace for many years.

Squanto treated the Pilgrims like honored guests in his native land. Though years earlier an Englishman had sold him as a slave, Squanto didn't hate all Englishmen. Instead, he treated the Pilgrims the way he would want to be treated. The Pilgrims couldn't have survived without him.

I SHALL NOT PASS THIS WAY AGAIN
author unknown

Through this toilsome world, alas!
Once and only once I pass;
If a kindness I may show,
If a good deed I may do
To a suffering fellow man,
Let me do it while I can.
No delay, for it is plain
I shall not pass this way again.

THE LITTLE RED HEN
retold by Jennifer Boudart

The little red hen lived next to the road by the farmer's house. Where she lived wasn't very fancy, but she loved it. She shared her home with her five baby chicks and her friends, the dog, the cat, and the duck.

The little red hen worked very hard. She kept the house and the yard neat and clean. There always seemed to be plenty of work to do in order to keep everything looking good.

Everyone liked having a clean house and good food on the table. When it came time to do the chores, though, the others always seemed to have something else to do. As soon as the hen would send her baby chicks out to play, the older animals always seemed to disappear, too. The little red hen did all the work herself. Her days were filled with making beds, cleaning, gardening, and cooking.

One day, the little red hen was sweeping her yard. When she looked down on the ground, she found some kernels of wheat. She put the kernels into her pocket for safe keeping. Then she went to look for the dog, cat, and duck. She found them by the pond. She showed them the kernels and asked, "Who will help me plant these?"

Her three friends looked at each other. Then they looked at the little red hen. "Not us," they said. "Right now we need to take a nap."

"I'll plant them myself," she told them. The little red hen returned to the garden and began digging. Soon her baby chicks came to see what she was doing. They told her they wanted to help. The little red hen and her five baby chicks pretended they were burying treasure. The game made the work go quickly. Soon they had planted all the kernels.

> A fake friend and a shadow attend only when the sun shines.
>
> ☙
>
> BENJAMIN FRANKLIN
> *Poor Richard's Almanac*

The little red hen visited the garden every day to watch the wheat grow. She made sure the young plants got plenty of sunshine and care.

One day she found her three friends leaning against the farmer's barn. The little red hen said, "There are weeds that are stopping the wheat from growing. Will you help me pull the weeds?"

"I can't," said the cat. "They're all dirty. Do you have any idea how long it takes me to wash my paws?"

The dog and the duck both had excuses, too. No one could help. "I'll just do it myself," said the little red hen. Then she walked back to the garden. Once again, her chicks joined her. They had a contest to see who could pull the most weeds. It was such fun that they finished in no time.

A dry spell kept the rain away for a week. The little red hen was worried about the wheat. If the plants didn't get some water soon, the tender stalks would wither and die. The only thing to do was bring water to the plants. She went looking for her friends. She found them on top of the hay pile. The hen looked up and said, "The summer heat is too strong for the wheat. Who will help me water the garden?"

The dog, the cat, and the duck looked at her. "We're busy writing a song and can't be bothered now," growled the dog. "Didn't you hear me playing my banjo?"

"I'll just water it myself," she said. The little red hen took her watering pail to the garden. Her chicks came to keep her company. The hen pretended to be a thundercloud and tried to sprinkle them with water. Before long, the whole garden had been watered.

The summer sun was very good, and the wheat grew fast. The little red hen and her chicks visited the garden every day. They lovingly tended to the wheat, and it grew strong and hardy. There was going to be a bumper crop!

Soon it was fall and the wheat turned golden brown. The little red hen knew what that meant. She found her friends playing cards under the farmer's wagon. The hen knelt down and said, "Who will help me harvest the wheat?"

The dog, the cat, and the duck kept their eyes on their cards. "Not us!" they mumbled. "Can't you see we're busy?"

The hen stood up and fixed her apron. "I'll harvest it myself," she said. The little red hen took her cutting tools to the garden. This time the five chicks were waiting for her. The family cut the wheat and tied it into bundles. They sang songs, and soon the hard work was done.

Even though she had already spent a great deal of time and energy on the garden, the little red hen knew the work was not finished. She often told her chicks that if a job was worth doing, it was worth doing well.

The little red hen went looking for her friends. She found them sitting by the road. "I need to have the wheat ground into flour," she said. "Who will help me carry it to the miller?"

The dog, the cat, and the duck looked way down the road. The miller was located several miles away. "Not us!" the trio said together. "It's too far for us to walk."

Once again, the little red hen would have to do it herself. She and her chicks left right away. They had a long journey ahead of them, and the chicks moved slowly. The trip seemed to go much faster when they pretended to be hobos traveling with their knapsacks across the country.

The little red hen returned home. She and the chicks were so tired that they soon fell asleep. That night everyone slept very well. The next morning, the little red hen went outside. Her friends were sunbathing on the roof. She called to them, "Who will help me bake bread with my flour?"

The dog, the cat, and the duck didn't even bother looking down. "It's a beautiful day. Who would want to be indoors baking bread?" observed the dog.

The hen shook her head. She thought, "Who would want to spend all day doing nothing?" She told the three, "I'll bake it myself." The little red hen went inside. Her chicks tried to make the bread dough for her. Flour was all over the floor and the chicks, too. They shaped the dough into a big loaf and pretended to be sculptors making a statue. Everyone was sorry to have to stop when the loaf was finished.

The smell of baking bread floated in the air. The dog, the cat, and the duck came and looked into the kitchen. Two baby chicks danced around the little red hen. She asked, "Who will help me eat this tasty, fresh bread?"

"We will!" squeaked all five of her chicks.

"We will!" cried the group in the doorway.

"Well," said the little red hen, "anyone who helped make this bread can have some. So, if you helped plant the wheat, water it, weed it, harvest it, take it to the miller, or bake the bread, raise your hand!" That night, six tummies got their fill of bread as a reward for work well done.

When everyone works together to get something accomplished, they feel satisfied in a job well done. And a bit of imagination transforms work into play!

THE SURPRISE
from Frog and Toad All Year
by Arnold Lobel

IT WAS OCTOBER.

The leaves had fallen off the trees.

They were lying on the ground.

"I will go to Toad's house," said Frog.

"I will rake all of the leaves that have fallen on his lawn. Toad will be surprised."

Frog took a rake out of the garden shed.

Toad looked out of his window. "These messy leaves have covered everything," said Toad. He took a rake out of the closet. "I will run over to Frog's house. I will rake all of his leaves. Frog will be very pleased."

Frog ran through the woods so that Toad would not see him.

Toad ran through the high grass so that Frog would not see him.

Frog came to Toad's house. He looked in the window. "Good," said Frog. "Toad is out. He will never know who raked his leaves."

Toad got to Frog's house. He looked in the window. "Good," said Toad. "Frog is not home. He will never guess who raked his leaves."

Frog worked hard. He raked the leaves into a pile. Soon Toad's lawn was clean. Frog picked up his rake and started home. Toad pushed and pulled on the rake. He raked the leaves into a pile. Soon there was not a single leaf in Frog's front yard. Toad took his rake and started home.

A wind came. It blew across the land. The pile of leaves that Frog had raked for Toad blew everywhere. The pile of leaves that Toad had raked for Frog blew everywhere.

When Frog got home, he said, "Tomorrow I will clean up the leaves that are all over my own lawn. How surprised Toad must be!"

When Toad got home, he said, "Tomorrow I will get to work and rake all of my own leaves. How surprised Frog must be!"

That night Frog and Toad were both happy when they each turned out the light and went to bed.

When you help someone, do it quietly and out of the kindness in your heart. Don't do it because you want everyone to know about your good deed.

THE WIZARD OF OZ
by L. Frank Baum

Dorothy and her dog Toto lived in rural Kansas. When a tornado hit Dorothy's home, she was whirled away into the magical land of Oz — a colorful and enchanted place where the animals, and even the flowers, talk. In Oz there is a good witch who greets Dorothy, but there is also a bad witch who chases her. The only way for Dorothy to return home is to follow the yellow brick road all the way to the great Wizard, who alone can grant her wish.

While traveling along the yellow brick road, Dorothy befriends the Tin Woodman, the Scarecrow, and the Cowardly Lion. In the scene that follows, the evil witch is hoping to put Dorothy into a deep sleep.

CHAPTER 8

*T*HEY WALKED ALONG listening to the singing of the bright colored birds and looking at the lovely flowers which now became so thick that the ground was carpeted with them. There were big yellow and white and blue and purple blossoms, great clusters of scarlet poppies, which were so brilliant in colour they almost dazzled Dorothy's eyes.

"Aren't they beautiful?" the girl asked, as she breathed in the spicy scent of the flowers.

"I suppose so," answered the Scarecrow. "When I have brains I shall probably like them better."

"If only I had a heart I should love them," added the Tin Woodman.

"I always did like flowers," said the Lion; "they seem so helpless and frail. But there are none in the forest so bright as these."

They now came upon more and more of the big scarlet poppies, and fewer and fewer of the other flowers; and soon they found themselves in the midst of a great meadow of poppies. Now it is well known that when there are so many of these flowers together their odour is so powerful that anyone who breathes it falls asleep, and if the sleeper is not carried away from the scent of the flowers he sleeps on and on forever. But Dorothy did not know this, nor could she get away from the bright red flowers that were everywhere about; so presently her eyes grew heavy and she felt she must sit down to rest and to sleep.

But the Tin Woodman would not let her do this.

"We must hurry and get back to the road of yellow brick before dark," he said; and the Scarecrow agreed with him. So they kept walking until Dorothy could stand no longer. Her eyes closed in spite of herself and she forgot where she was and fell among the poppies, fast asleep.

"What shall we do?" asked the Tin Woodman.

"If we leave her here she will die," said the Lion. "The smell of flowers is killing us all. I myself can scarcely keep my eyes open and the dog is asleep already."

It was true; Toto had fallen down beside his little mistress. But the Scarecrow and the Tin Woodman, not being made of flesh, were not troubled by the Scent of flowers.

"Run fast," said the Scarecrow to the Lion, "and get out of this deadly flower bed as soon as you can. We will bring the little girl with us, but if you should fall asleep you are too big to be carried."

So the Lion aroused himself and bounded forward as fast as he could go. In a moment he was out of sight.

"Let us make a chair with our hands, and carry her," said the Scarecrow. So they picked up Toto and put the dog in Dorothy's lap, and then they made a chair with their hands for the seat and their arms for the arms and carried the sleeping girls between them through the flowers.

On and on they walked, and it seemed that the great carpet of deadly flowers that surrounded them would never end. They followed the bend of the river, and at last came upon their friend the Lion, lying fast asleep among the poppies. The flowers had been too strong for the huge beast and he had given up, at last, and fallen only a short distance from the end of the poppy bed, where the sweet grass spread in beautiful green fields before them.

"We can do nothing for him," said the Tin Woodman, sadly; "for he is much too heavy to lift. We must leave him here to sleep on for ever, and perhaps he will dream that he has found courage at last."

"I'm sorry," said the Scarecrow. "The Lion was a very good comrade for one so cowardly. But let us go on."

They carried the sleeping girl to a pretty spot beside the river far enough from the poppy field to prevent her breathing any more of the poison of the flowers, and here they laid her gently on the soft grass and waited for the fresh breeze to waken her.

The Tin Woodman and Scarecrow were faithful friends to Dorothy. They carried her through the poppy field to make sure she got away from the poisonous flowers. When you are playing with other children, especially away from home, watch out for each other. If you are out playing with a friend and he gets hurt, make sure that he gets home safely and, when you get there, tell his parents what happened.

PINOCCHIO
by Carlo Collodi

In this episode from Pinocchio, *the wooden puppet is in search of his papa.*

CHAPTER 23

"PINOCCHIO? . . . Did you say Pinocchio?" repeated the puppet, jumping quickly to his feet. "I am Pinocchio!"

The Pigeon at this answer descended rapidly to the ground. He was larger than a turkey.

"Do you also know Geppetto?" he asked.

"Do I know him! He is my poor papa! Has he perhaps spoken to you of me? Will you take me to him? Is he still alive? Answer me for pity's sake: is he still alive?"

"I left him three days ago on the seashore."

"What was he doing?"

"He was building a little boat for himself, to cross the ocean. For more than three months that poor man has been going all round the world looking for you. Not having succeeded in finding you, he has now taken it into his head to go to the distant countries of the new world in search of you."

"How far is it from here to the shore?" asked Pinocchio breathlessly.

"More than six hundred miles."

"Six hundred miles? Oh, beautiful Pigeon, what a fine thing it would be to have your wings! . . ."

"If you wish to go, I will carry you there."

"How?"

"Astride on my back. Do you weigh much?"

"I weigh next to nothing. I am as light as a feather."

And without waiting for more, Pinocchio jumped at once on the Pigeon's back, and putting a leg on each side of him as men do on horseback, he exclaimed joyfully:

"Gallop, gallop, my little horse, for I am anxious to arrive quickly!"

The Pigeon took flight, and in a few minutes had soared so high that they almost touched the clouds. Finding himself at such an immense height, the puppet had the curiosity to turn and look down, but his head spun round, and he became so frightened that to save himself from the danger of falling, he wound his arms tightly round the neck of his feathered steed.

They flew all day. Toward evening the Pigeon said:

"I am very thirsty!"

"And I am very hungry!" rejoined Pinocchio.

"Let us stop at that dovecot for a few minutes, and then we will continue our journey that we may reach the seashore by dawn tomorrow."

Let us consider how we may spur one another on toward love and good deeds.

Hebrews 10:24

They went into a deserted dovecot, where they found nothing but a basin full of water and a basket full of vetch.

The puppet had never in his life been able to eat vetch: according to him, it made him sick and revolted him. That evening, however, he ate to repletion, and when he had nearly emptied the basket he turned to the Pigeon and said to him:

"I never could have believed that vetch was so good!"

"Be assured, my boy," replied the Pigeon, "that when hunger is real, and there is nothing else to eat, even vetch becomes delicious. Hunger knows neither caprice nor greediness."

Having quickly finished their little meal, they recommenced their journey and flew away. The following morning they reached the seashore.

The Pigeon placed Pinocchio on the ground, and not wishing to be troubled with thanks for having done a good action, flew quickly away and disappeared.

The shore was crowded with people who were looking out to sea, shouting and gesticulating.

"What has happened?" asked Pinocchio of an old woman.

"A poor father who has lost his son has gone away in a boat to search for him on the other side of the water, and today the sea is tempestuous

Everyday Graces

and the little boat is in danger of sinking."

"Where is the little boat?"

"It is out there in a line with my finger," said the old woman, pointing to a little boat which, seen at that distance, looked like a nutshell with a very little man in it.

Pinocchio fixed his eyes on it, and after looking attentively, he gave a piercing scream, crying:

"It is my papa! It is my papa!"

The boat meanwhile, beaten by the fury of the waves, at one moment disappeared in the trough of the sea, and the next came again to the surface. Pinocchio, standing on the top of a high rock, kept calling to his father by name, and making every kind of signal to him with his hands, his handkerchief, and his cap.

And although he was so far off, Geppetto appeared to recognize his son, for he also took off his cap and waved it, and tried by gestures to make him understand that he would have returned if it had been possible, but that the sea was so tempestuous that he could not use his oars or approach the shore.

Suddenly a tremendous wave rose and the boat disappeared. They waited, hoping it would come again to the surface, but it was seen no more.

"Poor man!" said the fishermen who were assembled on the shore, and murmuring a prayer, they turned to go home.

Just then they heard a desperate cry, and looking back they saw a little boy who exclaimed, as he jumped from a rock into the sea.

"I will save my papa!"

Pinocchio, being made of wood, floated easily and he swam like a fish. At one moment they saw him disappear under the water, carried down by the fury of the waves; and next he reappeared struggling with a leg or an arm. At last they lost sight of him and he was seen no more.

"Poor boy!" said the fishermen who were collected on the shore, and murmuring a prayer, they returned home.

Pinocchio was so excited to see his papa, and he wanted to help him so much, that he jumped into the water without noticing the tremendous waves. Sometimes, you may want to help a friend in a dangerous situation. But you must remember to assess the situation first or you may end up putting both yourself and your friend in danger. Sometimes you will need the help of adults or people who are trained to deal with emergency situations. Have your parents teach you how to call 911 for help.

5.
Good Ways to Lose Friends

IMPOSSIBLE!
by Gelette Burgess

There once was a Goop *(it is hard to believe*
    Such unpleasant behavior of you!)
Who always was wiping his nose on his sleeve;
    I hope that this Goop wasn't you!
He always was spitting (for fun, I suppose),
    I couldn't believe it of you!
And putting his fingers up into his nose;
    I KNOW that this Goop wasn't you!

Spitting in public is definitely not polite! If you have to remove something from your mouth, like a piece of gum, use a piece of tissue paper. If you need to cough or sneeze, turn your head away from other people and hold a tissue to your mouth. And putting your fingers into your nose will surely disgust your friends!

WHEN TO GO
by Gelett Burgess

When you go a-calling,
Never stay too late;
You will wear your welcome out
If you hesitate!
Just before they're tired of you,
Just before they yawn,
Before they think you are a Goop,

257

And wish that you were gone,
While they're laughing with you,
While they like you so,
While they want to keep you, —
That's the time to go!

When playing at a friend's house, don't overstay your welcome. Leave when your parents, or your friend's parents, say it's time to go. When it's time to go, don't whine or beg to stay. Politely say goodbye and leave promptly.

PRINCE DARLING
by Cabinet des Fées, retold by Karen Santorum

ONCE UPON A TIME there lived a king who was so good and kind that his subjects called him "the Good King." One day, when he was out hunting, a little white rabbit, which his dogs were chasing, sprang into his arms for shelter. The King gently stroked the frightened rabbit and said to it:

"Well, bunny, as you have come to me for protection, I will see that nobody harms you."

And he took it home to his palace and had it put in a pretty little house, with all sorts of good vegetables.

That night when he was alone in his chambers, a beautiful lady appeared before him; her long dress was as white as snow, and she had a crown of white roses upon her head. "I am the Spirit of Truth. I was passing through the woods when you were out hunting, and I wished to find out if you were really as good as everyone said. I took the shape of a little white rabbit and came to you for shelter, for I know that those who are merciful to the most helpless of creatures will be kinder still to their fellow-men. If you had refused to help me I would have known that you were wicked. I thank you for the kindness you showed me. It has made me your friend forever. You have only to ask, and I will grant you anything you want."

"Good Spirit," said the King, "you no doubt know all of my wishes. I have but one son whom I love very dearly, so dearly that I named him Prince Darling. Please do me the favor of becoming his friend."

"With all my heart," answered the Spirit. "I can make your son the handsomest prince in the world, or the richest, or the most powerful; choose whichever you like for him."

"I do not ask any of these things for him," replied the King, "but if you will make my son the kindest of princes, I shall indeed be grateful to you. What good would it do him to be rich, or handsome, or to possess all the kingdoms of the world if he were wicked? You know well he would still be unhappy and unloved. Only a good man can truly be content on this earth."

"You are a very wise king," answered the Spirit, "but it is not in my power to make Prince Darling a good man — unless he will help me. He must try hard and do his part to become good. I can only promise to give him good advice, to scold him for his faults, and to punish him if he will not correct himself."

The good King was satisfied with this promise; and very soon afterward he died.

Prince Darling was bereft at the loss, for he loved his father with all his heart. He would have willingly given all his treasures of gold and silver for more time with him.

Two days afterward, when the Prince had gone to bed, a beautiful woman dressed in white appeared to him and said:

"I promised your father that I would be your friend, and to keep my word I have come to bring you a present." At the same time she put a little gold ring upon his finger.

"Take great care of this ring," she said, "it is more precious than diamonds. Every time you do a bad deed it will tighten around your finger; but if, in spite of the pain it inflicts, you proceed to do more evil, you will lose my friendship, and I shall become your enemy." With those words she disappeared, leaving behind an astonished Prince Darling.

For some time he behaved so well that the ring never pained him.

One day, however, he went out hunting. His mood became cross when he could find no game. When he got home and went to his room, his little dog Bibi cheerfully ran to greet him. "Get away!" yelled the Prince. "I don't want you, leave me alone."

The poor little dog, wanting so much to please his master, playfully pulled at his cloak. This made the Prince even angrier, so he gave her a hard kick.

Instantly his ring became sharp-edged, and tightened so painfully that a drop of blood welled up from his skin. He was surprised, but only slightly ashamed of himself.

"The Spirit must be laughing at me now," he thought to himself. "What great wrong have I done by kicking this nagging animal? I am a powerful ruler of a great kingdom, and I should be able to control my own dog!"

"I am not making fun of you," said a voice, answering Prince Darling's thoughts. "You have committed three faults. First of all, you lost your temper because you could not have what you wanted. Second, you mistakenly assumed that all men and animals are made only to do your pleasure. Lastly, you were cruel to a poor animal who did nothing to deserve your ill treatment.

"I know your position is far above a little dog's — but if it were right that great people should mistreat all beneath them, I should at this moment beat you, or kill you, for a spirit is greater than a man. Listen well: the advantage in possessing a great empire is not to be able to do whatever one desires, but to do all the good that one possibly can."

The Prince saw how naughty he had been, and he promised to try and do better in the future. But he did not keep his word.

His ring squeezed him often, an uncomfortable twinge for small faults, but when he was really bad it made his finger bleed! After a while he tired of being constantly reminded of how naughty he was, so he threw the ring aside. "Finally, I am free of this curse!" he exclaimed.

Shortly thereafter, the Prince eyed a pretty young girl while riding through the village. He watched her as she kindly greeted everyone and cheerfully assisted those in need. "I must have her as my bride," he declared to himself. Her name was Celia, and she was indeed even more beautiful on the inside than the outside.

Thinking he was bestowing upon this poor girl the greatest honor she could ever imagine, he strode up to her and said, "I have decided to have you as my wife."

"Sire, I am only a shepherdess, and a poor girl. But, with all due respect, nevertheless I will not marry you."

"What! How dare you!" he sputtered, searching for something to say. "Do you dislike me?"

"No, my Prince," replied Celia, "You are most handsome, and obviously rich and powerful. But what good would riches and all the honor and prestige that you bestow be to me, if the terrible deeds I watched you do every day made me hate and despise you?"

Her speech was more than he could bear. "Take her to the tower and put her in shackles!" he screamed.

For days her admonition haunted him, but he was still in love with her.

Finally, he had had enough. He sent her an ultimatum: "Marry me or I will sell you into slavery in a foreign land."

At that very moment, a voice said: "I promised your father to give you good advice, and to punish you if you refused to follow it. You have ignored my counsel, and have gone your own evil way until you are now only a man on the outside. Inside, you are a monster — a horror to everyone who knows you. It is time for the fulfillment of my promise to your father. You will now take on the appearance of the animals whose ways you have imitated. Your head will be that of an angry lion, with the horns of a stubborn bull. Your body will be that of a wicked snake, and your feet like the paws of a greedy wolf." And with those words he took on the appearance of this horrible monster.

At the same instant, he found himself in a circus, chained up among all the other wild beasts for display. Feeling true remorse, he decided to show his repentance for his past behavior by being obedient and gentle.

It turned out to be a most difficult decision, for his master beat him and tormented him without cause. One day when his master was asleep, a tiger broke its chain and leapt at him in a rage. Prince Darling, who was witnessing this, at first felt pleased to think he would be free of his tormentor, but as the attack continued he changed his mind.

"I will return good for evil," he said to himself, "and save this wretched man's life." He had hardly wished this when his cage flew open and he rushed to his master's side. When the master saw the monster coming, he gave up all hope of surviving the attack, but his hopelessness turned to joy when the monster pounced on the tiger and killed it.

At that moment Prince Darling heard a voice. "A good action will not go unrewarded." He was turned into a beautiful white dove. White was the Spirit's favorite color, he remembered, and with that realization came the hope that he would win back her favor.

All he could think of now was the beautiful Celia. Off he flew to the castle to find her. He perched himself on the window of her cell and peered inside. The Prince was overjoyed to see her, but at the same time he was mortified by what his cruelty had caused. There she sat in shackles, dirty and malnourished, with a prison guard watching over her.

He flew to her side through the bars of the window, hoping to comfort her in some way. He lit onto her shoulder and for a long while caressed her check, cooing to show his affection. Celia was surprised and delighted by the tenderness of this lovely white dove. Though she did not believe the bird would understand, she said softly, "I accept the gift that

> Quarrels never could last long if one side only lay the wrong.
>
>
>
> BENJAMIN FRANKLIN
> *Poor Richard's Almanac*

you make of yourself. If you stay with me, I will love you always."

"I hope so, my sweet shepherdess!" exclaimed the Prince, who at that moment was turned back into human form. "You promised to love me always. Please tell me you mean what you said, or, if you'd rather, I shall have the Spirit turn me back into the dove which pleased you so much."

"You need not be afraid she will change her mind," said the Spirit, taking off the prison guard's cloak in which she had been disguised. "Celia has loved you ever since she first saw you, only she would not have the likes of the proud, rebellious young man you were. Now that you have repented and have placed the needs of your neighbors above yourself, you too are entitled to happiness. She may love you as much as she likes!"

Celia and Prince Darling threw themselves at the Spirit's feet in thanksgiving. Celia was overjoyed to hear that Prince Darling had amended his ways and had committed himself to her and her happiness. "I do promise to love him as long as I live!" she said to the Spirit.

"Rise, my children," said the Spirit, "and take my hand." And with that, they found themselves on the royal throne in front of a court astounded that the Prince had finally returned.

Celia and Prince Darling reigned for many years, and he was so determined to be a good king that he put his ring back on and never took it off again.

Prince Darling made many mistakes. He shouldn't have lost his temper; he shouldn't have mistreated his dog; and he shouldn't have been cruel to Celia. By mastering your emotions, you'll avoid many arguments, hard feelings, and embarrassing moments. More importantly, you'll behave in a way that is pleasing to God, your family, and your friends.

THE WATER BABIES
by Charles Kingsley

Tom used to clean chimneys. His work made him very dirty and his life was miserable because of his cruel master. When Tom escaped, he suddenly found himself in a quiet, happy place beneath the water. For the first time in years, he was clean! In this dreamy water-world, Tom plays with dragonflies, fish, and lobsters.

Chapter 3

NOW YOU MUST KNOW that all the things under the water talk; only not such a language as ours; but such as horses, and dogs, and cows, and birds talk to each other; and Tom soon learned to understand them and talk to them; so that he might have had very pleasant company if he had only been a good boy. But I am sorry to say, he was too like some other little boys, very fond of hunting and tormenting creatures for mere sport. Some people say that boys cannot help it; that it is nature, and only a proof that we are all originally descended from beasts of prey. But whether it is nature or not, little boys can help it, and must help it. For if they have naughty, low, mischievous tricks in their nature, as monkeys have, that is no reason why they should give way to those tricks like monkeys, who know no better. And therefore they must not torment dumb creatures; for if they do, a certain old lady who is coming will surely give exactly what they deserve.

But Tom did not know that; and he pecked and howked the poor water-things about sadly, till they were all afraid of him, and got out of his way, or crept into their shells; so he had no one to speak to or play with.

The water-fairies, of course, were very sorry to see him so unhappy, and longed to take him, and tell him how naughty he was, and teach him to be good, and to play and romp with him too: but they had been forbidden to do that. Tom had to learn his lesson for himself by sound and sharp experience, as many another foolish person has to do, though there may be many a kind heart yearning over them all the while, and longing to teach them what they can only teach themselves.

At last one day he found a caddis, and wanted it to peep out of its house: but its house-door was shut. He had never seen a caddis with a house-door before: so what must he do, the meddlesome little fellow, but pull it open, to see what the poor lady was doing inside. What a shame! How should you like to have any one breaking your bedroom-door in, to see how you looked when you were in bed? So Tom broke to pieces the door, which was the prettiest little grating of silk, stuck all over with shining bits of crystal; and when he looked in, the caddis poked out her head, and it had turned into just the shape of a bird's. But when Tom spoke to her she could not answer; for her mouth and face were tight tied up in a new night-cap of neat pink skin. However, if she didn't answer, all the other caddises did; for they held up their hands and shrieked like the cats in Struwelpeter: *"Oh, you nasty horrid boy; there you are at it again! And she had just laid herself up for a fortnight's sleep, and then she would have come out with such beautiful wings, and, flown about, and laid such lots of eggs: and now you have broken her door, and she can't mend it because her mouth is tied up for a fortnight, and she will die. Who sent you here to worry us out of our lives?"*

So Tom swam away. He was very much ashamed of himself, and felt all the naughtier; as little boys do when they have done wrong and won't say so.

Then he came to a pool full of little trout, and began tormenting them, and trying to catch them: but they slipped through his fingers, and jumped clean out of the water in their fright. But as Tom chased them, he came close to a great dark hover under an alder root, and out flushed a huge old brown trout ten times as big as he was, and ran right against him, and knocked all the breath out of his body; and I don't know which was the more frightened of the two.

Then he went on sulky and lonely, as he deserved to be; and under a bank he saw a very ugly dirty creature sitting, about half as big as himself, which had six legs, and a big stomach, and a most ridiculous head with two great eyes and a face just like a donkey's.

"Oh," said Tom, "you are an ugly fellow to be sure!" and he began making faces at him; and put his nose close to him, and halloed at him, like a very rude boy.

When, hey presto! all the thing's donkey-face came off in a moment, and out popped a long arm with a pair of pincers at the end of it, and caught Tom by the nose. It did not hurt him much; but it held him quite tight.

"Yah, ah! Oh, let me go!" cried Tom.

"Then let me go," said the creature. "I want to be quiet. I want to split."

Tom promised to let him alone, and he let go. "Why do you want to split?" said Tom.

"Because my brothers and sisters have all split, and turned into beautiful creatures with wings; and I want to split too. Don't speak to me. I am sure I shall split. I will split!"

Tom stood still, and watched him. And he swelled himself, and puffed, and stretched himself out stiff, and at last — crack, puff, bang — he opened all the way down his body, up to the top of his head.

And out of his inside came the most slender, elegant, soft creature, as soft and smooth as Tom: but very pale and weak, like a little child who has been a long time in a dark room. It moved its legs very feebly; and looked about it half ashamed, like a little girl when she goes for the first time into a ballroom; and then it began walking slowly up a grass stem to the top of the water.

Tom was so astonished that he never said a word: but he stared with all his eyes. And he went up to the top of the water too, and peeped out to see what would happen.

And as the creature sat in the warm bright sun, a wonderful change came over it. It grew strong and firm; the most lovely colours began to show on its body, blue and yellow and black, spots and bars and rings; out of its back rose four great wings of bright brown gauze; and its eyes grew so large that they filled all its head, and shone like ten thousand diamonds.

"Oh, you beautiful creature!" said Tom; and he put out his hand to catch it.

But the thing whirred up into the air, and hung poised on its wings a moment, and then settled down again by Tom quite fearless.

"No!" it said, "you cannot catch me. I am a dragon-fly now, the king of all the flies; and I shall dance in the sunshine, and hawk over the river, and catch gnats, and have a beautiful wife like myself. I know what I shall do. Hurrah!" And he flew away into the air, and began catching gnats.

"Oh! come back, come back," cried Tom, "you beautiful creature. I have no one to play with, and I am so lonely here. If you will but come back I will never try to catch you."

"I don't care whether you do or not," said the dragon-fly; "for you can't. But when I have had my dinner, and looked a little about this pretty place, I will come back, and have a little chat about all I have seen in my travels. Why, what a huge tree this is! And what huge leaves on it!"

It was only a big dock: but you know the dragonfly had never seen any but little water-trees; starwort, and milfoil, and water-crowfoot, and such like; so it did look very big to him. Besides, he was very short-sighted, as all dragon-flies are; and never could see a yard before his nose; any more than a great many other folks, who are not half as handsome as he.

The dragon-fly did come back, and chatted away with Tom. He was a little conceited about his fine looks and his large wings; but you know, he had been a poor dirty ugly creature all his life before; so there were great excuses for him. He was very fond of talking about all the wonderful things he saw in the trees and the meadows; and Tom liked to listen to him, for he had forgotten all about them. So in a little while they became great friends.

And I am very glad to say, that Tom learned such a lesson that day that he did not torment creatures for a long time after.

Tom's name-calling and tormenting of the other water creatures was wrong and showed his immaturity. The best way to make and build friendships is to be a good friend yourself. Cruelty makes people lonely, but kindness brings friendship. Speak kindly, remembering the old saying, "If you don't have anything nice to say, it's better not to say anything at all."

THE LOST PRINCESS
by George MacDonald

The Lost Princess *has taken an interesting turn — Rosamond has unknowingly traded places with another spoiled girl named Agnes. She finds herself at the humble home of a shepherd and shepherdess.*

CHAPTER 10

*T*HE SHEPHERDESS carried Rosamond home, gave her a warm bath in the tub in which she washed her linen, made her some bread and milk, and, after she had eaten it, put her to bed in Agnes's crib, where Rosamond slept all the rest of that day and all the following night.

When at last she opened her eyes, it was to see around her a far poorer cottage than the one she had left — very bare and uncomfortable indeed, she might well have thought. But she had come through such troubles of late, in the way of hunger and weariness and cold and fear, that she was not altogether in her ordinary mood of fault-finding, and so was able to lie in bed enjoying the thought that at length she was safe and was going to be fed and kept warm. The idea of doing anything in return for shelter and food and clothes did not, however, even cross her mind.

But the shepherdess was one of that plentiful number who can be wiser concerning other women's children than concerning their own. Such will often give you very tolerable hints as to how you ought to manage your children, and will find fault neatly enough with the system you are trying to carry out; but all their wisdom goes off in talking, and there is none left for doing what they have themselves said. There is one road talk never finds, and that is the way into the talker's own hands and feet.

The shepherdess came up to the bed, looked at the princess, and saw that she was better. But she did not like the girl much. There was no mark of a princess about her, and there never had been since she began to run alone. True, hunger had brought down her fat cheeks, but it had not turned down her impudent nose, or driven the sullenness and greed from her mouth. Nothing but the wise woman could do that — and not even she could do so without the aid of the princess herself. So the shepherdess thought what a poor substitute she had got for her own lovely Agnes — who was in fact equally repulsive, only in a way she had got used to; for the selfishness in her love had blinded her to the thin, pinched nose and the mean, self-satisfied mouth. However, it was well for the princess, sad as it is to say, that the shepherdess did not take to her, for then the shepherdess would most likely have done her only harm instead of good.

"Now, my girl," she said, "you must get up and do something. We can't keep idle folk here."

"I'm not a folk," said Rosamond; "I'm a princess."

"A pretty princess — with a nose like that! And all in rags too! If you tell such stories, I shall soon let you know what I think of you."

Rosamond then understood that merely calling herself a princess without having anything to show for it was of no use. She obeyed and rose, for she was hungry; she had to sweep the floor before she was given anything to eat.

The shepherd came in to breakfast and was kinder than his wife. He took Rosamond up in his arms and would have kissed her, but she took it as an insult from a man whose hands smelt of tar, and she kicked and screamed with rage. The poor man, finding he had made a mistake, set her down at once. But to look at the two, one might well have judged it condescension rather than rudeness in such a man to kiss such a child. For he was tall and almost stately, with a thoughtful forehead, bright eyes, eagle nose, and gentle mouth; the princess, on the other hand, was such as I have described her.

Not content with being set down and left alone, she continued to storm and scold at the shepherd, crying that she was a princess and would like to know what right he had to touch her! But he only looked down upon her from the height of his tall person with a kindly smile, regarding her as a spoiled little ape whose mother had flattered her by calling her a princess.

"Turn her out of doors, the ungrateful hussy!" cried his wife. "With your bread and your milk inside her ugly body, this is what she gives you for it! In truth, I'm paid for carrying home such an ill-bred tramp in my arms! My own poor angel Agnes! As if this ill-tempered toad were one hair like her!"

Upon hearing these words, the princess was beside herself, for those who are most given to abuse can least endure it. With fists and feet and teeth, as was her habit, she rushed at the shepherdess, whose hand was already raised to deal her a sound box on the ear, but at that moment a better-appointed minister of vengeance suddenly showed himself. Bounding in at the cottage door came one of the sheepdogs who was called Prince, and whom I shall not refer to with a which, because he was a very superior animal indeed, even for a sheepdog, which is the most intelligent of dogs.

Prince flew at the princess, knocked her down, and commenced shaking her so violently as to tear her miserable clothes to pieces. However, since he was used to mouthing little lambs, he took care not to hurt her much, though for her own good he left her a blue nip or two, by way of letting her imagine what biting might be. His master, knowing he would not injure her, thought it better not to call him off, and in half a minute he left her of his own accord and, casting a glance of indignant rebuke behind him as he went, walked slowly to the hearth, where he laid himself down with his tail toward her. The princess rose, terrified almost to death, and would have crept again into Agnes's crib for refuge, but the shepherdess cried, "Come, come, princess! I'll have no skulking to bed in the good daylight. Go and clean your master's Sunday boots there."

"I will not!" screamed the princess, and she ran from the house.

"Prince!" cried the shepherdess, and up jumped the dog and looked in her face, wagging his bushy tail.

"Fetch her back," she said, pointing to the door.

With two or three bounds Prince caught the princess, again threw her down, and, taking her by her clothes, dragged her back into the cottage and dropped her at his mistress's feet, where she lay like a bundle of rags.

"Get up," said the shepherdess.

Rosamond got up, as pale as death.

"Go and clean the boots."

"I don't know how."

"Go and try. There are the brushes, and yonder is the blacking pot."

Instructing her how to black boots, it occurred to the shepherdess what a fine thing it would be if she could teach this miserable little wretch, so forsaken and ill-bred, to be a good, well-behaved, respectable child. The shepherdess was hardly the woman to do it, but everything well meant is a help, and she had the wisdom to beg her husband to place Prince under her orders for a while and not take him to the hill as usual, so that he might help her get the princess in order.

When the husband was gone, and his boots, with the aid of the shepherdess's own finishing touches, were at last quite respectably brushed, the shepherdess told the princess that she might go and play for a while, only she must not go out of sight of the cottage door.

The princess went very gladly, but with the firm intention of getting out of sight by slow degrees and then at once taking to her heels. But no sooner was she over the threshold than the shepherdess said to the dog, "Watch her!" — and out the door shot Prince.

The moment she saw him, Rosamond threw herself on her face, trembling from head to foot. But the dog had no quarrel with her, and in the prostrate shape before him he saw no sign of the violence against which he always felt bound to protest in dog fashion; so he poked his nose under her, turned her over, and began licking her face and hands. When she saw that he meant to be friendly, her love for animals (which had had no indulgence for a long time now) came wide awake, and in a little while the two were romping and rushing about, the best friends in the world.

Do not be misled: "Bad company corrupts good character."

I CORINTHIANS 15:33

Having thus seen what she had considered an enemy change to a friend, Rosamond began to resume her former plan and crept cunningly farther and farther. At length she came to a little hollow and instantly rolled down into it. Finding then that she was out of sight of the cottage, she ran off at full speed.

But she had not gone more than a dozen paces when she heard a growling rush behind her, and the next instant she was on the ground with the dog standing over her, showing his teeth and glaring at her with his eyes. She threw her arms around his neck, and immediately he licked her face and let her get up. But the moment she would have moved a step farther from the cottage, there he was in front of her, growling and showing his teeth. She saw that attempting to escape was of no use, and she went back with him.

Thus was the princess provided with a dog for a private tutor — just the right sort for her.

Presently the shepherdess appeared at the door and called her. She would have disregarded the summons, but Prince did his best to let her know that, until she could obey herself, she must obey him. So she went into the cottage, and there the shepherdess ordered her to peel the potatoes for dinner. She sulked and refused. Here Prince could do nothing to help his mistress, but she did not have to go far to find another ally.

"Very well, Miss Princess!" she said, "we shall soon see how you like to go without when dinnertime comes."

Now the princess had very little foresight, and the idea of future hunger would have moved her little. But happily, from her game of romps with Prince, she had begun to be hungry already, and so the threat had force. She took the knife and began to peel the potatoes.

By slow degrees the princess improved a little. After a few more outbreaks of passion and a few more savage attacks from Prince, she had learned to try to restrain herself when she felt the passion coming on; while a few dinnerless afternoons entirely opened her eyes to the necessity of working in order to eat. Prince was her first counselor, and hunger was her second.

But a still better thing was that she soon grew very fond of Prince. Towards the gaining of her affections, he had three advantages: first, his nature was inferior to hers; next, he was a beast; and last, she was afraid of him. For so spoiled was she that she could more easily love what was below than what was above her, and a beast more easily than one of her own kind, and indeed could hardly have ever come to love anything much that she had not first learned to fear, and the white teeth and flaming eyes of the angry Prince were more terrible to her than anything had yet been, except those of the wolf, which she had now forgotten. Then again, Prince was such a delightful playfellow that so long as she neither lost her temper nor went against orders, she might do almost anything she pleased with him. In fact, such was his influence upon her that she who had scoffed at the wisest woman in the whole world and had derided the wishes of her own father and mother came at length to regard this dog as a superior being and to look up to him as well as love him. And this was best of all.

ANGER
by Charles and Mary Lamb

Anger in its time and place
May assume a kind of grace.
It must have some reason in it,
And not last beyond a minute.
If to further lengths it go,
It does into malice grow.

'Tis the difference that we see
'Twixt the serpent and the bee.
If the latter you provoke,
It inflicts a hasty stroke,
Puts you to some little pain,
But it never stings again.

Close in tufted bush or brake
Lurks the poison-swelled snake
Nursing up his cherished wrath;
In the purlieus of his path,
In the cold, or in the warm,
Mean him good, or mean him harm,
Wheresoever fate may bring you,
The vile snake will always sting you.

CHAPTER EIGHT

Good Manners
in School

1.
Working Hard

ABE LINCOLN'S EDUCATION
by Karen Santorum

ABRAHAM LINCOLN was the sixteenth President of our country. He served as president during the turbulent years from 1861 to 1865. The northern and southern states struggled against each other and we entered into the Civil War, which lasted four years. President Lincoln led our country throughout this difficult time, during which many thousands of Americans died.

When Abe Lincoln was just a child, he probably never dreamed he would become president. But the lessons he learned when he was growing up made him the well-spoken and courageous gentleman that we remember.

Abe Lincoln was born in Kentucky in 1809. He grew up in a one-room log cabin that his father built. It had a dirt floor, no windows, no bathroom, no playroom, and no bedrooms. Abe hunted birds, and his mother cooked them in the fireplace. But most of their food grew in the family garden. Often, Abe's dinner would consist of only a potato or nuts and berries.

Abe's parents slept on the floor near the fireplace. But Abe slept under a bearskin blanket, on cornstalks in the loft. The cabin roof leaked, and frequently Abe woke up sopping wet from the rain. Despite hardships, Abe always prayed and gave thanks to God for his blessings. Instead of complaining about what he did not have, he was thankful for what he did have.

Abe learned to work hard at an early age. He tended the farm, cared for the animals, helped chop wood, made furniture, and even helped spin thread and sew clothes. From sunrise to sunset, Abe was busy working. When he wanted to see a friend, he would walk for miles. This work ethic helped to shape Abe Lincoln into a great and honorable man.

Abe loved to learn. When he took breaks from his work he would read, for he liked nothing more than to sit under a shady tree and study. He had a very inquisitive mind and wanted to know everything. Unfortunately, books were scarce in the Lincoln home. His family had only the Bible and *Aesop's Fables*, which he read over and over again. Abe would walk for miles just to borrow books from his friends, such as *The Arabian Nights*, *Robinson Crusoe*, and *The Life of George Washington*.

The schools in the days of Abe Lincoln were far different from what we have now. Abe and his friends attended school in a one-room log cabin furnished with simple benches. Since the families needed their children to work the farms, school lasted only for a few months each year — that is, if they had a teacher. Often no teacher was available, so the school would be closed.

> Being ignorant is not so much a shame as being unwilling to learn.
>
> ❧
>
> BENJAMIN FRANKLIN
> *Poor Richard's Almanac*

Nonetheless, Abe became proficient in math, reading, and spelling. Because of his discipline and thirst for knowledge, he taught himself most of what he learned. Much of his reading was done after dark, when his farm work was done, and he strained his eyes to read by candlelight. Although Abe became well-educated through his own reading, the total amount of his life that he spent in a formal school was less than a year!

Paper was scarce in those days, so Abe would write in the dirt with a stick, or on wood with a piece of charcoal. When paper was available, he wrote with a bird's feather as a pen, dipping it in blackberry ink. Abe worked hard to help his family and to educate himself, overcoming limitations with courage and determination. His example shows us that by working hard, a determined student can accomplish anything.

Abe's example also reminds us that we learn best when we love the subjects we're studying. Look for books that interest you, and you'll find that learning can be entertaining.

MARIA
from Stories from Old-Fashioned Children's Books
edited by Andrew W. Tuer

Maria was a pretty girl,
But she could neither read nor spell,
And tho' she had so sweet a face,
She often got in sad disgrace.

She loved within the glass to look,
Rather than take her spelling-book.
To decorate and curl her hair,
Oft to the mirror she'd repair.
Soon she became exceedingly tall,
And did not go to school at all,
Now she begins to feel her need,
And wishes she could spell and read.

Does she attempt to write a line,
How sadly do her letters join,
Her diction is so incorrect,
Alas! she mourns her past neglect.

Nor will that season e'er return,
In early days ye children learn,
Strive to repeat your lessons well,
And ten to one but you excel.

GARRETT A. MORGAN: HERO OF PUBLIC SAFETY
by Karen Santorum

BACK IN 1923, Garrett A. Morgan watched cars and horse-drawn carriages try to make their way through busy intersections. Suddenly he realized that a traffic signal would help prevent accidents, and he was determined to make one.

Garret came from a poor family and had only an elementary school education, but he proved that hard work can overcome great adversity. The traffic light may be the most noticeable of his inventions, but it was only the first of his many successful ideas — ideas that have saved the lives of millions and left an indelible mark on the world.

On July 24, 1916, there was an explosion, causing a raging fire in a tunnel in Cleveland, Ohio. Because of the dangerous fumes, firemen could not rescue the thirty-two men trapped inside. But two brave souls wearing coverings over their heads charged into the thick smoke to certain doom — or so everyone thought.

After a few minutes, the two men reappeared with several of the survivors. Morgan and his brother had the courage and the confidence in Morgan's invention, the gas mask, to risk their lives in that daring rescue. As a result of his creativity, brave firemen today use gas masks to protect their lives and save others.

While many lives have been saved in fighting fires, even more lives were saved by Morgan's gas masks during World War I. Gas attacks were among the most frightening weapons ever launched on the battlefield. After horrible casualties, every soldier began carrying Morgan's invention in the event of a mustard gas attack. Fortunately, gas attacks were banned after the war.

Morgan's hard work and creativity inspired the gas mask, the traffic signal, and many other inventions. Creations like these require not only brilliant ideas, but the determination to see them through. After drawing pictures with detailed explanations of how his ideas would work, Morgan submitted them to the United States patent office. The patent office protects peoples' inventions so no one else can use them. He also had to develop, produce, and test his inventions. But his most difficult challenge was to get enough people to believe in his inventions to produce and market them.

Seeing an invention through can be a long and tiresome process. We owe a great deal to Garret A. Morgan — he saved many lives because of his determination and courage.

In spite of having only an elementary education, Garret Morgan was a very intelligent man. Most importantly, he was a hard worker. If you're smart but don't work hard, you'll never realize your potential. On the other hand, even if you are an "average" student, you can accomplish great things if you work hard.

> Do not squander time, for that's what life is made of.
>
>
>
> BENJAMIN FRANKLIN
> *Poor Richard's Almanac*

EARLY RISING
by Lady Flora Hastings

Get up, little sister: the morning is bright,
And the birds are all singing to welcome the light;
The buds are all opening: the dew's on the flower
If you shake but a branch, see there falls quite a shower.

By the side of their mothers, look under the trees,
How the young lambs are skipping about as they please;
And by all those rings on the water, I know,
The fishes are merrily swimming below.

The bee, I dare say, has been long on the wing
To get honey from every flower of the Spring
For the bee never idles, but labours; all day,
And thinks, wise little insect, work better than play.

The lark's singing gaily; it loves the bright sun,
And rejoices that now the gay Spring is begun;
For Spring is so cheerful, I think 'twould be wrong
If we did not feel happy to hear the lark's song.

Get up; for when all things are merry and glad,
Good children should never be lazy and sad;
For God gives us daylight, dear sister, that we
May rejoice like the lark, and may work like the bee.

Getting out of bed early is a good habit to develop. There's much you can accomplish in the morning hours. Rising early also provides you with a special time of peace and quiet while the world is waking up.

THE BOY WHO HATED SCHOOL
from The Education of Henry Adams *by Henry Adams*
adapted by Michael Lamb

HAVE YOU EVER WONDERED what it would be like to be the child or grandchild of the president of the United States? Do you think the grandchildren of the president always behave perfectly? Do they always show their best manners?

Henry Adams was the grandson of President John Quincy Adams. When he was seven years old his mother and he were staying at the home of his grandfather. Henry hated going to school. One morning he absolutely refused to leave the house. His poor mother bore the brunt of his terrible temper tantrum. She was simply unable to get him to budge.

It looked as though the child was going to win and have things his own way, when the former president's library door opened and the old man slowly made his way down the stairs. Putting on his hat, he took the boy's hand and without a word began to walk out the door. The boy thought that an old man of nearly eighty wouldn't trouble himself to walk nearly a mile in the hot sun to take a boy to school. He would have to stop and rest somewhere along the way, and that would give Henry a chance to make his escape; but the old man did not stop until the boy found himself seated inside the school. Only then did the former president release Henry's hand and depart.

This act may have made some boys dislike their grandfather forever, but Henry could never recall that it affected him in that way. The president had done this tough work with a certain intelligence. He had shown no temper, no irritation, no personal feeling, and used no force. During their long walk he had said nothing. The boy felt deep respect towards his grandfather. Eventually Henry developed a real love for learning. The boy who so disliked school went on to become one of America's greatest writers and one of Harvard's finest teachers.

Henry initially thought he hated school, but he ended up teaching for most of his life. Many children assume they don't like something before they've really tried it. This is especially true of school, studies, and spinach! Henry found that he loved learning, and he had his wise grandfather, the sixth president of the United States, to thank for this.

ALWAYS FINISH
author unknown

If a task is once begun
Never leave it till it's done.
Be the labor great or small,
Do it well or not at all.

2.
Classroom Courtesy

Miss Nelson Is Missing!
by Harry Allard

The kids in Room 207 were misbehaving again.
Spitballs stuck to the ceiling.
Paper planes whizzed through the air.
They were the worst-behaved class in the whole school.
"Now settle down," said Miss Nelson in a sweet voice.
But the class would not settle down.
They whispered and giggled.
They squirmed and made faces.
They were even rude during story hour.
And they always refused to do their lessons.
"Something will have to be done," said Miss Nelson.
The next morning Miss Nelson did not come to school.
"Wow!" yelled the kids. "Now we can *really* act up!"
They began to make more spitballs and paper planes.
"Today let's be just terrible!" they said.
"Not so fast!" hissed an unpleasant voice.
A woman in an ugly black dress stood before them.
"I am your new teacher, Miss Viola Swamp."
And she rapped the desk with her ruler.
"Where is Miss Nelson?" asked the kids.
"Never mind that!" snapped Miss Swamp.
"Open those arithmetic books!"
Miss Nelson's kids did as they were told.
They could see that Miss Swamp was a real witch.
She meant business.
Right away she put them to work.
And she loaded them down with homework.
"We'll have no story hour today," said Miss Swamp.
"Keep your mouths shut," said Miss Swamp.

"Sit perfectly still," said Miss Swamp.

"And if you misbehave, you'll be sorry," said Miss Swamp.

The kids in Room 207 had never worked so hard.

Days went by and there was no sign of Miss Nelson.

The kids *missed* Miss Nelson!

"Maybe we should try to find her," they said.

Some of them went to the police.

Detective McSmogg was assigned to the case.

He listened to their story.

He scratched his chin.

"Hmmmm," he said. "Hmmm."

"I think Miss Nelson is missing."

Detective McSmogg would not be much help.

Other kids went to Miss Nelson's house.

The shades were tightly drawn, and no one answered the door.

In fact, the only person they *did* see was the wicked Miss Viola Swamp, coming up the street.

"If she sees us, she'll give us more homework."

They got away just in time.

Maybe something *terrible* happened to Miss Nelson!

"Maybe she was gobbled up by a shark!" said one of the kids.

But that didn't seem likely.

"Maybe Miss Nelson went to Mars!" said another kid.

But that didn't seem likely either.

"I know!" exclaimed one know-it-all. "Maybe Miss Nelson's car was carried off by a swarm of angry butterflies!"

But that was the least likely of all.

The kids in Room 207 became very discouraged. It seemed that Miss Nelson was never coming back. And they would be stuck with Miss Viola Swamp forever.

They heard footsteps in the hall.

"Here comes the witch," they whispered.

"Hello, children," someone said in a sweet voice.

It was Miss Nelson!

"Did you miss me?" she asked.

"We certainly did!" cried all the kids.

"Where were you?"

"That's my little secret," said Miss Nelson.

"How about a story hour?"

"Oh yes!" cried the kids.

Miss Nelson noticed that during story hour no one was rude or silly.

"What brought about this lovely change?" she asked.

"That's *our* little secret," said the kids.

Back home Miss Nelson took off her coat and hung it in the closet (right next to an ugly black dress).

When it was time for bed she sang a little song. "I'll never tell," she said to herself with a smile.

P.S. Detective McSmogg is working on a new case.

He is *now* looking for Miss Viola Swamp.

Always respect your teachers. They are trying to teach you important subjects, and cannot do their work effectively unless all the students are following the rules. This is why you should sit still at your desk, pay attention to the lessons, and raise your hand if you would like to ask a question.

Tom Sawyer Learns His Lesson
from The Adventures of Tom Sawyer *by Mark Twain*
adapted by Michael Lamb

Tom Sawyer most certainly did not like Sunday school; but he did like Becky Thatcher. Becky was the daughter of Judge Thatcher and she was the prettiest girl in town. Tom would do just about anything to impress the judge or his daughter.

In those days, if children learned a verse or two from the Bible well, they were given small blue, red, or yellow tickets as an award. If you were able to accumulate one hundred tickets you could cash them in for a brand-new Bible. Now Tom Sawyer wasn't very interested in Sunday school or a new Bible, but he did find out that the school superintendent and Judge Thatcher would be visiting the class on the upcoming Sunday. Tom decided to prepare for a little showing off.

All week long he traded with other boys and girls to get their special tickets.

"Say Billy, How many tickets ya got?"

"Twelve."

"What'll you take for em?"

Tom showed Billy what he was offering in exchange. The goods were found to be acceptable, and another deal was completed. Tom traded two white marbles for 10 tickets. A jackknife was exchanged for 25 tickets. Before long, Tom had reached the grand total of 100 tickets. For the first time ever, Tom Sawyer couldn't wait until Sunday came.

When that fateful day finally arrived, Tom took his usual seat towards the back of the church. As the guest of honor, Judge Thatcher sat in the first pew and Becky was right next to him. The sunlight beamed through a great side window down onto the front row of seats. The way it shone on Becky's blonde hair and white dress caused her to resemble a glowing angel.

The superintendent strode up the center aisle and stopped just in front of the pulpit. There he made a short speech about the importance of learning sacred scripture. He then asked if any of the boys and girls had learned sufficient Bible verses to earn the 100 tickets necessary to receive the prize of a brand-new Bible. Tom rose from his seat. This was like a thunderbolt out of the sky. How had this boy come into all those tickets? It was simply preposterous that Tom Sawyer had suddenly become devoted to Biblical study. But there was no getting around it — here were the certified tickets. The other boys were eaten up with envy as they came to realize what Tom had been up to.

Tom was introduced to the Judge; but his tongue was tied and his breath would hardly come, partly because of the awful greatness of the man, but mainly because he was "her" parent. The Judge put his hand on Tom's head, called him a fine little man, and asked him his name. The boy stammered, gasped, and finally got out: "Tom."

"Oh no, not Tom — it is — Thomas. Thomas Sawyer, sir."

"That's it! That's a good boy. Fine boy. Fine mannerly little fellow." He then presented Tom with the new Bible, which was followed by another speech.

"Knowledge is worth more than anything in the world," said the Judge. "It's what makes great men and good men. You will be a great man and a good man someday yourself, Thomas, and then you'll look back and say, 'It's all owing to my precious Sunday school class — it's all owing to my dear teachers — it's all owing to the good superintendent, who encouraged me, and watched over me, and gave me a beautiful Bible — a splendid elegant Bible — to keep and have it all for my own, always — it's all owing to right bringing up! That is what you will say, Thomas."

The Judge then paused, took a deep breath, and gazed solemnly at Tom. "And now I'm sure you wouldn't mind telling all of us some of the things you have learned — no, I know you wouldn't — for we are proud of little boys who learn. Now, no doubt you know the names of all the twelve disciples. Won't you tell us the names of the first two that were appointed?"

Tom was tugging at a buttonhole and looking sheepish. He blushed, now, and his eyes fell. His mouth was as dry as a desert. He didn't expect this. No one told him there would be questions. His friends were now all smiling smugly.

"Now, I know you will tell me," said Judge Thatcher. "The names of the first two disciples were . . . "

Uncontrollably Tom blurted out, "David and Goliath." Let us draw the curtain of charity over the rest of the scene.

Tom Sawyer thought he could get away with cheating and look smart. He ended up being embarrassed in front of Becky and the rest of the class. Honesty and truthfulness are the traits that we greatly admire in others, and this is especially true in school.

LITTLE MEN
by Louisa May Alcott

Nat Blake is joining a school with twelve orphan boys. He has just gotten off the bus and climbed the steps onto the large porch of the "cheerful" house. When he enters the house, there are boys everywhere, playing games while on recess. Nat looks at the classrooms filled with maps, books, chalkboards, and desks. He waits patiently to meet his new teacher, Mrs. Jo Bhaer, and his classmates.

CHAPTER 1

"PLEASE, SIR, is this Plumfield?" asked a ragged boy of the man who opened the great gate at which the omnibus left him.

"Yes, who sent you?"

"Mr. Laurence. I have got a letter for the lady."

"All right; go up to the house, and give it to her; she'll see to you, little chap."

The man spoke pleasantly, and the boy went on, feeling much cheered by the words. Through the soft spring rain that fell on sprouting grass and budding trees, Nat saw a large square house before him — a hospitable-looking house, with an old-fashioned porch, wide steps, and lights shining in many windows. Neither curtains nor shutters hid the cheerful glimmer; and, pausing a moment before he rang, Nat saw many little shadows dancing on the walls, heard the pleasant hum of young voices, and felt that it was hardly possible that the light and warmth and comfort within could be for a homeless "little chap" like him.

"I hope the lady *will* see me," he thought; and gave a timid rap with the great bronze knocker, which was a jovial griffin's head.

A rosy-faced servant-main opened the door and smiled as she took the letter which he silently offered. She seemed used to receiving strange boys, for she pointed to a seat in the hall, and said, with a nod,

"Sit there and drip on the mat a bit, while I take this in to the misses."

Nat found plenty to amuse him while he waited, and stared about him curiously, enjoying the view, yet glad to do so unobserved in the dusky recess by the door.

The house seemed swarming with boys, who were beguiling the rainy twilight with all sorts of amusements. There were boys everywhere, upstairs and downstairs and in the lady's chamber, apparently, for various open doors showed pleasant groups of big boys, little boys, and middle-sized boys in all stages of evening relaxation, not to say effervescence. Two large rooms on the right were evidently schoolrooms, for desks, maps, blackboards, and books were scattered about. An open fire burned on the hearth, and several indolent lads lay on their backs before it, discussing a new cricket-ground, with such animation that their boots waved in the air. A tall youth was practicing on the flute in one corner, quite undisturbed by the racket all about him. Two or three others were jumping over the desks, pausing, now and then, to get their breath, and laugh at the droll sketches of a little wag who was caricaturing the whole household on a blackboard.

In the room on the left a long supper-table was seen, set forth with great pitchers of new milk, piles of brown and white bread, and perfect stacks of the shiny gingerbread so dear to boyish souls. A flavour of toast was in the air, also suggestions of baked apples, very tantalizing to one hungry little nose and stomach.

The hall, however, presented the most inviting prospect of all, for a brisk game of tag was going on in the upper entry. One landing was devoted to marbles, the other to checkers, while the stairs were occupied by a boy reading, a girl singing lullaby to her doll, two puppies, a kitten, and a constant succession of small boys sliding down the banisters, to the great detriment of their clothes, and danger to their limbs.

So absorbed did Nat become in this exciting race, that he ventured farther and farther out of his corner; and when one very lively boy came down so swiftly that he could not stop himself, but fell off the banisters, with a crash that would have broken any head but one rendered nearly as hard as a cannon-ball by eleven years of constant bumping, Nat forgot himself, and ran up to the fallen rider, expecting to find him half-dead.

The doors of wisdom
are never shut.

BENJAMIN FRANKLIN
Poor Richard's Almanac

The boy, however, only winked rapidly for a second, then lay calmly looking up at the new face with a surprised "Hullo!"

"Hullo!" returned Nat, not knowing what else to say, and thinking that form of reply both brief and easy.

"Are you a new boy?" asked the recumbent youth, without stirring.

"Don't know yet."

"What's your name?"

"Nat Blake."

"Mine's Tommy Bangs; come up and have a go, will you?" And Tommy got upon his legs like one suddenly remembering the duties of hospitality.

"Guess I won't, till I see whether I'm going to stay or not," returned Nat, feeling the desire to stay increase every moment.

"I say, Demi, here's the new one. Come and see to him," and the lively Thomas returned to his sport with unabated relish.

At his call, the boy reading on the stairs looked up with a pair of big brown eyes, and after an instant's pause, as if a little shy, he put the book under his arm, and came soberly down to greet the newcomer, who found something very attractive in the pleasant face of this slender, mild-eyed boy.

"Have you seen Aunt Jo?" he asked, as if that was some sort of important ceremony.

"I haven't seen anybody yet but you boys; I'm waiting," answered Nat.

"Did Uncle Laurie send you?" proceeded Demi, politely, but gravely.

"Mr. Laurence did."

"He is Uncle Laurie; and he always sends nice boys."

Nat looked gratified at the remark, and smiled, in a way that made his thin face very pleasant. He did not know what to say next, so the two stood staring at one another in friendly silence, till the little girl came up with her doll in her arms. She was very like Demi, only not so tall, and had a rounder, rosier face, and blue eyes.

"This is my sister Daisy," announced Demi, as if presenting a rare and precious creature.

The children nodded to one another; and the little girl's face dimpled with pleasure, as she said, affably,

"I hope you'll stay. We have such good times here, don't we, Demi?"

"Of course we do, that's what Aunt Jo has Plumfield for."

"It seems a very nice place indeed," observed Nat, feeling that he must respond to these amiable young persons.

"It's the nicest place in the world, isn't it, Demi?" said Daisy, who evidently regarded her brother as an authority on all subjects.

"No; I think Greenland, where the icebergs and seals are, is more interesting. But I'm fond of Plumfield, and it is a very nice place to be in," returned Demi, who was interested just now in a book on Greenland. He was about to offer to show Nat the pictures and explain them, when the servant returned, saying, with a nod toward the parlour-door,

"All right; you are to stop."

"I'm glad; now come to Aunt Jo." And Daisy took him by the hand with a pretty protective air, which made Nat feel at home at once.

Demi returned to his beloved book, while his sister led the newcomer into a back room, where a stout gentleman was frolicking with two little boys on the sofa, and a thin lady was just finishing the letter which she seemed to have been re-reading.

"Here he is, Aunty!" cried Daisy.

"So this is my new boy? I'm glad to see you, my dear, and hope you'll be happy here," said the lady, drawing him to her, and stroking back the hair from his forehead with a kind hand and a motherly look, which made Nat's lonely little heart yearn toward her.

She was not at all handsome, but she had a merry sort of face, that never seemed to have forgotten certain childish ways and looks, any more than her voice and manner had; and these things, hard to describe but very plain to see and feel, made her a genial, comfortable kind of person, easy to get on with, and generally "jolly," as boys would say. She saw the little tremble of Nat's lips as she smoothed his hair, and her keen eyes grew softer, but she only drew the shabby figure nearer and said, laughing, "I am Mother Bhaer, that gentleman is Father Bhaer, and these are the two little Bhaers. Come here, boys, and see Nat."

The three wrestlers obeyed at once; and the stout man, with a chubby child on each shoulder, came up to welcome the new boy. Rob and Teddy merely grinned at him, but Mr. Bhaer shook hands, pointed to a low chair near the fire, and said, in a cordial voice,

"There is a place all ready for thee, my son, sit down and dry they wet feet at once."

"Wet? So they are! My dear, off with your shoes this minute, and I'll have some dry things ready for you in a jiffy," cried Mrs. Bhaer, bustling about so energetically, that Nat found himself in the cozy little chair, with dry socks and warm slippers on his feet, before he would have had time to say Jack Robinson, if he had wanted to try. He said "Thank you, ma'am," instead; and said it so gratefully, that Mrs. Bhaer's eyes grew soft again, and she said something merry, because she felt so tender, which was a way she had.

"These are Tommy Bangs's slippers; but he never will remember to put them on in the house so he shall not have them. They are too big; but that's all the better, you can't run away from us so fast as if they fitted."

"I don't want to run away, ma'am." And Nat spread his grimy little hands before the comfortable blaze with a long sigh of satisfaction.

"That's good! Now I am going to toast you well, and try to get rid of that ugly cough. How long have you had it, dear?" asked Mrs. Bhaer, as she rummaged in her big basket for a strip of flannel.

"All winter. I got a cold, and it wouldn't get better, some-how."

"No wonder living in that damp cellar with hardly a rag to his poor dear back!" said Mrs. Bhaer, in a low tone to her husband, who was looking at the boy with a skillful pair of eyes, that marked the thin temples and feverish lips, as well as the hoarse voice and frequent fits of coughing that shook the bent shoulders under the patched jacket.

> How much better to get wisdom than gold, to choose understanding rather than silver!
>
>
>
> PROVERBS 16:16

"Robin, my man, trot up to Nursery, and tell her to give thee the cough-bottle and the liniment," said Mr. Bhaer, after his eyes had exchanged telegrams with his wife's.

Nat looked a little anxious at the preparations, but forgot his fears, in a hearty laugh, when Mrs. Bhaer whispered to him, with a droll look.

"Hear my rogue Teddy trying to cough. The syrup I'm going to give you has honey in it; and he wants some."

Little Ted was red in the face with his exertions by the time the bottle came, and was allowed to suck the spoon, after Nat had manfully taken a dose, and had the bit of flannel put about his throat.

These first steps toward a cure were hardly completed, when a great bell rang, and a loud tramping through the hall announced supper. Bashful Nat quaked at the thought of meeting many strange boys, but Mrs. Bhaer held out her hand to him, and Rob said, patronizingly, "Don't be 'fraid; I'll take care of you."

Twelve boys, six on a side, stood behind their chairs, prancing with impatience to begin, while the tall flute-playing youth was trying to curb their ardour. But no one sat down, till Mrs. Bhaer was in her place behind the teapot, with Teddy on her left, and Nat on her right.

"This is our new boy, Nat Blake. After supper you can say, How do you do? Gently, boys, gently."

As she spoke everyone stared at Nat, and then whisked into their seats, trying to be orderly, and failing utterly. The Bhaers did their best to have the lads behave well at meal times, and generally succeeded pretty well, for their rules were few and sensible, and the boys, knowing that they tried to make things easy and happy, did their best to obey.

It can be scary when you are new in a school. The boys' polite behavior made Nat feel at ease. Like Tommy Bangs, when you meet others for the first time, greet them and introduce yourself. Find out their names and where they're from, and make them feel welcome.

ANNE OF GREEN GABLES
by Lucy Maud Montgomery

Anne Shirley tries hard to behave in school. Unfortunately, she always loses her temper when a particular trait of hers is made fun of . . .

CHAPTER 15

THE AVONLEA SCHOOL was a whitewashed building low in the eaves and wide in the windows, furnished inside with comfortable substantial old-fashioned desks that opened and shut, and were carved all over their lids with the initials and hieroglyphics of three generations of school-children. The schoolhouse was set back from the road and behind it was a dusky fir wood and a brook where all the children put their bottles of milk in the morning to keep cool and sweet until dinner hour.

Marilla had seen Anne start off to school on the first day of September with many secret misgivings. Anne was such an odd girl. How would she get on with the other children? And how on earth would she ever manage to hold her tongue during school hours?

Things went better than Marilla feared, however. Anne came home that evening in high spirits.

"I think I'm going to like school here," she announced. "I don't think much of the master, though. He's all the time curling his moustache and making eyes at Prissy Andrews. Prissy is grown-up, you know. She's sixteen and she's studying for the entrance examination into Queen's Academy at Charlottetown next year. Tillie Boulter says that the master is *dead gone* on her. She's got a beautiful complexion and curly brown hair and she does it up so elegantly. She sits in the long seat at the back and he sits there, too, most of the time to explain her lessons, he says. But Ruby Gillis says she saw him writing something on her slate and when Prissy read it she blushed as red as a beet and giggled; and Ruby Gillis says she doesn't believe it had anything to do with the lesson."

"Anne Shirley, don't let me hear you talking about your teacher in that way again," said Marilla sharply. "You don't go to school to criticize the master. I guess he can teach you something and it's your business to learn. And I want you to understand right off that you are not to come home telling tales about him. That is something I won't encourage. I hope you were a good girl."

"Indeed I was," said Anne comfortably. "It wasn't so hard as you might imagine, either. I sit with Diana. Our seat is right by the window and we can look down to the Lake of Shining Waters. There are a lot of nice girls in school and we had scrumptious fun playing at dinner time. It's so nice to have a lot of little girls to play with. But of course I like Diana best and always will. I adore Diana. I'm dreadfully far behind the others. They're all in the fifth book and I'm only in the fourth. I feel that it's kind of a disgrace. But there's not one of them has such an imagination as I have and I soon found that out. We had reading and geography and Canadian History and dictation today. Mr. Phillips said my spelling was disgraceful and he held up my slate so that everybody could see it, all marked over. I felt so mortified, Marilla; he might have been politer to a stranger, I think. Ruby Gillis gave me an apple and Sophia Sloane lent me a lovely pink card with 'May I see you home?' on it. I'm to give it back to her tomorrow. And Tillie Boulter let me wear her bead ring all the afternoon. Can I have some of those pearl beads off the old pincushion in the garret to make myself a ring? And oh Marilla, Jane Andrews told me that Minnie MacPherson told her that she heard Prissy Andrews tell Sara Gillis that I had a very pretty nose. Marilla, that is the first compliment I have ever had in my life and you can't imagine what a strange feeling it gave me. Marilla, have I really a pretty nose? I know you'll tell me the truth."

"Your nose is well enough," said Marilla shortly. Secretly she thought Anne's nose was a remarkably pretty one; but she had no intention of telling her so.

That was three weeks ago and all had gone smoothly so far. And now, this crisp September morning, Anne and Diana were tripping blithely down the Birch Path, two of the happiest little girls in Avonlea.

"I guess Gilbert Blythe will be in school today," said Diana. "He's been visiting his cousins over in New Brunswick all summer and he only came home Saturday night. He's aw'fly handsome, Anne. And he teases the girls something terrible. He just torments our lives out."

Diana's voice indicated that she rather liked having her life tormented out than not.

"Gilbert Blythe?" said Anne. "Isn't it his name that's written up on the porch wall with Julia Bell's and a big 'Take Notice' over them?"

"Yes," said Diana, tossing her head, "but I'm sure he doesn't like Julia Bell so very much. I've heard him say he studied the multiplication table by her freckles."

"Oh, don't speak about freckles to me," implored Anne. "It isn't delicate when I've got so many. But I do think that writing take-notices up on the wall about the boys and girls is the silliest ever. I should just like to see anybody dare to write my name up with a boy's. Not, of course," she hastened to add, "that anybody would."

Anne sighed. She didn't want her name written up. But it was a little humiliating to know that there was no danger of it.

"Nonsense," said Diana, whose black eyes and glossy tresses had played such havoc with the hearts of Avonlea schoolboys that her name figured on the porch walls in half a dozen take-notices. "It's only meant as a joke. And don't you be too sure your name won't ever be written up. Charlie Sloane is dead gone on you. He told his mother — his mother mind you — that you were the smartest girl in school. That's better than being good-looking."

"No, it isn't," said Anne, feminine to the core. "I'd rather be pretty than clever. And I hate Charlie Sloane. I can't bear a boy with goggle eyes. If anyone wrote my name up with his I'd never get over it, Diana Barry. But it is nice to keep head of your class."

"You'll have Gilbert in your class after this," said Diana, "and he's used to being head of his class, I can tell you. He's only in the fourth book although he's nearly fourteen. Four years ago his father was sick and had to go out to Alberta for his health and Gilbert went with him. They were there three years and Gil didn't go to school hardly any until they came back. You won't find it so easy to keep head after this, Anne."

"I'm glad," said Anne quickly. "I couldn't really feel proud of keeping ahead of little boys and girls of just nine or ten. I got up yesterday spelling 'ebullition.' Josie Pye was head and, mind you, she peeped in her book. Mr. Phillips didn't see her — he was looking at Prissy Andrews —

but I did. I just swept her a look of freezing scorn and she got as red as a beet and spelled it wrong after all."

"Those Pye girls are cheats all round," said Diana indignantly, as they climbed the fence of the main road. "Gertie Pye actually went and put her milk bottle in my place in the brook yesterday. Did you ever? I don't speak to her now."

When Mr. Phillips was in the back of the room hearing Prissy Andrews' Latin Diana whispered to Anne, "That's Gilbert Blythe sitting right across the aisle from you, Anne. Just look at him and see if you don't think he's handsome."

Anne looked accordingly. She had a good chance to do so, for the said Gilbert Blythe was absorbed in stealthily pinning the long yellow braid of Ruby Gillis, who sat in front of him, to the back of her seat. He was a tall boy, with curly brown hair, roguish hazel eyes and a mouth twisted into a teasing smile. Presently Ruby Gillis started up to take a sum to the master; she fell back into her seat with a little shriek, believing that her hair was pulled out by the roots. Everybody looked at her and Mr. Phillips glared so sternly that Ruby began to cry. Gilbert had whisked the pin out of sight and was studying his history with the soberest face in the world; but when the commotion subsided he looked at Anne and winked with inexpressible drollery.

> You may delay, but time will not; Lost time is never seen again.
>
>
>
> BENJAMIN FRANKLIN
> *Poor Richard's Almanac*

"I think your Gilbert Blythe is handsome," confided Anne to Diana, "but I think he's very bold. It isn't good manners to wink at a strange girl."

But it was not until the afternoon that things really began to happen.

Mr. Phillips was back in the corner explaining a problem in algebra to Prissy Andrews and the rest of the scholars were doing pretty much as they pleased, eating green apples, whispering, drawing pictures on their slates, and driving crickets, harnessed to strings, up and down the aisle. Gilbert Blythe was trying to make Anne Shirley look at him and failing utterly, because Anne was at that moment totally oblivious, not only of the very existence of Gilbert Blythe, but of every other scholar in Avonlea school and of Avonlea school itself. With her chin propped on her hands and her eyes fixed on the blue glimpse of the Lake of Shining Waters that the west window afforded, she was far away in a gorgeous dreamland, hearing and seeing nothing save her own wonderful visions.

Gilbert Blythe wasn't used to putting himself out to make a girl look at him and meeting with failure. She should look at him, that red-haired Shirley girl with the little pointed chin and the big eyes that weren't like the eyes of any other girl in Avonlea school.

Gilbert reached across the aisle, picked up the end of Anne's long red braid, held it out at arm's length and said in a piercing whisper, "Carrots! Carrots!"

Then Anne looked at him with a vengeance!

She did more than look. She sprang to her feet, her bright fancies fallen into cureless ruin. She flashed one indignant glance at Gilbert from eyes whose angry sparkle was swiftly quenched in equally angry tears.

"You mean, hateful boy!" she exclaimed passionately. "How dare you!"

And then — Thwack! Anne had brought her slate down on Gilbert's head and cracked it — slate, not head — clear across.

Avonlea school always enjoyed a scene. This was an especially enjoyable one. Everybody said, "Oh" in horrified delight. Diana gasped. Ruby Gillis, who was inclined to be hysterical, began to cry. Tommy Sloane let his team of crickets escape him altogether while he stared open-mouthed at the tableau.

Mr. Phillips stalked down the aisle and laid his hand heavily on Anne's shoulder.

"Anne Shirley, what does this mean?" he said angrily.

Anne returned no answer. It was asking too much of flesh and blood to expect her to tell before the whole school that she had been called "carrots." Gilbert it was who spoke up stoutly.

"It was my fault, Mr. Phillips. I teased her."

Mr. Phillips paid no heed to Gilbert.

"I am sorry to see a pupil of mine displaying such a temper and such a vindictive spirit," he said in a solemn tone, as if the mere fact of being a pupil of his ought to root out all evil passions from the hearts of small imperfect mortals. "Anne, go and stand on the platform in front of the blackboard for the rest of the afternoon."

If another child teases you during class time, wait until the teacher is done with the lesson and discuss the problem with him. Interruptions like yelling or hitting disrupt the class environment and make the teacher's job more difficult.

THE LETTERS AT SCHOOL
by Mary Mapes Dodge

One day the letters went to school,
    And tried to learn each other;
They got so mixed 't was really hard
    To pick out one from t' other.

A went in first, and Z went last;
    The rest all were between them —
K, L and M, and N, O, P —
    I wish you could have seen them!

B, C, D, E, and J, K, L,
    Soon jostled well their betters;
Q, R, S, T — I grieve to say —
    Were very naughty letters.

Of course, ere long, they came to words —
    What else could be expected?
Till E made D, J, C, and T
    Decidedly dejected.
Now, through it all, the Consonants
    Were rudest and uncouthest,
While all the pretty Vowel girls
    Were certainly the smoothest.

And simple U kept far from Q,
 With face demure and moral,
"Because," she said, "we are, we two,
 So apt to start a quarrel!"

But spiteful P said, "Pooh for U!"
 (Which made her feel quite bitter),
And, calling O, L, E to help,
 He really tried to hit her.

Cried A, "Now E and C, come here!
 If both will aid a minute,
Good P will join in making peace,
 Or else the mischief's in it."

And smiling E, the ready sprite,
 Said, "Yes, and count me double."
This done, sweet peace shone o'er the scene,
 And gone was all the trouble!

Meanwhile, when U and P made up,
 The cons'nants looked about them,
And kissed the Vowels, for, you see,
 They could not do without them.

PIPPI LONGSTOCKING
by Astrid Lindgren

We return once again to the story of Pippi Longstocking. She was the girl who lived all alone with no parents to teach her what to do. In this scene, her friends Tommy and Annika encourage her to go to school.

CHAPTER 4

OF COURSE Tommy and Annika went to school. Each morning at eight o'clock they trotted off, hand in hand, swinging their schoolbags.

At that time Pippi was usually grooming her horse or dressing Mr. Nilsson in his little suit. Or else she was taking her morning exercises, which meant turning forty-three somersaults in a row. Then she would sit down on the kitchen table and, utterly happy, drink a large cup of coffee and eat a piece of bread and cheese.

Tommy and Annika always looked longingly toward Villa Villekulla as they started off to school. They would much rather have gone to play with Pippi. If only Pippi had been going to school too; that would have been something else again.

"Just think what fun we could have on the way home from school," said Tommy.

"Yes, and on the way to school too," said Annika.

The more they thought about it the worse they felt to think that Pippi did not go to school, and at last they determined to try to persuade her to begin.

"You can't imagine what a nice teacher we have," said Tommy artfully to Pippi one afternoon when he and Annika had come for a visit at Villa Villekulla after they had finished their homework.

"If you only knew what fun it is in school!" Annika added. "I'd die if I couldn't go to school."

Pippi sat on a hassock, bathing her feet in a tub. She said nothing but just wiggled her toes for a while so that the water splashed around every-where.

"You don't have to stay so very long," continued Tommy. "Just until two o'clock."

"Yes, and besides, we get Christmas vacation and Easter vacation and summer vacation," said Annika.

Pippi bit her big toe thoughtfully but still said nothing. Suddenly, as if she had made some decision, she poured all the water out on the kitchen floor, so that Mr. Nilsson, who sat near her playing with a mirror, got his pants absolutely soaked.

"It's not fair!" said Pippi sternly without paying any attention to Mr. Nilsson's puzzled air about his wet pants. "It is absolutely unfair! I don't intend to stand it!"

"What's the matter now?" asked Tommy.

"In four months it will be Christmas, and then you'll have Christmas vacation. But I, what'll I get?" Pippi's voice sounded sad. "No Christmas vacation, not even the tiniest bit of a Christmas vacation," she complained. "Something will have to be done about that. Tomorrow morning I'll begin school."

Tommy and Annika clapped their hands with delight. "Hurrah! We'll wait for you outside our gate at eight o'clock."

"Oh, no," said Pippi. "I can't begin as early as that. And besides, I'm going to ride to school."

And ride she did. Exactly at ten o'clock the next day she lifted her horse off the porch, and a little later all the people in the town ran to their windows to see what horse it was that was running away. That is to say, they thought he was running away, but it was only Pippi in a bit of a hurry to get to school.

She galloped wildly into the schoolyard, jumped off the horse, tied him to a tree, and burst into the schoolroom with such a noise and a clatter that Tommy and Annika and all their classmates jumped in their seats.

"Hi, there," cried Pippi, waving her big hat. "Did I get here in time for pluttifikation?"

Tommy and Annika had told their teacher that a new girl named Pippi Longstocking was coming, and the teacher had already heard about Pippi in the little town. As she was a very pleasant teacher, she had decided to do all she could to make Pippi happy in school.

Pippi threw herself down on a vacant bench without having been invited to do so, but the teacher paid no attention to her heedless way. She simply said in a very friendly voice, "Welcome to school, little Pippi. I hope that you will enjoy yourself here and learn a great deal."

"Yes, and I hope I'll get some Christmas vacation," said Pippi. "That is the reason I've come. It's only fair, you know."

"If you would first tell me your whole name," said the teacher, "then I'll register you in school."

"My name is Pippilotta Delicatessa Window-shade Mackrelmint Efraim's Daughter Longstocking, daughter of Captain Efraim Longstocking, formerly the Terror of the Sea, now a cannibal king. Pippi is really only a nickname, because Papa thought that Pippilotta was too long to say."

"Indeed?" said the teacher. "Well, then we shall call you Pippi too. But now," she continued, "suppose we test you a little and see what you know. You are a big girl and no doubt know a great deal already. Let us begin with arithmetic. Pippi, can you tell me what seven and five are?"

Pippi, astonished and dismayed, looked at her and said, "Well, if you don't know that yourself, you needn't think I'm going to tell you."

All the children stared in horror at Pippi, and the teacher explained that one couldn't answer that way in school.

"I beg your pardon," said Pippi contritely. "I didn't know that. I won't do it again."

"No, let us hope not," said the teacher. "And now I will tell you that seven and five are twelve."

"See that!" said Pippi. "You knew it yourself. Why are you asking then?"

The teacher decided to act as if nothing unusual were happening and went on with her examination.

"Well now, Pippi, how much do you think eight and four are?"

"Oh, about sixty-seven," hazarded Pippi.

"Of course not," said the teacher. "Eight and four are twelve."

"Well now, really, my dear little woman," said Pippi, "that is carrying things too far. You just said that seven and five are twelve. There should be some rhyme and reason to things even in school. Furthermore, if you are so childishly interested in that foolishness, why don't you sit down in a corner by yourself and do arithmetic and leave us alone so we can play tag?"

The teacher decided there was no point in trying to teach Pippi any more arithmetic. She began to ask the other children the arithmetic questions.

"Can Tommy answer this one?" she asked. "If Lisa has seven apples and Axel has nine apples, how many apples do they have together?"

"Yes, you tell, Tommy," Pippi interrupted, "and tell me too, if Lisa gets a stomach-ache and Axel gets more stomach-ache, whose fault is it and where did they get hold of the apples in the first place?"

The teacher tried to pretend that she hadn't heard and turned to Annika. "Now, Annika, here's an example for you: Gustav was with his schoolmates on a picnic. He had a quarter when he started out and seven cents when he got home. How much did he spend?"

"Yes, indeed," said Pippi, "and I also want to know why he was so extravagant, and if it was pop he bought, and if he washed his ears properly before he left home."

The teacher decided to give up arithmetic altogether. She thought maybe Pippi would prefer to learn to read. So she took out a pretty little card with a picture of an ibex on it. In front of the ibex's nose was the letter "i."

"Now, Pippi," she said briskly, "you'll see something jolly. You see here an ibex. And the letter in front of this ibex is called i."

"That I'll never believe," said Pippi. "I think it looks exactly like a straight line with a little fly speck over it. But what I'd really like to know is, what has the ibex to do with the fly speck?"

The teacher took out another card with a picture of a snake on it and

It is ill-manners to silence a fool, and cruelty to let him go on.

BENJAMIN FRANKLIN
Poor Richard's Almanac

told Pippi that the letter on that was an s.

"Speaking of snakes," said Pippi, "I'll never, ever forget the time I had a fight with a huge snake in India. You can't imagine what a dreadful snake it was, fourteen yards long and mad as a hornet, and every day he ate up five Indians and then two little children for dessert, and one time he came and wanted me for dessert, and he wound himself around me — uhhh! — but I've been around a bit, I said, and hit him in the head, bang, and then he hissed uiuiuiuiuiuiuiuitch, and then I hit him again, and bingo! he was dead, and, indeed, so that is the letter s — most remarkable!"

Pippi had to stop to get her breath. And the teacher, who had now begun to think that Pippi was an unruly and troublesome child, decided that the class should have drawing for a while. Surely Pippi could sit still and be quiet and draw, thought the teacher. She took out paper and pencils and passed them out to the children.

"Now you may draw whatever you wish," she said and sat down at her desk and began to correct homework. In a little while she looked up to see how the drawing was going. All the children sat looking at Pippi, who lay flat on the floor, drawing to her heart's content.

"But, Pippi," said the teacher impatiently, "why in the world aren't you drawing on your paper?"

"I filled that long ago. There isn't room enough for my whole horse on that little snip of a paper," said Pippi. "Just now I'm working on his front legs, but when I get to his tail I guess I'll have to go out in the hall."

The teacher thought hard for a while. "Suppose instead we all sing a little song," she suggested.

All the children stood up by their seats except Pippi; she stayed where she was on the floor. "You go ahead and sing," she said. "I'll rest myself a while. Too much learning breaks even the healthiest."

But now the teacher's patience came to an end. She told all the children to go out into the yard so she could talk to Pippi alone.

When the teacher and Pippi were alone, Pippi got up and walked to the desk. "Do you know what?" she said. "It was awfully jolly to come to school to find out what it was like. But I don't think I care about going to school any more, Christmas vacation or no Christmas vacation. There's altogether too many apples and ibexes and snakes and things like that. It makes me dizzy in the head. I hope that you, Teacher, won't be sorry."

But the teacher said she certainly was sorry, most of all because Pippi wouldn't behave decently; and that any girl who acted as badly as Pippi did wouldn't be allowed to go to school even if she wanted to.

"Have I behaved badly?" asked Pippi, much astonished. "Goodness,

I didn't know that," she added and looked very sad. And nobody could look as sad as Pippi when she was sad. She stood silent for a while, and then she said in a trembling voice, "You understand, Teacher, don't you, that when you have a mother who's an angel and a father who is a cannibal king, and when you have sailed on the ocean all your whole life, then you don't know just how to behave in school with all the apples and ibexes."

Then the teacher said she understood and didn't feel annoyed with Pippi any longer, and maybe Pippi could come back to school when she was a little older. Pippi positively beamed with delight. "I think you are awfully nice, Teacher. And here is something for you."

Out of her pocket Pippi took a lovely little gold watch and laid it on the desk. The teacher said she couldn't possibly accept such a valuable gift from Pippi, but Pippi replied, "You've got to take it; otherwise I'll come back again tomorrow, and that would be a pretty how-do-you-do."

Then Pippi rushed out to the schoolyard and jumped on her horse. All the children gathered around to pat the horse and see her off.

> Lazy hands make a man poor, but diligent hands bring wealth.
>
>
>
> PROVERBS 10:4

"You ought to know about the schools in Argentina," said Pippi, looking down at the children. "That's where you should go. Easter vacation begins three days after Christmas vacation ends, and when Easter vacation is over there are three days and then it's summer vacation. Summer vacation ends on the first of November, and then you have a tough time until Christmas vacation begins on November 11. But you can stand that because there are at least no lessons. It is strictly against the law to have lessons in Argentina. Once in a while it happens that some Argentine kid sneaks into a closet and sits there studying a lesson, but it's just too bad for him if his mother finds him. Arithmetic they don't have at all in the schools, and if there is any kid who knows what seven and five are he has to stand in the corner all day — that is, if he's foolish enough to let the teacher know that he knows. They have reading on Friday, and then only if they have some books, which they never have."

"But what do they do in school?" asked one little boy.

"Eat caramels," said Pippi decidedly. "There is a long pipe that goes from a caramel factory nearby directly into the schoolroom, and caramels keep shooting out of it all day long so the children have all they can do to eat them up."

"Yes, but what does the teacher do?" asked one little girl.

"Takes the paper off the caramels for the children, of course," said Pippi. "You didn't suppose they did it themselves, did you? Hardly. They don't even go to school themselves — they send their brothers." Pippi waved her big hat.

"So long, kids," she cried gaily. "Now you won't see me for a while. But always remember how many apples Axel had or you'll be sorry."

With a ringing laugh Pippi rode out through the gate so wildly that the pebbles whirled around the horse's hoofs and the windowpanes rattled in the schoolhouse.

Good behavior at school is essential for everyone to learn their lessons. It's disrespectful to talk back to your teachers or interrupt as Pippi did. When you behave poorly, don't make excuses or blame others; take responsibility for your actions and apologize.

DEAR STUDENTS
from Pope John Paul II

HOLD SCHOOL IN ESTEEM! Return to it joyfully; consider it a great gift, a fundamental right which, of course, also involves duties.

Think of all your contemporaries in many countries of the world who have no education at all. *Illiteracy is a plague, a heavy "handicap,"* which comes in addition to that of hunger and other miseries. With illiteracy, not only is some aspect of the economy and political life at issue, but the *very dignity of the human being*. The right to education is the right to be fully human.

Best wishes, then, dear students!

Chapter Nine

Good Sportsmanship

Good Sportsmanship

Lou Gehrig's Good Example
by Karen Santorum

ONE OF THE GREATEST baseball players who ever lived was Lou Gehrig. He played for the New York Yankees in the 1920s. He was a starting first baseman, and he never missed a game in fourteen years! Until recently, this was the longest record in sports — no misses out of a total of 2,130 games. This streak showed Lou's dedication. Injuries, including broken fingers and even a concussion, did not stop him. For this reason he was called the "Iron Horse." He was tough and extremely talented, playing in seven World Series.

Not even Babe Ruth could hit a baseball as hard as Lou. The opposing team's fielders would always move way back when Lou came up to bat. Despite this, Lou remained humble, never seeking the limelight. He considered himself just another batter on the team. But in 1934, he led the American League with the most home runs, the best batting average, and the most runs batted in. All of Lou's teammates, and even the players on opposing teams, respected Lou because he played like a gentleman.

His colleagues held Lou in high esteem for his good sportsmanship. If he was ever impolite, he would apologize and shake hands with the opposing player. Once, Lou tried to break up a double play by crashing into the player on the other team. The next day, as soon as Lou saw this player, he immediately went up to him, offered to shake hands, and said,

"I'm sorry I went into you so hard yesterday. I shouldn't have done it."

Sadly, in 1939, Lou was diagnosed with a serious life-threatening muscle disease that forced him to permanently retire from baseball. Even though Lou was given only a few years to live, he accepted the news with grace, saying in his retirement speech: "Fans, for the past two weeks, you have been reading about a bad break I got. Yet today, I consider myself the luckiest man on the face of the earth."

Less than two years later, Lou died at the young age of thirty-eight. He was respected by his teammates and loved by the fans not simply for his great talents, but for his kindness and gentleness.

Stan the Man: Baseball's Gentleman
by Michael Lamb

SOMETIMES IF A PLAYER makes a great play on the field, his teammates will yell, "You da man!" From 1941 to 1963, the St. Louis Cardinals had a tremendous baseball player who really was "the man." His name was Stan Musial, but everyone called him Stan the Man.

Stan Musial grew up in the coal-mining town of Donora, Pennsylvania. He learned the value of hard work at an early age. Musial became one of baseball's greatest hitters, winning the National League batting championship seven times and getting 3,630 hits in his career. He was named to the league all-star team twenty-four times and is a member of the Baseball Hall of Fame.

Anger is never without a reason but seldom with a good one.

BENJAMIN FRANKLIN
Poor Richard's Almanac

In 1962, Stan Musial was forty-two years old. Many baseball experts thought that his career was finished. Stan simply ignored the comments of sportswriters who thought he was too old. Musial knew he could still play and he was determined to prove it. During that season, Stan met President John F. Kennedy, who was about the same age. President Kennedy said, "They tell me you're too old to play ball and I'm too young to be president. I have a hunch we'll both fool 'em."

Stan went on to bat .330 that year, a tremendous achievement. He was able to say, "Mr. President, it looks like we're both doing a pretty good job now."

Stan was not called "the Man" because of his outstanding hitting or fielding or even his durability. He was given this name because he was a gentleman. He hustled on every play, always sought to do his best, and he never tried to show up his opponents. He didn't argue with umpires and he respected his coaches and managers. He was a star player, but it never went to his head. He always remained a humble man.

Stan Musial was baseball's shining example of what good sportsmanship is all about. There is a statue of Stan (the Man) Musial outside the baseball stadium in St. Louis. The inscription on it reads, "Here stands baseball's perfect warrior, here stands baseball's perfect knight." That says it all.

Be like Stan the Man. Respect your coaches, teammates, and opponents. Always be humble — don't brag about yourself. Encourage your teammates. Even if someone makes a bad play, respond with "good effort" or "way to hustle."

A SMILE
author unknown

Let others cheer the winning man,
There's one I hold worth while;
'Tis he who does the best he can,
Then loses with a smile.
Beaten he is, but not to stay
Down with the rank and file;
That man will win some other day,
Who loses with a smile.

THE RACE FOR THE SILVER SKATES
from Hans Brinker, or The Silver Skates *by Mary Mapes Dodge*
adapted by Michael Lamb

HOLLAND IS A LOVELY COUNTRY, a land of windmills and tulips. It is also a land of water — clear lakes, beautiful canals, and great dikes that hold back the sea. In winter the canals of Holland's cities freeze over. The lakes too become a glassy sheet of ice. It is then that this country becomes a land of skaters.

There is hardly anyone in Holland who doesn't love skating. The Dutch people will skate to work and skate back home. They skate to the market and skate to church. On weekends, families enjoy skating together on the frozen ponds. The girls skate gracefully and the boys love to race. This is a story about one of those skaters and the race to win the silver skates.

Ah, the silver skates! Now that was a prize. A great race was to be held in honor of the mayor's birthday. A pair of beautiful silver skates would be awarded to the best boy and girl skaters. Children from all over Holland entered the race. Among these young skaters were Hans Brinker and his sister Gretel. Hans Brinker was a solid, well-built boy with honest eyes. Gretel was a pretty young girl with a dancing light in her eyes, and her cheeks looked like a bed of pink and white blossoms when the wind blows. They were graceful and speedy skaters. Hans and his sister both wanted to win the silver skates. All winter they glided along the frozen canals, practicing for the big race. There were other fine young skaters too: Katrinka, Annie, Hilda, Carl Schummel and Peter Van Holp. All of them were busy preparing for the day of the race.

At last the great day arrived. The racing course was blocked off and the children eagerly began to line up for the race. The frozen canals glistened in the bright sunlight. Flags and banners of many colors lined the crowded raceway. All were excited that the race for the silver skates would soon begin. The first to race would be the girls. The bugle sounded and the girls sprang forward, bending in perfect balance. Each flashing stroke seemed longer than the last. There were shouts of cheering as the girls neared the finish. Who would be first? Not Katrinka, nor Annie, nor Hilda, but Gretel — Gretel Brinker, the fastest sprite who ever skated. The town crier lifted his voice to announce the winner, but he could not be heard as the news rang through the crowd. Gretel had won the silver skates!

Hans was very happy for his sister. With natural pride, he turned to see if Peter Van Holp had seen Gretel win the race. Peter was not looking at them at all. He was kneeling, bending his saddened face low and working hurriedly at his skate strap. Hans rushed beside him at once. "Are you in trouble my friend?"

"Ah Hans, yes, my fun is over. I tried to tighten my skate strap and it broke in two."

"My friend," said Hans, at the same time pulling off a skate, "you must use my strap!"

"Not I indeed, Hans Brinker," cried Peter, looking up, "though I thank you warmly. Go to your post, my friend. The bugle will sound in a minute."

"Peter," pleaded Hans, "you have called me your friend. Take this strap quickly! There is not an instant to lose! I shall not skate this time. There will be other races." Hans slipped his strap into Peter's skate. "There," said Hans, "the skate is almost on."

"You are a noble fellow, Hans!" cried Peter. He then sprang to his post just as the bugle sounded.

Peter skated well — so well, in fact, that he won the race and the famous silver skates. But Hans Brinker also won. He won the everlasting friendship of Peter and the respect of the entire town. He was truly a noble fellow and the prize he won was greater than any other.

THE BATTLE OF HECTOR AND AJAX
from The Iliad *by Homer*
adapted by Michael Lamb

THE GREEKS AND THE TROJANS had been fighting for seven years. Many brave men had died on both sides. The two armies were growing very tired of war. Each side prayed for peace. The gods heard their prayers. Apollo, the sun god, favored the Trojans. Athena, the goddess of wisdom, loved the Greeks. The two gods met high above the soft white clouds on Mount Olympus to find a way to end the war.

"The mighty Hector is the bravest of the Trojans," said Apollo. "Have the Greeks find a champion to battle alone with Hector, and let that decide the outcome of this war." Athena agreed with Apollo's plan and sped down from Olympus to give this message to the Greek chieftains. Apollo in turn gave the news to the mighty Hector.

The Greeks could not decide who to choose as their champion. Many of the bravest Greek chieftains wanted to go up against Hector. Finally, the wisest of the Greeks, an old man named Nestor, had an idea. "Let each man write down his name and place it in a jar. I will then ask the help of the gods and pick a name out of the jar. The one whose name is chosen will be our champion."

All the great Greek warriors placed their names in the jar. Nestor then pulled out the name of Ajax, a man of tremendous strength and courage. Ajax was proud to represent his country and battle the Trojan hero. "I fear no force on earth," said Ajax. "Tell Hector to come and have this battle begin so that the war may finally end."

Soon the two great warriors faced each other. Hector's silver armor gleamed in the sunlight. His helmet was crowned with dark brown horsehairs and his shield was brightly polished. Ajax had huge muscles in his arms and shoulders. The helmet of Ajax was made of bronze and was topped with a red plume. He carried a great shield made of six layers of bull's hide and a seventh layer of brass. Ajax looked at Hector and called out, "As I am, I come to prove my might; now let us begin the fight."

Hector then threw his spear. It passed through the shield's six layers of bull's hide, but the layer of brass stopped it. Ajax, with incredible force, hurled his spear at Hector. It shot through Hector's shield, barely missing him. Then, like two fierce mountain lions, they charged each other. Hector was cut on his neck but bravely continued to fight. The ferocious battle continued with javelins and swords until darkness fell and they could fight no more. Neither man had won the contest, but they both had done their best. "Let us stop this battle," said Hector, "that we may happily meet again another day." Both men agreed to end the fight, and each of them gave the other a fine gift. Hector gave Ajax a beautiful silver sword, while Ajax presented Hector with a golden buckle filled with a large purple jewel. So it was that Hector said, "Ajax and Hector have met in battle but not in hate; and each brave foe left in his soul a friend." Thus, the two great warriors who had battled so fiercely left as friends.

When you compete, try hard and do your best. Respect your opponent and play fair. When the contest is over, shake your opponent's hand and congratulate him for his effort. You may enter the battle as foes, but you should try to leave as friends.

THE MAN WHO WAS BRAVE ENOUGH NOT TO FIGHT
by Michael Lamb

THERE ARE MANY STORIES written about great heroes and heroines who fight and defeat an evil enemy. Sometimes, though, the bravest person is the one who has the courage *not* to fight. Jackie Robinson was a fighter. He grew up amid the rough street gangs of Pasadena, California. Robinson used his great athletic skills to earn a college scholarship to U.C.L.A., where he would star in football, basketball, track, and baseball. Jackie Robinson was a fierce competitor who always gave his best. People who saw him compete knew they were watching one of America's finest young athletes. He would achieve great things in the world of sports. He was the first black man to play major league baseball. This was a task that required him to be brave enough not to fight.

In 1947, Branch Rickey was the general manager of the Brooklyn Dodgers baseball team. In those days blacks were not allowed to play baseball in the major leagues. It didn't matter how good the black players were, major league baseball was strictly a white man's game. Branch Rickey believed this was unfair. If America was truly "the land of the free," then Rickey believed that all Americans, no matter what color their skin, should get a fair chance. Branch Rickey decided he was going to change things. He planned to have a black man play for his baseball team. Branch Rickey knew that this man would have to be more than just a great ballplayer. He would also need to be a man who was strong enough to take all the meanness and racial insults that would come his way. He needed a man who would be both a baseball star and a gentleman. He thought Jackie Robinson was the right man, but he had to be sure.

Jackie Robinson was called. The general manager told Jackie that he knew he was good enough to play for the Dodgers. But did Robinson have the courage not to fight back, if he was insulted or spat upon, or if a pitcher threw a ball at his head? He asked Robinson to promise not to fight back. He told him that especially during his first two years on the team, Robinson needed to set an example. He couldn't fight hate with hate, or trade insult for insult. Jackie Robinson looked calmly at Rickey and told him that he was strong enough not to fight back. He told him that he could keep that promise. Rickey knew he had picked the right man.

No one in the history of sports faced the kind of challenge that Jackie Robinson did. Six players on the Dodgers threatened to quit if Robinson played. Players from opposing teams and their fans called him awful names. When he stepped up to bat some pitchers would deliberately throw the ball at his head. Runners would try to stick their spikes in his ankles. He received letters filled with hatred and racial insults, and some people and groups even threatened to kill Robinson. Deep inside, Jackie Robinson was hurt and angry. But he suffered it all silently. He kept his promise. He was brave enough not to fight.

In 1947, Jackie Robinson of the Brooklyn Dodgers won the National League Rookie of the Year Award. Although he had been treated in the worst way, he acted in the best way. He was a gentleman who rose above the people who tried to degrade him. Jackie Robinson's self-control and silent courage opened the door to countless other black athletes who would play professional sports. There are times for fighting and times for enduring. Jackie Robinson endured and so has his legacy.

When people taunt you, the natural response is to treat them poorly in return. But people who have good manners don't insult others, even when they are insulted. Jackie Robinson's story shows what can be accomplished when we are brave enough not to fight and strong enough to control our tongue and our temper.

GALLANT IN DEFEAT, GRACIOUS IN VICTORY: THE SURRENDER OF ROBERT E. LEE
by Michael Lamb

IT WAS PALM SUNDAY AFTERNOON, April 9, 1865. General Robert E. Lee knew that the situation was hopeless. The commander of the Confederate Army of Northern Virginia had decided to surrender. It was a difficult decision, but Lee was certain it was the right one.

Lee saddled up his horse, Traveler, and slowly rode out between the lines of his army to meet the Union general, Ulysses S. Grant. Some of the gray-clothed rebel soldiers cheered as he passed; others simply bowed their heads. He slowly passed through the Union lines, dismounted, and walked up the steps of the McLean house where he would meet General Grant.

Grant arrived shortly. The two men were introduced. Grant thought about how difficult it must be for Lee to surrender after fighting so bravely for so long. "I met you once before, General Lee," he said, "when we were serving in Mexico. I have always remembered your appearance and I think I should have recognized you anywhere."

"Yes, I know I met you on that occasion" replied Lee.

The two men talked a little longer and then Lee said, "I suppose, General Grant, that the object of our meeting is fully understood, to determine upon what terms you would receive the surrender of my army."

The two men then discussed the surrender terms. General Grant was as kind and generous as he could possibly be to the rebel commander.

Lee was willing to accept all of Grant's conditions and had only one main concern: as politely as possible he asked the Union commander if his men would be permitted to retain their horses. This was very important because without their horses these southern soldiers would be unable to properly tend to their farms. Grant graciously replied that he would allow all the men to take their animals home with them. "This will have a very happy effect upon my army," replied Lee.

The two generals then signed the surrender document. Lee shook hands with Grant and went outside to mount his horse. Grant also went outside. He and his men respectfully removed their hats for the opposing general. From atop his horse, Traveler, Lee looked back at Grant and silently raised his hat in a final salute. He then began the slow ride back to his troops. As his men gathered around him, many had tears in their eyes, as did Lee. "You will all be paroled and go to your homes," he said.

> Do not repay evil with evil or insult with insult, but with blessing.
>
> ❧
>
> 1 PETER 3:9

The great general then said his final goodbye to his courageous army. The surrender had been fair, the terms acceptable. The two men in the best gentlemanly fashion had just ended one of history's bloodiest wars.

Although his troops had won the war, Grant didn't gloat over his victory. He was fair and kind to the defeated rebel army. And Robert E. Lee was gallant even in defeat. Lee's main concern was for his men, their families, and their farms. Both men respected each other. Winners and losers should try to act as Robert E. Lee and Ulysses S. Grant did on that fateful day.

ABE LINCOLN, CHAMPION WRESTLER
from Abraham Lincoln *by Carl Sandburg*
adapted by Michael Lamb

EVERYONE KNOWS that Abe Lincoln was the sixteenth president of the United States. Most everyone knows that he freed the slaves and preserved the union. But hardly anyone knows that "Honest Abe" was one very tough wrestler. As a matter of fact, he could be called a champion wrestler. Here's how it all happened.

In the summer of 1831 Abe Lincoln was living in the small town of New Salem, Illinois. He worked in Denton Offut's country store stacking shelves and waiting on customers. Lincoln was a hard worker who was reliable and honest. "Best darn worker I've ever had," said Offut. Denton was always bragging about Lincoln. Abe was six-foot-four and weighed 185 pounds. He was a big man who, according to Offut, was the best wrestler in the whole state of Illinois.

A fellow from a neighboring town came into the store one day, claiming that his friend, Jack Armstrong, was the area's champion wrestler. He bet Offut ten dollars that Lincoln couldn't throw Armstrong down. Denton Offut took that bet and spread the word that the wrestling match would be held in a few days, right next to his country store.

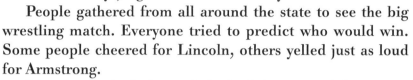

People gathered from all around the state to see the big wrestling match. Everyone tried to predict who would win. Some people cheered for Lincoln, others yelled just as loud for Armstrong.

Lincoln stood calmly, ready for Jack Armstrong's first move. Armstrong was shorter but heavier and more muscular than Abe. He tried to charge in low and grab Lincoln's legs. Abe used his long arms to hold Armstrong back. Jack kept trying to pounce on Lincoln, but was not succeeding in doing anything but tiring himself out.

They continued to grab, pull, and clutch at each other for nearly an hour. Lincoln was still pretty fresh, but Armstrong was wearing down. Suddenly, Abe twisted Armstrong into his favorite hold and threw him down. In a few seconds Abe Lincoln had his opponent's shoulders pinned to the ground. The match was over — or was it? Some of Jack's friends threatened Lincoln. Armstrong quickly got up and pushed his friends back, saying that Lincoln had "fought fair" and that Abe was "the best feller that ever broke into this settlement." He then gave Lincoln a firm handshake. The two men became close friends and would remain so for the rest of their lives.

Many years later, when President Abraham Lincoln had led the Northern states to victory over the South during the bloody Civil War, he tried to act as friendly as possible to the defeated Southern states. This was his purpose when he said, "with malice toward none; with charity for all." It was a lesson he had learned many years earlier.

Good sportsmanship is important in all areas of life. Lincoln learned that you can befriend your foes if there is mutual respect. This is why he could treat the Southern states in a kind-hearted way after the Civil War, something that many Northerners had trouble accepting. That's what made Abraham Lincoln a great champion and leader.

CHAPTER TEN

Writing Letters and Invitations

1.
Letters

HOW THE FIRST LETTER WAS WRITTEN
from Just So Stories *by Rudyard Kipling*
adapted by Karen Santorum

ONCE UPON a time, there was a primitive, Neolithic man who lived in a Cave. He wore very few clothes. He couldn't read or write, but he didn't want to. And except when he was hungry, he was quite happy. His name was Tegumai, which means, "Man-who-does-not-put-his-foot-forward-in-a-hurry." And his wife's name was Teshumai, which means, "Lady-who-asks-too-many-questions." And his little girl's name was Taffimai, which means, "Small-person-without-any-manners-who-ought-to-be-spanked." But I'm going to call her Taffy.

One day Tegumai and Taffy went down to the river to spear fish. Tegumai's spear was made of wood, and before he had caught any fish he broke it by jabbing it down too hard on the bottom of the river. They were miles from home and Tegumai had forgotten to bring any extra spears. "Here's a fine kettle of fish!" said Tegumai. "It will take me half the day to mend this."

"There's your big black spear at home," said Taffy. "Let me run back to the Cave and ask Mummy to give it me."

"It's too far for your chubby little legs," said Tegumai. "We must make the best of a bad job." He sat down and took out a little leather mending-bag and began to mend the spear.

"I say, Daddy," said Taffy, "it's awful that you and I don't know how to write, isn't it? If we did we could send a message for a new spear."

Just then a Stranger-man came along the river, but he belonged to a far tribe, and he did not understand one word of Tegumai's language. He stood on the bank and smiled at Taffy. Tegumai began mending his spear.

"Come here," said Taffy, "Do you know where my Mummy lives?"

319

The Stranger-man said, "Um!"

"Silly!" said Taffy, and she stamped her foot, because she saw a shoal of very big carp going up the river just when her Daddy couldn't use his spear.

"Don't bother grown-ups," said Tegumai, so busy with his spear-mending that he did not turn around.

The Stranger-man thought, "This is a very wonderful child. She stamps her foot at me and she makes faces. She must be the daughter of the noble Chief who is so great that he won't take any notice of me." So he smiled more politely than ever.

"Now," said Taffy, "I want you to go to my Mummy and ask for Daddy's spear."

The Stranger-man thought, "This is a very, very wonderful child. She waves her arms and she shouts at me, but I don't understand a word of what she says. But if I don't do what she wants, I greatly fear that that haughty Chief will be angry." He got up and twisted a big flat piece of bark off a birch tree and gave it to Taffy. He did this to show that he meant no harm.

"Oh!" said she. "Now I see! You want my Mummy's address? Of course, I can't write, but I can draw pictures if I've anything sharp to scratch with. Please lend me the shark's tooth off your necklace," and she put up her little hand and pulled at the beautiful bead and seed and shark-tooth necklace round his neck.

He immediately gave Taffy the shark's tooth, and she lay down flat on her tummy and said, "Now I'll draw you some beautiful pictures! First I'll draw Daddy fishing. It isn't very like him; but Mummy will know, because I've drawn his spear all broken. Well, now I'll draw the other spear that he wants. It looks as if it was sticking in Daddy's back, but that's because this piece of bark isn't big enough. That's the spear I want you to fetch; so I'll draw a picture of me 'splaining to you. My hair doesn't stand up like I've drawn, but it's easier to draw that way."

The Stranger-man smiled. He thought, "There must be a big battle that's going to be fought, and this extraordinary child is telling me to call all the great Chief's tribe to help him. He *is* a great Chief, or he would have noticed me."

"Look," said Taffy, drawing very hard, "now I've drawn you, and I've put the spear that Daddy wants into your hand, just to remind you that you're to bring it."

When she finished, the Stranger-man looked at the picture and nodded very hard. He said to himself, "If I do not fetch this great Chief's tribe to help him, he will be slain. I will run and get help for him." He raced into the bushes, with the birch-bark in his hand.

The Stranger-man hurried away with the picture and ran for several miles, till quite by accident he found Teshumai at the door of her Cave talking to some other Neolithic ladies. Taffy looked just like Teshumai, so the Stranger-man smiled politely and handed Teshumai the birch-bark. As soon as Teshumai saw the picture she screamed and flew at the Stranger-man. The other Neolithic ladies at once knocked him down and sat on him. "It's as plain as the nose on this Stranger-man's face," she said. "He has stuck my Tegumai all full of spears, and frightened poor Taffy so that her hair stands all on end; and not content with that, he brings me a horrid picture of how it was done. Look!"

"Most shocking!" said the Neolithic ladies, and they filled the Stranger-man's hair with mud and they beat upon the Tribal Drums and called together all chiefs of the Tribe of Tegumai. Then off they went to find Tegumai.

When they saw him alive, the Head Chief of the Tribe took Tegumai by the topknot feathers and shook him severely. "Explain! Explain! Explain!" he cried.

"Goodness' sakes alive!" said Tegumai. "Let go of my topknot. Can't a man break his carp-spear without the whole countryside descending on him?"

"I don't believe you've brought my Daddy's spear after all," said Taffy. "And what *are* you doing to my nice Stranger-man?" They were thumping him till his eyes turned round and round. He could only gasp and point at Taffy.

"Where are the bad people who speared you, my darling?" said Teshumai.

"There weren't any," said Tegumai. "My only visitor this morning was the poor fellow that you are trying to choke."

"He came with a horrible picture," said the Head Chief. "A picture that showed you were full of spears."

"Errr — umm, I'd better 'splain that I gave him that picture," said Taffy.

"You!" said the Tribe of Tegumai all together. "Small-person-without-any-manners-who-ought-to-be-spanked! You?"

"Taffy dear, I'm afraid we're in for a little trouble," said her Daddy.

She explained what she drew and for a long time nobody said anything, till the Head Chief laughed; then the Stranger-man laughed; then Tegumai laughed; then all the Tribe laughed more and louder. The only people who did not laugh were Teshumai and all the Neolithic ladies.

Then the Head Chief of the Tribe of Tegumai cried and sang, "Oh Small-person-without-any-manners-who-ought-to-be-spanked, you've hit upon a great invention! Some day men will call it writing. At present it is only pictures, and, as we have seen today, pictures are not always properly understood. But a time will come when we shall make letters — twenty-six of 'em — and we shall be able to read as well as to write, and then we shall say exactly what we mean without any mistakes."

But from that very day to this (and I suppose it is all Taffy's fault), very few children have ever liked learning to read or write. Most of them prefer to draw pictures and play about with their daddies — just like Taffy.

Letter-writing allows us to communicate joy, love, news, and ideas to people we care about. There are many reasons for writing — to say "thank you," to say "I'm thinking of you," to wish a sick friend a speedy recovery, to offer congratulations, to wish someone happy birthday, and so much more. Even if you can't write yet, you can send letters full of pictures that will one day grow into words.

Write Right!
by Gelette Burgess

If you were writing with your nose,
You'd *have* to curl up, I suppose,
And lay your head upon your hand;
But now, I cannot understand,
For you are writing with your pen!
So sit erect, and smile again!
You need not scowl because you write,
Nor hold your fingers *quite* so tight!
And if you gnaw the holder so,
They'll take you for
a Goop, you know!

When writing letters, use your best handwriting, good grammar and spelling, and keep the paper neat and clean. This sends the message that you care enough about the person to whom you are writing to take the time to send a thoughtfully written letter.

How to Write a Letter
by Elizabeth Turner

Maria intended a letter to write,
But could not begin (as she thought) to indite;
So went to her mother with pencil and slate,
Containing "Dear Sister," and also a date.

"With nothing to say, my dear girl, do not think
Of wasting your time over paper and ink;
But certainly this is an excellent way,
To try with your slate to find something to say."

"I will give you a rule," said her mother, "my dear;
Just think for a moment your sister is here,
And what would you tell her? Consider, and then,
Though silent your tongue, you can speak with your Pen."

Thomas Jefferson Writes to a Little Boy

Thomas Jefferson, the third president of the United States, was known as a "man of letters." He read widely and was an excellent writer. He made use of his intelligence and writing skill when he drafted our Declaration of Independence, one of history's most famous documents. He also wrote many letters dealing with a variety of subjects, for Jefferson knew something about nearly everything.

This letter was written by Jefferson to a small boy who had been named after him. The boy was the son of Jefferson's friend, Samuel Smith.

Monticello, February 21, 1825

To Thomas Jefferson Smith:

THIS LETTER will, to you, be as one from the dead. The writer will be in the grave before you can weigh its counsels. Your affectionate and excellent father has requested that I address to you something which might possibly have a favorable influence on the course of life you have to run, and I too, as a namesake, feel an interest in that course. Few words will be necessary, with good dispositions on your part. Adore God. Reverence and cherish your parents. Love your neighbor as yourself. Be just. Be true. Murmur not at the ways of Providence. So shall the life into which you have entered, be the portal to one of eternal and ineffable bliss. And if to the dead it is permitted to care for the things of this world, every action of your life will be under my regard.

Farewell.

You can try to write a letter yourself, following the pattern of this one. Include the date, a greeting, your message, and your signature.

When you were very young, did your parents take some of your notes and put them on the refrigerator? Your letters are your own creation and mean a lot to the people who receive them. A letter enables you to put your innermost thoughts on paper, which can be saved and read over and over again.

The following letter is a good example of how our writing can leave people with a gift to cherish. A husband wrote it to his wife during the Civil War.

SULLIVAN BALLOU'S LETTER

July 14, 1861
Camp Clark, Washington

My Very Dear Sarah,

THE INDICATIONS are very strong that we should move in a few days — perhaps tomorrow. Lest I should not be able to write again, I feel impelled to write a few lines that may fall under your eye when I am no more. . . .

I have no misgivings about or lack of confidence in the cause in which I am engaged, and my courage does not halt or falter. I know how American Civilization now leans upon the triumph of the Government, and how great a debt we owe to those who went before us through the blood and suffering of the Revolution. And I am perfectly willing — to lay down all my joys in this life, to help maintain this government and to pay that debt. . . .

Sarah, my love for you is deathless; it seems to bind me with mighty cables that nothing but Omnipotence could break; and yet my love of country comes over me like a strong wind and bears me unresistibly on with all those chains to the battlefield.

The memories of the blissful moments I have spent with you come creeping over me, and I feel most gratified to God and to you that I've enjoyed them for so long. And how hard it is for me to give them up and burn to ashes the hopes of future years, when, God willing, we may have still lived and loved together, and see our boys grown up to honorable manhood, around us. I have, I know, but few and small claims upon Divine Providence, but something whispers to me — perhaps it is the wafted prayer of my little Edgar, that I shall return to my loved ones unharmed. If I do not, my dear Sarah, never forget how much I loved you, and when my last breath escapes me on the battlefield, it will whisper your name.

Forgive my many faults, and the many pains I have caused you. How thoughtless, how foolish I have often times been. How gladly I would wash out with my tears every little spot upon your happiness. . . . But Oh Sarah! If the dead can come back to this earth and flit unseen around those they loved, I shall always be near you; in the gladdest days and the darkest nights. . . . *Always — Always,* and if there be a soft breeze upon your cheek, it shall be my breath, as the cool air fans your throbbing temple, it shall be my spirit passing by. Sarah do not mourn me dead; think I am gone and wait for thee, for we shall meet again. . . .

Yours Affectionately,
Sullivan

Sullivan Ballou was killed one week later, in the battle of Bull Run.

PRESIDENT LINCOLN'S LETTER TO MRS. BIXBY
from Abraham Lincoln *by Carl Sandburg*

To LINCOLN'S DESK in September had come a request from Massachusetts Governor Andrew on behalf of a widow living at 15 Dover Street, Boston. She had sent her five sons into the Union armies and all had been killed in action, according to the information he had received from his state adjutant general, William Schoulder.

On request of the War Department, Schoulder made an investigation and officially certified the names, regiments, and dates of deaths of Mrs. Bixby's five sons. This document came to Lincoln in mid-October. He could have then written a letter to Mrs. Bixby and made it public for campaign purposes. Instead, he waited. As on occasion with certain speeches or letters, he probably wrote a first draft of the letter and later changed the phrasing. On November 21 he dated the letter and sent it through the War Department to Schoulder. He addressed it "Mrs. Bixby, Boston, Massachusetts." Her first name, Lydia, and her address in Boston, were not given. Schoulder received the letter in an envelope addressed to himself and copied it. On Thanksgiving Day the Adjutant General took a holiday dinner and a present of money raised among good people of Boston and delivered them at 15 Dover Street to Mrs. Bixby, along with Lincoln's letter to her.

> I have been shown in the files of the War Department a statement of the Adjutant General of Massachusetts, that you are the mother of five sons who have died gloriously on the field of battle.
>
> I feel how weak and fruitless must be any words of mine which should attempt to beguile you from the grief of a loss so overwhelming. But I cannot refrain from tendering to you the consolation that may be found in the thanks of the Republic they died to save.
>
> I pray that our Heavenly Father may assuage the anguish of your bereavement, and leave you only the cherished memory of the loved and lost, and the solemn pride that must be yours, to have laid so costly a sacrifice upon the altar of Freedom.
>
> Yours, very sincerely and respectfully,
> A Lincoln.

Later research revealed that, of the five Bixby boys, Charles died in action at Fredericksburg, and Oliver met death at Petersburg. Henry was reported killed at Gettysburg, but had actually been taken prisoner, and was later exchanged and returned to his mother in good health. George, too, was taken prisoner, secured his release by enlisting as a Confederate soldier, and was on record as having "deserted to the enemy." Edward Bixby became homesick and had periods of insanity. The order for his discharge was issued, but the worried boy had already deserted the Army and gone to sea as a sailor.

Despite this, President Lincoln's letter was an important gesture to Mrs. Bixby. When someone is in pain, it is good to let her know you care by writing a brief note.

THOMAS JEFFERSON'S LETTER
TO PETER CARR

Paris, August 19, 1785

Dear Peter,

I RECEIVED, by Mr. Mazzei, your letter of April the 20th. I am much mortified to hear that you have lost so much time; and that, when you arrived in Williamsburg, you were not at all advanced from where you were when you left Monticello. Time now begins to be precious to you. Every day you lose will retard a day your entrance on that public stage whereon you may begin to be useful to yourself. However, the way to repair the loss is to improve the future time. I trust, that with your dispositions, even the acquisition of science is a pleasing employment. I can assure you, that the possession of it is, what (next to an honest heart) will above all things render you dear to your friends, and give you fame and promotion in your own country.

When your mind shall be well improved with science, nothing will be necessary to take you in the highest points of view, but to pursue the interests of your country, the interests of your friends, and your own interests also, with the purest integrity, the most chaste honor. The defect of these virtues can never be made up by all the other acquirements of body and mind. Make these, then, your first object.

Give up money, give up fame, give up science, give the earth itself and all it contains, rather than do an immoral act. And never suppose, that in any possible situation, or under any circumstances, it is best for you to do a dishonorable thing, however slightly so it may appear to you. Whenever you are to do a thing, though it can never be known but to yourself, ask yourself how you would act were all the world looking at you, and act accordingly. Encourage all your virtuous dispositions, and exercise them whenever an opportunity arises; being assured that they will gain strength by exercise, as a limb of the body does, and that exercise will make them habitual. From the practice of the purest virtue, you may be assured you will derive the most sublime comforts in every moment of life, and in the moment of death.

If ever you find yourself environed with difficulties and perplexing circumstances, out of which you are at a loss how to extricate yourself, do what is right, and be assured that that will extricate you the best out of the worst situations. Though you cannot see, when you take one step, what will be the next, yet follows truth, justice, and plain dealing, and never fear their leading you out of the labyrinth, in the easiest manner possible. The knot which you thought a Gordian one, will untie itself before you.

Nothing is so mistaken as the supposition, that a person is to extricate himself from a difficulty, by intrigue, by an injustice. This increases the difficulties tenfold; and those, who pursue these methods, get themselves so involved at length, that they can turn no way but their infamy becomes more exposed. It is of great importance to set a resolution, not to be shaken, never to tell an untruth. There is no vice so mean, so pitiful, so contemptible; and he who permits himself to tell a lie once, finds it much easier to do it a second and third time, till at length it becomes habitual; he tells lies without attending to it, and truths without the world's believing him. This falsehood of the tongue leads to that of the heart, and in time depraves all of its good dispositions.

> The first Degree of Folly is to conceit one's self wise; the second to profess it; the third to despise counsel.
>
>
>
> BENJAMIN FRANKLIN
> *Poor Richard's Almanac*

Thomas Jefferson wrote to Peter as if he were speaking with him. Writing in this way will give your letters a personal touch.

2.
Invitations

ALICE'S DINNER PARTY
from Through the Looking Glass *by Lewis Carroll*
adapted by Michael Lamb

ALICE HAD BEEN MADE A QUEEN. What's more, she was now sitting directly between the Red Queen and the White Queen. As they looked at each other, there was an uncomfortable silence for a minute or two.

The Red Queen broke the silence by saying to the White Queen, "I invite you to Alice's dinner party this afternoon." The White Queen smiled feebly and said, "And I invite you."

"I didn't know I was to have a party at all," said Alice; "but if there is to be one, I think I ought to invite the guests." "We gave you the opportunity of doing it," the Red Queen remarked: "but I daresay you've not had many lessons in manners yet?"

I think we must agree with Alice here: the person who has the party should do the inviting! The Red Queen and the White Queen are the ones who need lessons in manners, not Alice.

Invitations should include everything the invited guests will need to know, such as for whom the party is being held, the date and time, the place, who is giving the party, and any other necessary information. If the invitation says "R.S.V.P.," that means you should send your reply, or call the phone number listed, to let the host know whether you'll be able to attend. It is polite to respond in a timely way, so that the person giving the party knows how many guests to prepare for.

Christopher Robin Gives Pooh a Party, and We Say Good-bye
from Winnie the Pooh *by A. A. Milne*

ONE DAY when the sun had come back over the Forest, bringing with it the scent of May, and all the streams of the Forest were tinkling happily to find themselves their own pretty shape again, and the little pools lay dreaming of the life they had seen and the big things they had done, and in the warmth and quiet of the Forest the cuckoo was trying over his voice carefully and listening to see if he liked it, and woodpigeons were complaining gently to themselves in their lazy comfortable way that it was the other fellow's fault, but it didn't matter very much; on such a day as this Christopher Robin whistled in a special way he had, and Owl came flying out the Hundred Acre Wood to see what was wanted.

"Owl," said Christopher Robin, "I am going to give a party."

"You are, are you?" said Owl.

"And it's to be a special sort of party, because it's because of what Pooh did when he did what he did to save Piglet from the flood.

"Oh, that's what it's for, is it," said Owl.

"Yes, so will you tell Pooh as quickly as you can, and all the others, because it will be tomorrow."

"So will you go and tell them, Owl?"

Owl tried to think of something very wise to say, but couldn't, so he flew off to tell the others. And the first person he told was Pooh.

"Pooh," he said, "Christopher Robin is giving a party."

"Oh!" said Pooh. And then seeing that Owl expected him to say something else, he said, "Will there be those little cake things with pink sugar icing?"

Owl felt that it was rather beneath him to talk about little cake things with pink sugar icing, so he told Pooh exactly what Christopher Robin had said, and flew off to Eeyore.

"A party for Me?" thought Pooh to himself. "How grand!" And he began to wonder if all the other animals would know that it was a special Pooh Party, and if Christopher Robin had told them about *The Floating*

Bear and the *Brain of Pooh* and all the wonderful ships he had invented and sailed on, and he began to think how awful it would be if everybody had forgotten about it, and nobody quite knew what the party was for; and the more he thought like this, the more the party got muddled in his mind, like a dream when nothing goes right. And the dream began to sing itself over in his head until it became a sort of song. It was an

Anxious Pooh Song.

3 Cheers for Pooh!
(For Who?)
For Pooh —
(Why what did he do?)
I thought you knew;
He saved his friend from a wetting!
3 Cheers for Bear!
(For where?)
For Bear —
He couldn't swim,
But he rescued him!
(He rescued who?)
Oh, listen, do!
I am talking of Pooh —
(Of who?)
Of Pooh!
(I'm sorry I keep forgetting)
Well, Pooh was a Bear of Enormous Brain
(Just say it again!)
Of Enormous brain —
(Of enormous what?)
Well, he ate a lot,
And I don't know if he could swim or not,
But he managed to float
On a sort of boat
(On a sort of what?)
Well, a sort of pot —
So now let's give him three hearty cheers
(So now let's give him three hearty whiches?)
And hope he'll be with us for years and years,
And grow in health and wisdom and riches!

3 Cheers for Pooh!
(For who?)
For Pooh —
3 Cheers for Bear!
(For where?)
For Bear —
3 Cheers for the Wonderful Winnie-the-Pooh!
(Just tell me, Somebody — WHAT DID HE DO?)

While this was going on inside him, Owl was talking to Eeyore.

"Eeyore," said Owl, "Christopher Robin is giving a party."

"Very interesting," said Eeyore. "I suppose they will be sending me down the odd bits which got trodden on. Kind and Thoughtful. Not at all, don't mention it."

"There is an Invitation for you."

"What's that like?"

"An Invitation!"

"Yes, I heard you. Who dropped it?"

"This isn't anything to eat, it's asking you to the party. Tomorrow."

Eeyore shook his head slowly.

"You mean Piglet. The little fellow with the excited ears. That's Piglet. I'll tell him."

"No, no!" said Owl, getting quite fussy. "It's you!"

"Are you sure!"

"Of course I'm sure. Christopher Robin said 'All of them! Tell all of them.'"

"All of them," said Owl sulkily.

"Ah!" said Eeyore. "A mistake, no doubt, but still, I shall come. Only don't blame me if it rains."

But it didn't rain. Christopher Robin had made a long table out of some long pieces of wood, and they all sat around it. Christopher Robin sat at one end, and Pooh sat at the other, and between them on one side were Owl and Eeyore and Piglet, and between them on the other side were Rabbit and Roo and Kanga. And all Rabbit's fields-and-relations spread themselves about on the grass, and waited hopefully in case anybody spoke to them, or dropped anything, or asked them the time.

It was the first party to which Roo had ever been, and he was very excited. As soon as they had sat down he began to talk.

"Hallo, Pooh!" he squeaked.

"Hallo, Roo!" said Pooh.

Roo jumped up and down in his seat for a little while and then began again.

"Hallo, Piglet!" he squeaked.

Piglet waved a paw at him, being too busy to say anything.

"Hallo, Eeyore!" said Roo.

Eeyore nodded gloomily at him. "It will rain soon, you see if it doesn't," he said.

Roo looked to see if it didn't, and it didn't, so he said "Hallow, Owl!" — and Owl said "Hallo, my little fellow, in a kindly way, and went on telling Christopher Robin about an accident which had nearly happened to a friend of his whom Christopher Robin didn't know, and Kanga said to Roo, "Drink up your milk first, dear, and talk afterwards." So Roo, who was drinking his milk, tried to say that he could do both at once . . . and had to be patted on the back and dried for quite a long time afterwards.

When they had all nearly eaten enough, Christopher Robin banged on the table with his spoon, and everybody stopped talking and was very silent, except Roo who was just finishing a loud attack of hiccups and trying to look as if it was one of Rabbit's relations.

"This party," said Christopher Robin, "is a party because of what someone did, and we all know who it was, and it's his party, because of what he did, and I've got a present for him and here it is." Then he felt about a little and whispered, "Where is it?"

While he was looking, Eeyore coughed in an impressive way and began to speak.

"Friends," he said, "including oddments, it is a great pleasure, or perhaps I had better say it has been a pleasure so far, to see you at my party. What I did was nothing. Any of you — except Rabbit and Owl and Kanga — would have done the same. Oh, and Pooh. My remarks do not, of course, apply to Piglet and Roo, because they are too small. Any of you would have done the same. But it just happened to be Me. It was not, I need hardly say, with an idea of getting what Christopher Robin is looking for now" — and he put his front leg to his mouth and said in a loud whisper, "Try under the table" — "that I did what I did — but because I feel that we should all do what we can to help. I feel that we should all —"

"H-hup!" said Roo accidentally.

"Roo, dear!" said Kanga reproachfully.

"Was it me?" asked Roo, a little surprised.

"What's Eeyore talking about?" Piglet whispered to Pooh.

"I don't know," said Pooh rather dolefully.

"I thought this was *your* party."

"I thought it was *once*. But I suppose it isn't."

"I'd sooner it was yours than Eeyore's," said Piglet.

"So would I," said Pooh.

"H-hup!" said Roo again.

"AS — I — WAS — SAYING," said Eeyore loudly and sternly, "as I was saying when I was interrupted by various Loud Sounds, I feel that — "

"Here it is!" cried Christopher Robin excitedly. "Pass it down to silly old Pooh. It's for Pooh."

"For Pooh?" said Eeyore.

"Of course it is. The best bear in all the world."

"I might have known," said Eeyore. "After all, one can't complain. I have my friends. Somebody spoke to me only yesterday. And was it last week or the week before that Rabbit bumped into me and said 'Brother!' The Social Round. Always something going on."

Nobody was listening, for they were all saying "Open it, Pooh," "What is it, Pooh?" "I know what it is," "No, you don't," and other helpful remarks of this sort. And of course Pooh was opening it as quickly as ever he could, but without cutting the string, because you never know when a bit of string might be Useful. At last it was undone.

When Pooh saw what it was, he nearly fell down, he was so pleased. It was a Special Pencil Case. There were pencils in it marked "B" for Bear, and pencils marked 'HB" for Helping Bear, and pencils marked "BB" for Brave Bear. There was a knife for sharpening the pencils, and india-rubber for rubbing out anything which you had spelt wrong, and a ruler for ruling lines for the words to walk on, and inches marked on the ruler in case you wanted to know how many inches anything was, and Blue Pencils and Red Pencils and Green Pencils for saying special things in blue and red and green. And all these lovely things were in little pockets of their own in a Special Case which shut with a click when you clicked it. And they were all for Pooh.

"Oh!" said Pooh.

"Oh, Pooh!" said everybody else except Eeyore.

"Thank-you," growled Pooh.

But Eeyore was saying to himself, "This writing business. Pencils and what-not. Over-rated, if you ask me. Silly stuff. Nothing in it."

Later on, when they had all said "Good-bye" and "Thank-you" to Christopher Robin, Pooh and Piglet walked home thoughtfully together in the golden evening, and for a long time they were silent.

"When you wake up in the morning, Pooh," said Piglet at last, "what's the first thing you say to yourself?"

"What's for breakfast?" said Pooh. "What do you say, Piglet?'

"I say, I wonder what's going to happen exciting today?" said Piglet.

Pooh nodded thoughtfully.

"It's the same thing," he said.

As we said earlier, a good invitation will provide the invited guests with all the information they need for the party, in order to prevent misunderstandings. In this case, Eeyore mistakenly believed the party was for him!

One more thing: when you are sending out invitations, either mail them or place them in people's mailboxes. Don't hand them out in school unless everyone is invited. This will prevent any hurt feelings.

CHAPTER ELEVEN

Church, Weddings, and Funerals

1.
Church

HOW TO ORDER THYSELF IN CHURCH
by Francis Seager
adapted by Karen Santorum

When you go to church you shall repair,
Kneeling or standing, to God say your prayer,
All things of your mind please set apart,
Earnestly praying, to God lift up your heart.

A contrite heart He will not despise,
Which He does count a sweet sacrifice.
Tell Him your sins, show and confess,
Asking for them grace and forgiveness.

He is the physician who knows your painful sore,
He will heal you and lovingly your soul restore.
Ask then in faith, not doubting to have;
The things you desire, you shall from Him receive.

If they be lawful of God to require,
He will hear you and grant your desire,
More merciful He is than a pen can express,
The author and giver here of all goodness.

"All you that labor and burdened be,
I will refresh you in coming in love to Me."
These are Christ's words, the Scripture is plain,
Spoken to all of you who suffer pain.

Our wills to His word then let us frame,
The heavenly home where we hope to live and claim.
When you come to church remember to be good,
Sit quietly, don't fidget, and act as you should.

While you're there don't talk of any matter,
Don't play with another or whisper or chatter.
Be prayerful yourself in an orderly way,
When visiting church you're there to pray.

Each thing has its time, consider the place,
For that is a token of virtue and grace.
The Lord does call it the house of prayer,
And it's not to be used as is the fair.

A church is a place where people go to worship God. People assemble for a holy service to give thanks and offer prayers to Him. During this time of devotion, sit quietly in a reverent manner. Try not to allow your thoughts to wander; instead, direct them toward God. Pray to Him from your heart — talk to Him as a friend — and tell Him that you love Him. When people sing a song, try to join in. If you do not know the words, just smile and hum — your voice will be pleasing to God.

NOT TO WALK IN CHURCH
by Richard West
adapted by Karen Santorum

Please sit quietly in church, and don't walk about,
For it is most unsightly, without any doubt.
It's fit at a fair, or in some busy town,
But not in God's house so don't walk up and down.

We go to church to hear sermons, orations,
And we say prayers for the soul's recreations.
We're not in a playhouse or ship on the sea,
Despising the reverence to God's Majesty.

Please be most attentive to what you shall find,
For God's word is light so please keep that in mind.
Do all this with duty and loving heart,
And God will reward you so well for your part.

Do not let your tongue be talking or tattling,
Nor allow things of yours to be a-prattling,
Nor let your eyes wander, nor cast them about,
For in your devotion there will be great doubt.

> I will praise the
> LORD all my life;
> I will sing praise
> to my God as
> long as I live.
>
> PSALM 146:2

Remember that when you go to church, you are in God's house. When you are at another person's house you should treat it respectfully, and this is especially true for God's house!

ALL FOR YOU
author unknown

All for You, dear God.
Everything I do,
Or think,
Or say,
The whole day long.
Help me to be good.

2.
Weddings

A wedding takes place when a man and woman love each other and promise to live the rest of their lives together in a sacred union. The ceremony is followed by a party to celebrate the happy moment — the start of a new life for the couple.

A lot of preparation goes into the wedding ceremony and reception. So make sure you wear a suit and tie, or a pretty dress, to show your respect for the occasion. Be on your best behavior — act as good as you look!

THE LEGEND OF LOHENGRIN
by Michael Lamb

A LONG TIME AGO in the days of knights, lords, ladies, and castles there were seven brothers who were enchanted by a wicked sorceress and turned into swans. Their father Parzival, the Knight of the Holy Grail, eventually rescued them. Parzival used the sacred grail cup to turn the swans back into handsome boys. The oldest boy was named Lohengrin. He grew to become a brave and noble knight. On his shield was painted a flying swan to remind him what he had been and how his father had saved him from the spell of the sorceress. His fame was known all over Germany and he was called the Knight of the Swan.

A beautiful princess, who was named Elsa, sent a messenger to Lohengrin to ask for help. The same evil sorceress who had enchanted Lohengrin as a boy was tormenting Elsa. Lohengrin agreed to help Elsa and arrived at her castle in a boat drawn by swans. He rescued Elsa and was so taken by her beauty and goodness that he married her. They lived happily together for many years.

The German musician and composer Richard Wagner wrote an opera about the legend of Lohengrin. The most famous song from that opera is called "Lohengrin's Wedding March." It is better known as "Here Comes the Bride." This song is still played quite often at weddings as the bride walks down the aisle.

When the wedding march is played, everyone stands and quietly watches the beautiful bride walk to the altar. This is a big moment for the bride and groom, so it is very important to pay close attention.

Now, the next time you hear "Here Comes the Bride," you will know that it is really the wedding march from Lohengrin!

The Wedding of Lorna Doone
by R. D. Blackmore, adapted by Michael Lamb

JOHN RIDD had loved Lorna Doone from that first day when he saw her in the Doone Glen. Now, at last, they would be married. It had not been easy. The Doones' were a clan of thieves and murderers who for years had terrorized all of Exmoor. Their reputation was known and feared throughout seventeenth-century England. The local people trembled at the mere mention of their name. Years earlier they had killed John Ridd's father. Lorna, though, was different. She was sweet and kind. She hated the violence and greed of the Doones. Lorna Doone was as purely good as her kinfolk were evil, and she loved John as much as he loved her.

But, Lorna had been told since childhood that she was promised to Carver Doone and must marry him. Carver was the cruelest and the most ruthless of all the Doones. He hated John Ridd and he wanted Lorna more than anything, For many years John had fought and feuded with the Doones until they were finally beaten and peace had seemingly returned to Exmoor. Carver Doone, however, had escaped the destruction of the Doones' fortress. He had ridden through the Doone-gate, spurred his great black horse, and swore the deadliest of oaths. He passed into the darkness of the night and for a while he was forgotten.

Indeed, all the terrors and trials of the past were now almost a distant memory; this was Lorna Doone's wedding day. She was gloriously beautiful, so much so that John was almost afraid to glance at her. Her dress was of pure white, clouded with faint lavender. John stood there with joy and pride. He placed the ring on her finger. The parson blessed them and they gazed into each other's eyes. Lorna Doone was a vision of pure loveliness. Her eyes, which none on earth may ever equal, told a tale of hope, faith, and a heart's devotion.

The echo of a gunshot suddenly tore apart that happy moment and those lovely eyes were dim with death. A flood of blood came out upon the yellow wood of the altar steps. Lorna Doone had been shot. John lifted her up and tried to coax her to speak, but it was no good. The only sign of life remaining was the dripping of her bright red blood. She sighed a long sigh and grew dreadfully cold. Outside the church there were lilacs in blossom. Inside, Lorna lay dying in John Ridd's arms. In the terrible sadness of that moment John knew what he must do. He laid his wife in his mother's arms and went forth to find her killer.

> He that falls in love with himself will have no rivals.
>
> ❦
>
> BENJAMIN FRANKLIN
> *Poor Richard's Almanac*

Of course John knew who had done it. There was but one man upon earth, or under it, where the devil dwells, who could have done such a thing, Carver Doone. Ridd, unarmed and clothed in his wedding vest, rode his horse furiously toward Black Barrow Down. There in the distance, on a great black horse, riding hard was Carver Doone. John followed his enemy carefully, steadily, urging his horse onward.

Grabbing the limb of an oak, John charged Carver and knocked him from his horse. Before falling, Carver had fired his pistol. The shot had hit John and knocked him backwards. He took no heed of the bullet that had struck him and leaped upon Carver. There, in the middle of the swamp, the two men wrestled. With their strong muscles, they grabbed and tore at each other. Summoning all of his might, Ridd threw the dreaded Carver into the bog. Carver Doone had no strength left as he crawled towards Ridd with his beard all frothy like a mad dog, his eyes gleaming with hate.

"I will not harm thee any more," cried out John Ridd. "Carver Doone, thou art beaten, own it, thank God for it, and go thy way and repent."

Doone lunged out at Ridd in a last, desperate surge of evil — and fell into a soft arm of the bog. It was all over now. The black bog had Carver by the feet. He was steadily sinking as the sucking of the soft ground drew on him like the thirsty lips of death. Joint by joint he sank from sight. Carver Doone was dead at last.

Lorna Doone was not dead. Truly, she had lost a great deal of blood, but great care was given to her by the womenfolk and the county doctor, and she survived. Lorna Doone became, through God's grace, John Ridd's loving wife. Year by year her beauty grew with an equal growth of goodness, kindness, and true happiness. And if ever later in his life John Ridd felt sad or ill used, he could always bring himself out of it by remembering his blessing with two words, "Lorna Doone."

Thankfully, it's very rare for a bride to be shot at the altar! But bad manners can "kill" the beauty and joy of a couple's wedding day. In fact, families probably squabble over weddings more than any other other type of event. First, there are those who disapprove of the bride or the groom and make impolite comments. Then there are always a few who, like Carver Doone, are horribly jealous of or hateful towards the bride or groom. There are also problems that arise over the amount of money that goes into a wedding and reception. Lastly, there are the usual disagreements over who to invite, and there are always some who are offended over not being invited or not having a prominent role in the wedding.

Family squabbles are still too common at weddings, although they are seldom as serious as those recounted in this story. At weddings it is always best to remember that this is the bride and groom's day, and we should do everything we can to make it a special time for them.

3.
Funerals

The sadness of funerals is just the opposite of the joy of weddings. When someone attends a funeral, it is because someone has died. If you attend a funeral, make sure to tell your friend or the family who is grieving that you are sorry for their loss. You can also offer to help in some way or tell them that you will be praying for them.

THE DEATH OF LITTLE NELL
by Charles Dickens

SHE WAS DEAD. No sleep so beautiful and calm, so free from trace of pain, so fair to look upon. She seemed a creature fresh from the hand of God, and waiting for the breath of life; not one who had lived, and suffered death. Her couch was dressed with here and there some winter berries and green leaves, gathered in a spot she had been used to favor. "When I die, put near me something that has loved the light, and had the sky above it always." These were her words.

She was dead. Dear, gentle, patient, noble Nell was dead. Her little bird, a poor, slight thing the pressure of a finger would have crushed, was stirring nimbly in its cage, and the strong heart of its child-mistress was mute and motionless forever! Where were the traces of her early cares, her sufferings, and fatigues? All gone. Sorrow was dead, indeed, in her; but peace and perfect happiness were born, imagined in her tranquil beauty and profound repose.

And still her former self lay there, unaltered in this change. Yes! the old fireside had smiled upon that same sweet face; it had passed, like a dream, through haunts of misery and care; at the door of the poor schoolmaster on the summer evening, before the furnace fire upon the cold wet night, at the still bedside of the dying boy, there had been the same mild and lovely look. So shall we know the angels, in their majesty, after death.

Wish not so much to live long as to live well.

BENJAMIN FRANKLIN
Poor Richard's Almanac

The old man held one languid arm in his, and had the small hand tight folded to his breast for warmth. It was the hand she had stretched out to him with her last smile; the hand that had led him on through all their wanderings. Ever and again he pressed it to his lips; then hugged it to his breast again, murmuring that it was warmer now, and, as he said it, he looked in agony to those who stood around, as if imploring them to help her.

She was dead, and past all help, or need of help. The ancient rooms she had seemed to fill with life, even while her own was waning fast, the garden she had tended, the eyes she had gladdened, the noiseless haunts of many a thoughtful hour, the paths she had trodden, as it were, but yesterday, could know her no more.

"It is not," said the school-master, as he bent down to kiss her on the cheek, and gave his tears free vent, "it is not in this world that heaven's justice ends. Think what earth is, compared with the world to which her young spirit has winged its early flight, and say, if one deliberate wish, expressed in solemn tones above this bed, could call her back to life, which of us would utter it?"

She had been dead two days. They were all about her at the time, knowing that the end was drawing on. She died soon after day-break. They had read and talked to her in the earlier portion of the night; but, as the hours crept on, she sank to sleep. They could tell by what she faintly uttered in her dreams, that they were of her journeyings with the old man;

they were of no painful scenes, but of people who had helped them, and used them kindly; for she often said "God bless you!" with great fervor.

Waking, she never wandered in her mind but once, and that was at beautiful music, which, she said, was in the air. God knows. It may have been. Opening her eyes, at last, from a very quiet sleep, she begged that they would kiss her once again. That done, she turned to the old man, with a lovely smile upon her face, such, they said, as they had never seen, and could never forget, and clung, with both her arms, about his neck. She had never murmured or complained; but, with a quiet mind, and manner quite unaltered, save that she every day became more earnest and more grateful to them, faded like the light upon the summer's evening.

The child who had been her little friend, came there, almost as soon as it was day, with an offering of dried flowers, which he begged them to lay upon her breast. He told them of his dream again, and that it was of her being restored to them, just as she used to be. He begged hard to see her: saying, that he would be very quiet, and that they need not fear his being alarmed, for he had sat alone by his young brother all day long, when he was dead, and had felt glad to be so near him. They let him have his wish; and, indeed, he kept his word, and was, in his childish way, a lesson to them all.

Up to that time, the old man had not spoken once, except to her, or stirred from the bedside. But, when he saw her little favorite, he was moved as they had not seen him yet, and made as though he would have him come nearer. Then, pointing to the bed, he burst into tears for the first time, and they who stood by, knowing that the sight of this child had done him good, left them alone together.

Soothing him with his artless talk of her, the child persuaded him to take some rest, to walk abroad, to do almost as he desired him. And, when the day came, on which they must remove her, in her earthly shape, from earthly eyes forever, he led him away, that he might not know when she was taken from him. They were to gather fresh leaves and berries for her bed.

And now the bell, the bell she had so often heard by night and day, and listened to with solemn pleasure, almost as a living voice, rung its remorseless toll for her, so young, so beautiful, so good. Decrepit age, and vigorous life, and blooming youth, and helpless infancy — on crutches, in the pride of health and strength, in the full blush of promise, in the mere dawn of life — gather around her. Old men were there, whose eyes were dim and senses failing, grandmothers, who might have died ten years ago, and still been old, the deaf, the blind, the lame, the palsied, the living dead, in many shapes and forms, to see the closing of that early grave.

Along the crowded path they bore her now, pure as the newly fallen snow that covered it, whose day on earth had been as fleeting. Under that porch, where she had sat when heaven, in its mercy, brought her to that peaceful spot, she passed again, and the old church received her in its quiet shade.

This passage expresses deeply how the loss of a loved one can affect someone. Those still alive miss the person who has died terribly. When you say "I'm sorry," it means a great deal to your grieving friend or family.

Even when someone you know loses a pet, it can be a very sad time for him. Whenever death occurs, acknowledge the loss felt by the loved ones.

ANNE OF GREEN GABLES
by Lucy Maud Montgomery

CHAPTER 37

"MATTHEW — Matthew — what is the matter? Matthew, are you sick?"

It was Marilla who spoke, alarm in every jerky word. Anne came through the hall, her hands full of white narcissus, — it was long before Anne could love the sight or odor of white narcissus again, — in time to hear her and to see Matthew standing in the porch doorway a folded paper in his hand, and his face strangely drawn and gray. Anne dropped her flowers and sprang across the kitchen to him at the same moment as Marilla. They were both too late, before they could reach him Matthew had fallen across the threshhold.

He's fainted," gasped Marilla. "Anne, run for Martin — quick! He's at the barn."

Martin, the hired man, who had just driven home from the post office, started at once for the doctor, calling at Orchard Slope on his way to send Mr. and Mrs. Barry over. Mrs. Lynde was there on an errand. They found Anne and Marilla distractedly trying to restore Matthew to consciousness.

Mrs. Lynde pushed them gently aside, tried his pulse, laid her ear over his heart. She looked at their anxious faces sorrowfully and the tears came into their eyes.

"Oh, Marilla," she said gravely. "I don't think — we can do anything for him."

"Mrs. Lynde, you don't think — you can't think Matthew is — is — " Anne could not say the dreadful word, she turned sick and pallid.

"Child, yes, I'm afraid of it. Look at his face. When you've seen that look as often as I have you'll know what it means."

Anne looked at the still face and there beheld the seal of the Great Presence.

When the doctor came he said that death had been instantaneous and probably painless caused in all likelihood by some sudden shock. The secret of the shock was discovered to be in the paper Matthew had held and which Martin had brought from the office that morning. It contained an account of the failure of the Abbey Bank.

The news spread quickly through Avonlea, and all day friends and neighbors thronged Green Gables and came and went on errands of kindness for the dead and living. For the first time shy, quiet Matthew Cuthbert was a person of central importance; the white majesty of death had fallen on him and set him apart as one crowned.

When the calm night came softly down over Green Gables the old house was hushed and tranquil. In the parlor lay Matthew Cuthbert in his coffin, his long gray hair framing his placid face on which there was a little kindly smile as if he but slept, dreaming pleasant dreams. There were flowers about him — sweet old-fashioned flowers which his mother had planted in the homestead garden in her bridal days and for which Matthew had always had a secret, wordless love. Anne had gathered them and brought them to him, her anguished, tearless eyes burning in her white face. It was the last thing she could do for him.

The Barrys and Mrs. Lynde stayed with them that night. Diana, going to the east gable, where Anne was standing at her window, said gently:

"Anne dear, would you like to have me sleep with you tonight?"

"Thank you, Diana," Anne looked earnestly in her friend's face. "I think you won't misunderstand me when I say that I want to be alone. I'm not afraid. I haven't been alone one minute since it happened — and I want to be. I want to be quite silent and quiet and try to realize it. I can't realize it. Half the time it seems to me that Matthew can't be dead; and the other half it seems as if he must have been dead for a long time and I've had this horrible dull ache ever since."

Diana did not quite understand. Marilla's impassioned grief, breaking all the bounds of natural reserve and lifelong habit in its stormy rush, she could comprehend better than Anne's tearless agony. But she went away kindly, leaving Anne alone to keep her first vigil with sorrow.

Anne hoped that tears would come in solitude. It seemed to her a terrible thing that she could not shed a tear for Matthew, whom she had loved so much and who had been so kind to her, Matthew, who had walked with her last evening at sunset and was now lying in the dim room below with that awful peace on his brow. But no tears came at first, even when she knelt by her window in the darkness and prayed, looking up to the stars beyond the hills — no tears, only the same horrible dull ache of misery that kept on aching until she fell asleep, worn out with the day's pain and excitement.

In the night she awakened, with the stillness and the darkness about her, and the recollection of the day came over her like a wave of sorrow. She could see Matthew's face smiling at her as he had smiled when they parted at the gate that last evening — she could hear his voice saying, "My girl — my girl that I'm proud of." The tears came and Anne wept her heart out. Marilla heard her and crept in to comfort her.

There, there — don't cry so, dearie. It can't bring him back. It — it — isn't right to cry so. I knew that today, but I couldn't help it then. He'd always been such a good, kind brother to me — but God knows best.

"Oh, just let me cry, Marilla," sobbed Anne. "The tears don't hurt me like that ache did. Stay here for a little while with me and keep your arm round me — so. I couldn't have Diana stay, she's good and kind and sweet — but it's not her sorrow — she's outside of it and she couldn't come close enough to my heart to help me. It's our sorrow — yours and mine. Oh, Marilla, what will we do without him?"

"We've got each other, Anne. I don't know what I'd do if you weren't here — if you'd never come. Oh, Anne, I know I've been kind of strict and harsh with you maybe — but you mustn't think I didn't love you as well as Matthew did, for all that. I want to tell you now when I can. It's never been easy for me to say things out of my heart, but at times like this it's easier. I love you as dear as if you were my own flesh and blood and you've been my joy and comfort ever since you came to Green Gables."

Two days afterwards they carried Matthew Cuthbert over his homestead threshold and away from the fields he had tilled and the orchards he had loved and the trees he had planted, and then Avonlea settled back to its usual placidity and even at Green Gables affairs slipped into their old groove and work was done and duties fulfilled with regularity as before, although always with the aching sense of "loss in all familiar things." Anne, new to grief, thought it almost sad that it could be so — that they could go on in the old way without Matthew. She felt something like shame and remorse when she discovered that the sunrises behind the firs and the pale pink buds opening in the garden gave her the old inrush of gladness when she saw them — that Diana's visits were pleasant to her and that Diana's merry words and ways moved her to laughter and smiles — that, in brief, the beautiful world of blossom and love and friendship had lost none of its power to please her fancy and thrill her heart, that life still called to her with many insistent voices.

"It seems like disloyalty to Matthew, somehow, to find pleasure in these things now that he has gone," she said wistfully to Mrs. Allan one evening when they were together in the manse garden. "I miss him so much — all the time — and yet, Mrs. Allan, the world and life seem very beautiful and interesting to me after all. Today Diana said something funny and I found myself laughing. I thought when it happened I could never laugh again. And it somehow seems as if I oughtn't to."

> There is a time for everything, and a season for every activity under heaven: a time to be born and a time to die, a time to plant and a time to uproot, a time to kill and a time to heal, a time to tear down and a time to build, a time to weep and a time to laugh, a time to mourn and a time to dance.
>
>
>
> ECCLESIASTES 3:1–4

"When Matthew was here he liked to hear you laugh and he liked to know that you found pleasure in the pleasant things around you," said Mrs. Allan gently. "He is just away now; and he likes to know it just the same. I am sure we should not shut our hearts against the healing influences that nature offers us. But I understand your feeling. I think we all experience the same thing. We resent the thought that anything can please us when someone we love is no longer here to share the pleasure with us, and we almost feel as if we were unfaithful to our sorrow when we find our interest in life returning to us."

"I went down to the graveyard to plant a rosebush on Matthew's grave this afternoon," said Anne dreamily. I took a slip of the little white Scotch rosebush his mother brought out from Scotland long ago; Matthew always liked those roses the best — they were so small and sweet on their thorny stems. It made me feel glad that I could plant it by his grave — as if I were doing something that must please him in taking it there to be near him. I hope he has roses like them in heaven. Perhaps the souls of all those little white roses he has loved so many summers were all there to meet him. I must go home now. Marilla is all alone and she gets lonely at twilight."

It can be frightening when you are with someone who is sick or dying, especially if it's someone you love the way Anne loved Matthew. During those times, do your best to help out in whatever way you can, and remember that it's all right to cry and grieve and even feel angry. Everyone deals with death and sorrow differently. Like Anne, it's good to remember things that you did with the person who died, as well as things that he said.

If you do attend a funeral, it will probably be uncomfortable for you. The room will be filled with a lot of older people, many dressed in black (the color that symbolizes mourning or sadness), and many will be crying. It's all right if you feel awkward. Your parents will help you know what to do.

Most Christians will have the body of the deceased person laid out at a funeral home for a few days prior to the funeral. This is to give people the opportunity to say their final goodbyes. Most people will kneel at the casket and say a prayer. This is a solemn time, and a time to remember all the good things about the deceased loved one.

Christian funeral services take place in a church, and they are similar to a church service, with Scripture readings and prayers. After the service, people follow the hearse (the long black car that transports the coffin) to the graveyard. More prayers are said, and flowers are placed on the burial site.

Jewish funerals are different. Both the funeral and burial take place as soon as possible after the person dies. There is no viewing. You may hear the words "sitting shiva." This is a seven-day period of quietness, when the Jewish family mourns the death of their deceased. During this time, extended family and friends visit, bringing kosher foods but not gifts.

When you lose a close friend or family member, it can be extremely painful at first. With time, your heartache will diminish, but you will always miss your loved one.

CHAPTER TWELVE

Kindness towards Animals

Kindness towards Animals

You might wonder, why should there be a chapter about animals in a book about manners? Aren't good manners about being kind to other people? Yes, but they don't stop there. A kind person will always be gentle with animals. When you practice kindness towards animals, you are cultivating good qualities within yourself.

HURT NO LIVING THING
by Christina Rossetti

Hurt no living thing:
Ladybird, nor butterfly,
Nor moth with dusty wing,
Nor cricket chirping cheerily,
Nor grasshopper so light of leap,
Nor dancing gnat, nor beetle fat,
Nor harmless worms that creep.

THE HISTORY OF A GOLDFINCH
from Stories from Old-Fashioned Children's Books
edited by Andrew W. Tuer

A FOOLISH, silly boy — I hope no little girl would have thought of such a thing, or if she did I should be ashamed of her — took it into his head that a poor bird which had fallen into his power would look *very pretty* after his feathers were plucked off. To work he went, the poor bird did not complain, and he plucked every feather except the wings;

and to make the bird look the prettier as he called it, he got some warm paste and with it stuck a piece of red cloth upon the poor creature's head, and then let it go. Whilst he was admiring the victim of his cruelty, his father, who abhorred it, seeing him very attentive to the wicked work that he had been about, called him and questioned him in a kind manner, how he could be so cruel to an innocent creature that never injured him? The boy "did not," he said, "think any harm in it — he thought it looked pretty," and added that "he had not hurt the bird." Upon this, the father called him in the same mild way, for had he scolded, it would not have been so effectual, and plucking some of the hair from the young gentleman's head asked if *it hurt him?*

The boy cried and said that it hurt him very sadly indeed. The father then plucked some more, the pain of which made the boy cry very loud. "Now then," says the father, "learn in future to be more tender to your fellow creatures; for if such a small portion of hair which I have plucked from your head has occasioned you such pain as to make you cry so bitterly, what must you think of the pain which the poor little defenceless bird was put to, when without any provocation you plucked the feathers from its whole body! Go from my presence, you cruel wicked boy, and never let me see your face till you are sensible of your monstrous crime!"

This punishment had such effect upon the son that, as he himself not long since told me, he never could abide to be cruel to little innocent creatures ever afterwards.

BLACK BEAUTY
by Anna Sewell

Black Beauty is about a beautiful black horse who knows the joy of being loved and cared for, as well as the pain of being mistreated. In this scene, Black Beauty describes her current master, Reuben Smith.

CHAPTER 25

I MUST NOW SAY a little about Reuben Smith, who was left in charge of the stables when York went to London. No one more thoroughly understood his business than he did, and when he was all right, there could not be a more faithful or valuable man. He was gentle and very clever in his management of horses, and could doctor them almost as well as a farrier, for he had lived two years with a veterinary surgeon. He was a first-rate driver; he could take a four-in-hand, or a tandem, as easily as a pair. He was a handsome man, a good scholar, and had very pleasant manners. I believe everybody liked him; certainly the horses did; the only wonder was, that he should be in an under situation, and not in the place of a head coachman like York: but he had one great fault, and that was the love of drink. He was not like some men, always at it; he used to keep steady for weeks or months together; and then he would break out and have a "bout" of it, as York called it, and be a disgrace to himself, a terror to his wife, and a nuisance to all that had to do with him. He was, however, so useful, that two or three times York had hushed the matter up, and kept it from the Earl's knowledge; but one night, when Reuben had to drive a party home from a ball, he was so drunk that he could not hold the reins, and a gentleman of the party had to mount the box and drive the ladies home. Of course this could not be hidden, and Reuben was at once dismissed; his poor wife and little children had to turn out of the pretty cottage by the Park gate and go where they could. Old Max told me all this, for it happened a good while ago; but shortly before Ginger and I came Smith had been taken back again. York had interceded for him with the Earl, who is very kind-hearted, and the man had promised faithfully that he would never taste another drop as long as he lived there. He had kept his promise so well that York thought he might be safely trusted to fill his place whilst he was away, and he was so clever and honest, that no one else seemed so well fitted for it.

The heart of a fool is in his mouth, but the mouth of a wise man is in his heart.

BENJAMIN FRANKLIN
Poor Richard's Almanac

It was now early in April, and the family was expected home some time in May. The light brougham was to be fresh done up, and as Colonel Blantyre was obliged to return to his regiment, it was arranged that Smith should drive him to the town in it, and ride back; for this purpose he took the saddle with him, and I was chosen for the journey. At the station the Colonel put some money into Smith's hand and bid him good-bye, saying, "Take care of your young mistress, Reuben, and don't let Black Auster be hacked about by any random young prig that wants to ride him — keep him for the lady."

We left the carriage at the maker's, and Smith rode me to the White Lion, and ordered the ostler to feed me well and have me ready for him at four o'clock. A nail in one of my front shoes had started as I came along, but the ostler did not notice it till just about four o'clock. Smith did not come into the yard till five, and then he said he should not leave till six, as he had met with some old friends. The man then told him of the nail, and asked if he should have the shoe looked to.

"No," said Smith, "that will be all right till we get home."

He spoke in a very loud off-hand way, and I thought it very unlike him, not to see about the shoe, as he was generally wonderfully particular about loose nails in our shoes. He did not come at six, nor seven, nor eight, and it was nearly nine o'clock before he called for me, and then it was with a loud rough voice. He seemed in a very bad temper, and abused the ostler, though I could not tell what for.

The landlord stood at the door and said, "Have a care, Mr. Smith!" but he answered angrily with an oath; and almost before he was out of the town he began to gallop, frequently giving me a sharp cut with his whip, though I was going at full speed. The moon had not yet risen, and it was very dark. The roads were stony, having been recently mended; going over them at this pace, my shoe became looser and when we were near the turnpike gate it came off.

If Smith had been in his right senses, he would have been sensible of something wrong in my pace; but he was too madly drunk to notice anything.

Beyond the turnpike was a long piece of road, upon which fresh stones had just been laid; large sharp stones, over which no horse could be driven quickly without risk of danger. Over this road, with one shoe gone, I was forced to gallop at my utmost speed, my rider meanwhile cutting into me with his whip, and with wild curses urging me to go still faster. Of course my shoeless foot suffered dreadfully; the hoof was broken and split down to the very quick, and the inside was terribly cut by the sharpness of the stones.

This could not go on; no horse could keep his footing under such circumstances, the pain was too great. I stumbled, and fell with violence on both my knees. Smith was flung off by my fall, and owing to the speed: I was going at, he must have fallen with great force. I soon recovered my feet and limped to the side of the road, where it was free from stones. The moon had just risen above the hedge, and by its light I could see Smith lying a few yards beyond me. He did not rise, he made one slight effort to do so, and then there was a heavy groan. I could have groaned too, for I was suffering intense pain both from my foot and knees; but horses are used to bear their pain in silence. I uttered no sound, but I stood there and listened. One more heavy groan from Smith; but though he now lay in the full moonlight, I could see no motion. I could do nothing for him nor myself, but, oh! how I listened for the sound of horse, or wheels, or footsteps. The road was not much frequented, and at this time of the night we might stay for hours before help came to us. I stood watching and listening. It was a calm sweet April night; there were no sounds, but a few low notes of a nightingale, and nothing moved but the white clouds near the moon, and a brown owl that flitted over the hedge. It made me think of the summer nights long ago, when I used to lie beside my mother in the green pleasant meadow at Farmer Grey's.

THE COW
by Robert Louis Stevenson

The friendly cow all red and white,
I love with all my heart:
She gives me cream with all her might,
To eat with apple tart.
She wanders lowing here and there,
And yet she cannot stray,
All in the pleasant open air,
The pleasant light of day;
And blown by all the winds that pass
And wet with all the showers,
She walks among the meadow grass
And eats the meadow flowers.

Animals provide us with nourishment and protection; cows give us meat and milk, sheep give us wool for clothing, dogs provide protection. In the Bible, God allows man to take the life of animals for food and clothing.

While we are raising animals for our benefit, we must always provide for their health, shelter, and comfort. This means feeding, washing, brushing, and doing everything necessary to keep the animals healthy.

THE SWALLOW
by Christina Rossetti

Fly away, fly away over the sea,
Sun-loving swallow, for summer is done;
Come again, come again, come back to me,
Bringing the summer and bringing the sun.

We can learn so much by watching animals — to nurture our little ones, to be peaceful and content, and to praise God by jumping and singing and laughing.

THE LION
from Stories from Old-Fashioned Children's Books
edited by Andrew W. Tuer

HERE IS A GREAT LION! The king of beasts! And look how that little lamb skips around him. He could eat up the lamb in a moment, but he is too noble and generous to hurt the poor harmless lamb because it is in his power. Oh! what a noble animal! So you, my dear child, when you catch a bird, or butterfly, or any little creature, remember the lion, and do not hurt it because you have caught it; but let it go again and be happy, and then everybody will call you a good child and love you.

Be compassionate towards animals. Don't remove birds' nests from trees — they are home and shelter for a family of birds. Imagine if wild animals turned around and destroyed your home!

THE STORY OF DOCTOR DOLITTLE
by Hugh Lofting

CHAPTER I

ONCE UPON A TIME, many years ago — when our grandfathers were little children — there was a doctor, and his name was Dolittle — John Dolittle, M.D. "M.D." means that he was a proper doctor and knew a whole lot.

He lived in a little town called Puddleby-on-the-Marsh. All the folks, young and old, knew him well by sight. And whenever he walked down the street in his high hat everyone would say, "There goes the Doctor! He's a clever man." And the dogs and the children would all run up and follow behind him; and even the crows that lived in the church tower would caw and nod their heads.

The house he lived in, on the edge of the town, was quite small, but his garden was very large and had a wide lawn and stone seats and weeping willows hanging over. His sister, Sarah Dolittle, was housekeeper for him, but the Doctor looked after the garden himself.

He was very fond of animals and kept many kinds of pets. Besides the goldfish in the pond at the bottom of his garden, he had rabbits in the pantry, white mice in his piano, a squirrel in the linen closet, and a hedgehog in the cellar. He had a cow with a calf too and an old lame horse — twenty-five years of age — and chickens and pigeons and two lambs and many other animals. But his favorite pets were Dab-Dab, the duck; Jip, the dog; Gub-Gub, the baby pig; Polynesia, the parrot; and the owl, Too-Too.

His sister used to grumble about all these animals and said they made the house untidy. And one day when an old lady with rheumatism came to see the Doctor, she sat on the hedgehog, who was sleeping on the sofa, and never came to see him anymore, but drove every Saturday all the way to Oxenthorpe, another town ten miles off, to see a different doctor.

Then his sister, Sarah Dolittle, came to him and said, "John, how can you expect sick people to come and see you when you keep all these animals in the house? It's a fine doctor who would have his parlor full of hedgehogs and mice!

"That's the fourth person these animals have driven away. Squire Jenkins and the Parson say they wouldn't come near your house again — no matter how sick they are. We are getting poorer every day. If you go on like this, none of the best people will have you for a doctor."

"But I like the animals better than the best people," said the Doctor.

"You are ridiculous," said his sister and walked out of the room.

So, as time went on, the Doctor got more and more animals, and the people who came to see him got less and less. Till at last he had no one left — except the cat's-meat man, who didn't mind any kind of animals. But the cat's-meat man wasn't very rich and he only got sick once a year — at Christmastime, when he used to give the Doctor sixpence for a bottle of medicine.

Sixpence a year wasn't enough to live on even in those days long ago; and if the Doctor hadn't had some money saved up in his money box, no one knows what would have happened.

And he kept on getting still more pets, and of course it cost a lot to feed them. And the money he had saved up grew littler and littler.

Then he sold his piano and let the mice live in a bureau drawer. But the money he got for that too began to go, so he sold the brown suit he wore on Sundays and went on becoming poorer and poorer.

And now, when he walked down the street in his high hat, people would say to one another, "There goes John Dolittle, M.D. There was a time when he was the best-known doctor in the West Country. Look at him now. He hasn't any money and his stockings are full of holes!"

But the dogs and the cats and the children still ran up and followed him through the town — the same as they had done when he was rich.

We can learn from Dr. Dolittle that kindness toward animals is a wonderful quality. But we also have responsibilities toward animals. We should only take in animals that we have time and energy to care for.

ROBIN REDBREAST
by William Blake

A Robin Redbreast in a Cage
Puts all Heaven in a Rage.

A Skylark wounded in the wing,
A Cherubim does cease to sing.

He who shall hurt the little Wren
Shall never be belov'd by Men.

The wanton Boy that kills the Fly
Shall feel the Spider's enmity.

A truth that's told with bad intent
Beats all the Lies you can invent.

SAINT KEVIN AND THE BLACKBIRDS
retold by Jenny Schroedel

MANY, MANY YEARS AGO, in Ireland, there lived a young man named Kevin who could venture into the wildest forests and never feel alone. Even at night, when the trees quivered in the wind and fallen branches snapped beneath the paws of creatures he could not see, he was never afraid.

Every year, Kevin retreated to a little hut in the forest where he would spend all of Lent praying, reading the Bible, and pondering God's deep, wide love. He snacked only on berries and nettles that grew from the trees around him, and he drank a little water every now and then. Each morning, as he prayed, he stretched his arms through an opening in the hut, his palms empty and waiting.

Ask the animals, and they will teach you, or the birds of the air, and they will tell you. . . . In the LORD's hand is the life of every creature and the breath of all mankind.

JOB 12:7, 10

One day as he prayed this way, a blackbird dropped a twig in his open palm. Kevin froze. Then, the blackbird returned with another twig, and then another. Before Kevin's very eyes, she was building a nest in his hands.

And so he stood, day after day, as she wove a nest of stalks, cotton-tails, and twigs. She lined her nest with a silky sheet of grass, tucked her wings around herself, and fell asleep. Kevin groaned. But he did not move.

One morning, Kevin was startled awake by the joyful singing of the blackbird's mate. Kevin's eyes focused on the nest in his hand. There he spotted five sea-green, brown-flecked eggs. His hand trembled.

Kevin stood breathlessly still. He did not even wiggle his big toe, and he did not scratch his nose, although he desperately wanted to. His knees were stiff, his arms ached, and his fingers were turning blue.

On the thirteenth morning the father blackbird's song ceased. Kevin heard muted chirping coming from one of the eggs. For hours, the baby bird wriggled inside, struggling to peck its way out. Finally, the egg cracked open, and out tumbled the first baby bird, shell bits still clinging to its body. And then Kevin heard more cracking as the other eggs began to break open.

Kevin was so touched by the miracle that took place in the palm of his hand that he never did move until the last baby bird was strong enough to fly off on its own. He lived to be 120 years old, and he is remembered all over the world for his patient prayers and brave gentleness.

THE PASTURE
by Robert Frost

I'm going out to clean the pasture spring;
I'll only stop to rake the leaves away
(And wait to watch the water clear, I may):
I sha'n't be gone long. — You come too.

I'm going out to fetch the little calf
That's standing by the mother. It's so young,
It totters when she licks it with her tongue.
I sha'n't be gone long. — You come too.

Taking care of animals teaches us not only about compassion, but also about the value of hard work.

I Walk My Dog at Daybreak
by Jack Prelutsky

I walk my dog at daybreak,
and again right after school.
It's often inconvenient,
but I'm sticking to the rule.
I feed the fish and parakeets,
my hungry cats as well,
then tidy up the litter box
before it starts to smell.
I tend to all the rabbits,
turtles, gerbils, frog, and snake,
and clean the little messes
they inevitably make.
The finches' cage needs freshening,
especially the tray,
and then there are the elephants —
I'm giving them away.

Having a pet is a big responsibility. You have to feed it, brush and bathe it, walk it, clean up after it, and take it to the vet for check-ups. Weigh this responsibility before considering a pet of your own. Pets need a lot of love and care and should never be neglected.

CHAPTER THIRTEEN

Respecting Our Country

1.
Good Citizenship

AMERICA THE BEAUTIFUL
by Katharine Lee Bates

O beautiful for spacious skies,
    For amber waves of grain,
For purple mountain majesties
    Above the fruited plain!
America! America!
    God shed His grace on thee
And crown thy good with brotherhood
    From sea to shining sea!
O beautiful for pilgrim feet,
    Whose stern, impassioned stress
A thoroughfare for freedom beat
    Across the wilderness!
America! America!
    God mend thine every flaw,
Confirm thy soul in self-control,
    Thy liberty in law!
O beautiful for heroes proved
    In liberating strife,
Who more than self their country loved,
    And mercy more than life!
America! America!
    May God thy gold refine,
Till all success be nobleness
    And every gain divine!

O beautiful for patriot dream
    That sees beyond the years
Thine alabaster cities gleam
    Undimmed by human tears!
America! America!
    God shed His grace on thee,
And crown thy good with brotherhood
    From sea to shining sea!

Our country is like no other. America was founded on godly principles, and because of the sacrifices of those who came before us, we are able to live in freedom. As you get older you will learn about and appreciate the strengths and uniqueness of our great country. These are some of the freedoms that you benefit from right now:

Blessed is the nation whose God is the LORD.

PSALM 33:12

1) When you are with your friends, there are probably children of many faiths — Catholic, Protestant, Jewish, Muslim, Buddhist. In our country, we are free to practice many different religions. It's not this way in many other countries. In fact, in some parts of the world, people are jailed and tortured for their faith.

2) We have a president and political leaders in our country who are chosen by the people and represent the people. In other countries, some of the leaders only care about themselves — not the people.

3) You may belong to a group like the Brownies or Boy Scouts. When you get older, you can belong to many different kinds of groups. In many countries, people aren't free to form these kinds of associations.

4) When you are with your family and friends, you can freely talk about your opinions. Believe it or not, in some countries, expressing certain opinions will land you in jail.

These are just a few examples of the freedoms we enjoy in America. Never take your freedoms for granted, because if you do, you may lose them.

IN FLANDERS FIELDS
by John McCrae

In Flanders fields the poppies blow
Between the crosses, row on row,
    That mark our place; and in the sky
    The larks, still bravely singing, fly
Scarce heard amid the guns below.
We are the Dead. Short days ago
We lived, felt dawn, saw sunset glow,
    Loved and were loved, and now we lie
    In Flanders fields.
Take up our quarrel with the foe:
To you from failing hands we throw
    The torch; be yours to hold it high.
    If ye break faith with us who die
We shall not sleep, though poppies grow
    In Flanders fields.

REPLY TO "IN FLANDERS FIELDS"
by John Mitchell

Oh! sleep in peace where poppies grow;
The torch your falling hands let go
Was caught by us, again held high,
A beacon light in Flanders sky
That dims the stars to those below.
You are our dead, you held the foe,
And ere the poppies cease to blow,
We'll prove our faith in you who lie
    In Flanders Fields.
Oh! rest in peace, we quickly go
To you who bravely died, and know
In other fields was heard the cry,
For freedom's cause, of you who lie,
So still asleep where poppies grow,
In Flanders Fields.
As in rumbling sound, to and fro,
The lightning flashes, sky aglow,

The mighty hosts appear, and high
Above the din of battle cry,
Scarce heard amidst the guns below,
Are fearless hearts who fight the foe,
And guard the place where poppies grow.
Oh! sleep in peace, all you who lie
   In Flanders Fields.
And still the poppies gently blow,
Between the crosses, row on row.
The larks, still bravely soaring high,
Are singing now their lullaby
To you who sleep where poppies grow
In Flanders Fields.

Never forget all of the lives that were sacrificed in the defense of our country. In your prayers at night, remember to thank God for all of those men and women who gave their lives for our freedom. Learn to be a good and faithful citizen. Fly an American flag proudly outside your home, study our country's heroes and history, place your hand over your heart during the national anthem, and salute the American flag. As you get older, excercise your right to vote and do your part to preserve the American dream for generations to come. Pray to God for protection, and for him to continue to bless our country with peace and prosperity.

ABRAHAM LINCOLN WALKS AT MIDNIGHT
by Vas Lindsay

(In Springfield, Illinois)

It is portentous, and a thing of state
That here at midnight, in our little town
A mourning figure walks, and will not rest,
Near the old courthouse pacing up and down,
Or by his homestead, or in shadowed yards
He lingers where his children used to play,
Or through the market, on the well-worn stones
He stalks until the dawn stars bum away.
A bronzed, lank man! His suit of ancient black,
A famous high top-hat and plain, worn shawl

Make him the quaint great figure that men love,
The prairie lawyer, master of us all.
He cannot sleep upon his hillside now.
He is among us — as in times before!
And we who toss and lie awake for long
Breathe deep, and start, to see him pass the door.
His head is bowed. He thinks on men and kings.
Yea, when the sick world cries, how can he sleep?
Too many peasants fight, they know not why;
Too many homesteads in black terror weep.
The sins of all the warlords burn his heart.
He sees the dreadnoughts scouring every main.
He carries on his shawl-wrapped shoulders now
The bitterness, the folly, and the pain.
He cannot rest until a spirit-dawn
Shall come; the shining hope of Europe free:
The league of sober folk, the Workers' earth,
Bringing long peace to Comland, Alp and Sea.
It breaks his heart that kings must murder still,
That all his hours of travail here for men
Seem yet in vain. And who will bring white peace
That he may sleep upon his hill again?

This poem describes how a great leader lived each moment with the weight of the country on his shoulders. Freedom requires hard work and sacrifice to preserve.

THE MESSENGER WHO INSULTED WALLACE
from The Scottish Chiefs *by Jane Porter*
adapted by Michael Lamb

WALLACE and the chiefs of Scotland were met in a council of war, when a messenger arrived from the English King Edward and his allies. The messenger was Sir Hugh de Spencer, a Southron knight. Wallace was standing when he entered, and so were the chieftains, but at his appearance they sat down. Wallace remained standing. "I come to the leader of this rebellion, William Wallace, to receive an answer to the terms granted by the goodness of my master to this misled kingdom," said the messenger.

"Sir Knight," replied the noble Wallace, "when the English lords delegate a messenger to me who knows how to respect the country to which he is sent and the men of his own country, then I shall give my reply."

The messenger stood there, proud as could be, and retorted, "Do you know, proud Scot, whom you dare talk to in this way? I am the nephew of the lord high constable of England."

"That impresses no one here," said Wallace.

"Sir, this insult — "

"Must be put up with!" cried Wallace. "You have insulted this country and these men of Scotland, to which you were sent on an errand of peace. Because you are young and foolish, we forgive you and permit you safely to return to those who sent you." With that, the boastful knight turned away and was escorted back to his own lands.

Sell not virtue to purchase wealth, nor liberty to purchase power.

Benjamin Franklin
Poor Richard's Almanac

William Wallace was one of Scotland's greatest heroes. His bravery, honesty, and love for his country were legendary. Here we see how a true patriot like William Wallace not only loves and respects his own country, but also respects people of other lands, even his enemies. The English messenger insulted Wallace and the Scots; that is why his message of peace wasn't heard. A person who truly loves his country respects others who equally love their country.

2.
Respecting the American Flag

The American flag is more than a political symbol. It represents the courage, dignity, honor, and immense sacrifices of all those who came before us — those who fought and gave their lives so that we can live in a country that attempts to provide freedom, justice, and opportunity for all. That's why we should treat it with the utmost respect.

THE FLAG GOES BY
by Henry Holcomb Bennett

> Hats off!
> Along the street there comes
> A blare of bugles, a ruffle of drums,
> A flash of color beneath the sky:
> Hats off!
> The flag is passing by!
>
> Blue and crimson and white it shines,
> Over the steel-tipped, ordered lines.
> Hats off!
> The colors before us fly;
> But more than the flag is passing by.
>
> Sea-fights and land-fights, grim and great,
> Fought to make and to save the State;
> Weary marches and sinking ships;
> Cheers of victory on dying lips;
>
> Days of plenty and years of peace;
> March of a strong land's swift increase;

Equal justice, right and law,
Stately honor and reverend awe;

Sign of a nation, great and strong
Toward her people from foreign wrong:
Pride and glory and honor — all
Live in the colors to stand or fall.

    Hats off!
Along the streets there comes
A blare of bugles, a ruffle of drums;
And loyal hearts are beating high:
    Hats off!
The flag is passing by!

FLAG ETIQUETTE

1. The flag should be flown from sunrise until sunset. It should not be flown in bad weather. When you raise the flag, do it briskly with pride and take it down with respect. Do not allow it to touch the ground.
2. When the flag is displayed on a wall or window it should be with the blue star area to the upper left. Except as a distress signal, never hang the flag upside down.
3. Always carry the flag waving high and free.
4. When a flag passes you in a parade or when it is raised or lowered, place your hand over your heart and face the flag.
5. Always keep your flag clean and neat, and repair it carefully when it is damaged.

THE PLEDGE OF ALLEGIANCE
by James B. Upham and Francis Bellamy in 1882
amended by Congress in 1923 and 1954

> I pledge allegiance to the flag
> Of the United States of America,
> And to the republic
> For which it stands —
> One nation, under God,
> Indivisible —
> With liberty and justice for all.

When you say "The Pledge of Allegiance," you should place your hand over your heart, face the flag, and stand attentively as you recite it.

THE STAR-SPANGLED BANNER
by Francis Scott Key

Oh, say can you see, by the dawn's early light,
What so proudly we hailed at the twilight's last gleaming?
Whose broad stripes and bright stars, thro' the perilous fight,
O'er the ramparts we watched, were so gallantly streaming.
And the rockets' red glare, the bombs bursting in air,
Gave proof through the night that our flag was still there.
Oh, say does that star-spangled banner yet wave
O'er the land of the free and the home of the brave?

On the shore dimly seen, thro' the mists of the deep,
Where the foe's haughty host in dread silence reposes,
What is that which the breeze, o'er the towering steep,
As it fitfully blows, half conceals, half discloses?
Now it catches the gleam of the morning's first beam,
In full glory reflected, now shines on the stream;
'Tis the star-spangled banner; oh, long may it wave
O'er the land of the free and the home of the brave.

And where is that band who so vauntingly swore
That the havoc of war and the battle's confusion
A home and a country should leave us no more?

Their blood has wash'd out their foul footsteps' pollution.
No refuge could save the hireling and slave
From the terror of flight or the gloom of the grave:
And the star-spangled banner in triumph doth wave
O'er the land of the free and the home of the brave.

Oh, thus be it ever when free men shall stand,
Between their loved homes and the war's desolation;
Blest with vict'ry and peace, may the heav'n-rescued land
Praise the Power that has made and preserved us a nation!
Then conquer we must, when our cause it is just,
And this be our motto: "In God is our trust";
And the star-spangled banner in triumph shall wave
O'er the land of the free and the home of the brave.

Francis Scott Key wrote this beautiful poem on September 14, 1814. In 1931, "The Star-Spangled Banner" became our national anthem, the official song of our country. When you're at an event where "The Star-Spangled Banner" is sung, place your hand over your heart, face the flag, and sing the song as well as you can.

ACKNOWLEDGMENTS

ROFOUND GRATITUDE is due everyone who helped me with this book. First and foremost, I offer my heartfelt thanks to my dear husband, Rick, who is the most loving, supportive, and generous husband in the world. This book would not have been possible without your support. Life with you is a wonderful journey, and I love sharing all our days together. In addition, I could not have done this book without our wonderful children, Elizabeth, John, Daniel, Sarah Maria, Peter, Patrick, and Bella. They were all a tremendous help in their own ways. My older children were a big help sifting through the stories, and they provided lots of good advice from a child's perspective. We had immense fun deciding what stories we should include, and why others should not be included! My little ones provided immense amounts of joy with all of their smiles and hugs! Thanks for all of your little acts of kindness that brighten all of my days. You are the inspiration behind this book. I love you all so much.

I will be forever grateful to my dear parents, Ken and Betty Lee Garver, who taught my siblings and me the importance of being pleasant and thoughtful so family life would be happy. As a family of twelve children, this was a valuable lesson that has kept us close through the years. Thank you, Mom and Dad, for serving others with complete selflessness. Thank you to all of my dear brothers, sisters, in-laws, and friends for all of your love and friendship through the years. It is a blessing walking through life with all of you. Special thanks to Nancy Garver, my wonderful sister-in-law and scheduler extraordinaire! You're the best! I'm grateful to my brilliant brother-in-law, Michael Lamb. He is extraordinarily well read, and I think he remembers every detail of every story he has ever read in his entire life! Thank you, Mike, for all of your help with the chapter on sportsmanship, and also your knowledge and assistance with other sections of the book.

I am also very thankful to my dear friends Mark and Leanne Rodgers, who care deeply about the issue of civility in our culture and were a great source of inspiration and good ideas. Thank you, Susie and Walt Twetten, for watching my children on many occasions while I was working on the book. You are dear friends, and Rick and I will never forget all of your thoughtfulness.

I am grateful to Bill Bennett, who encouraged me from the start. When the book was just an idea, he provided valuable wisdom and guidance. The staff at the Library of Congress was impressive with their knowledge of old and rare books. Heartfelt thanks to Maria Wusinich for her assistance and research as I began this project. I cannot thank Al Regnery enough for believing in this book. He saw it not just as a book, but rather as part of a mission to help restore some civility to our culture.

I am extremely grateful to my editors: Vigen Guroian, author and professor at Loyola College in Baltimore, Maryland; and Jeff Nelson, the publisher of ISI Books. Thank you for all of the commas, periods, deletions, clarifications, ideas, and valuable suggestions! It was a joy working with you. You were so generous with your time, and for that, I am extremely grateful.

I also want to thank Sam Torode, an incredibly talented artist, editor, and young father, whose graceful illustrations are a gift to the children who will read this book, as well as to their parents, who will share in their delight.

And finally, this book would not have been possible without the people at ISI Books. They are some of the finest that I have ever met. They are all hard-working, professional, and completely dedicated to this project. I want to acknowledge with deepest appreciation especially Doug Schneider, Lindsay Wheeler, Sandy Callender, Bethany Torode, and Jenny Schroedel for all of their suggestions and wisdom during the publishing process. Thank you for all of your encouragement and for sharing my vision.

Finally, my greatest thanks goes to Jesus Christ, the Light of the World, for giving me strength through the long nights as I worked after tucking my children into bed, and for giving me the honor of serving Him through this work.

—KAREN SANTORUM

PERMISSIONS

Index of Titles

Chapter Two: Using Words Wisely

Chapter Three: Table Manners

CHAPTER FOUR: WASHING AND DRESSING

CHAPTER EIGHT: GOOD MANNERS IN SCHOOL